Japanese Multinationals in China

China is poised to gain global importance as a growth engine for the world economy on a par with Europe and the USA. Meanwhile, Japanese multinational enterprises are increasingly active in relocating to China their R&D and capital- and knowledge-intensive production for both export-platform and target market reasons. It is at the juncture of the growing impact of China-related activities of Japanese corporations on the transformation of Japanese management philosophies, and on the transformation of the Japanese economy more generally, that this book is situated.

As Japanese corporations re-align activities to increasingly accommodate the growing importance of China as a business location, inter-regional expansion will integrate more deeply the Chinese economy within their global strategies, business structures and decision-taking. By presenting current research and thinking on the significance of corporate Japan's growing engagement with China, the book explores the following imminent questions: What is China's future position in the global corporate activities of Japanese firms? How has China's investment profile changed and how and with what purpose do Japanese firms enforce their Chinese presence? The book sheds light on the implications for European businesses and policy-makers of the consequences of deepening integration of these two economic powerhouses.

This book was published as a special issue of *Asia Pacific Business Review*.

Sierk A. Horn is Senior Lecturer in Japanese Studies at the University of Leeds.

Adam R. Cross is Senior Lecturer in International Business and Director of the Centre for Chinese Business and Development at the University of Leeds.

Japanese Multinationals in China

Edited by Sierk A. Horn and Adam R. Cross

Routledge
Taylor & Francis Group
LONDON AND NEW YORK

First published 2010 by Routledge
2 Park Square, Milton Park, Abingdon, Oxon, OX14 4RN

Simultaneously published in the USA and Canada
by Routledge
52 Vanderbilt Avenue, New York, NY 10017

Routledge is an imprint of the Taylor & Francis Group, an informa business

First issued in paperback 2013

Typeset in Times by Value Chain, India

British Library Cataloguing in Publication Data
A catalogue record for this book is available from the British Library

ISBN13: 978-0-415-44002-8 (hbk)
ISBN13: 978-0-415-84541-0 (pbk)

CONTENTS

Abstracts vi

Notes on contributors ix

Introduction
Japanese management at a crossroads? The changing role of China in the transformation of corporate Japan 1
Sierk A. Horn and Adam R. Cross

1 The rise of the Japanese multinational enterprise: then and now 25
P.J. Buckley

2 The evolution of Japanese investment in China: from toys to textiles to business process outsourcing 38
A. Delios, P.W. Beamish and X. Zhao

3 The transformation of Japan Post into a global player 61
T. Goydke

4 Pre-clusterization in emerging markets: the Toyota group's entry process in China 83
F. Hatani

5 Product adoption and innovation diffusion: the case of Japanese marketing to China 102
S.A. Horn

6 Why Japanese multinationals failed in the Chinese mobile phone market: a comparative study of new product development in Japan and China 123
T. Marukawa

7 The impact of workgroup commitment on organizational citizenship behaviour, absenteeism and turnover intention: the case of Germany and China 144
J. Felfe and W.H. Yan

8 Competitiveness, localization and Japanese companies in China: realities and alternate approaches 162
H. Itagaki

Conclusions and Implications
9 The changing role of China in the transformation of corporate Japan 174
Adam R. Cross and Sierk A. Horn

Index 188

Abstracts

INTRODUCTION

Japanese management at a crossroads? The changing role of China in the transformation of corporate Japan

Sierk A. Horn and Adam R. Cross

This introduction to *Japanese Multinationals in China*, argues that better understanding is needed of how the economic rise of China is influencing the transformation of corporate Japan. After examining key trends in the evolution of Sino-Japanese business relations, we consider potential triggers of corporate transformation under the headings of marketing and distribution, inter-corporate networks and human resources management. Each of these areas is discussed in the context of increasing engagement of Japanese firms with the Chinese economy and the ability of Japanese firms to transfer sources of competitive advantage to this emerging market.

The rise of the Japanese multinational enterprise: then and now

P.J. Buckley

Japanese multinational enterprises (MNEs) have evolved since the1980s when they first came to prominence. The rise and degree of their success are not uniform stories and Japanese MNEs vary greatly by size, sector and administrative heritage. This Chapter discusses these issues and argues that the degree of integration of Japanese MNEs with world capital markets is low and their management styles and innovation systems are idiosyncratic. Pressures on Japanese MNEs to increase flexibility and openness have resulted in unusual hybrid structures.

The evolution of Japanese investment in China: from toys to textiles to business process outsourcing

A. Delios, P.W. Beamish and X. Zhao

The nature of Japanese firms' international activity in China underwent substantive change between 1995 – 2006. Japanese companies now compete in many more regions in China and have shifted their investment strategies in various provinces and municipalities to reflect new competitive realities. This creates substantial opportunities and challenges to scholars and practitioners alike. The challenge is to develop a nuanced understanding of sub-national variations in Japanese firms' strategies in China. The opportunities come from deepening research in three areas of scholarly endeavour: (1) subsidiary development and multinational firm strategy; (2) institutions and international business; and (3) offshoring, outsourcing and international business theory.

The transformation of Japan Post into a global player
T. Goydke

The privatisation of Japan Post has been a cornerstone of recent Japanese government reform policy. However, little scholarly attention has been given to the expansion of Japan Post into the global express delivery market. This study compares the privatisation and internationalisation of Japan Post with Deutsche Post to 2007. Similarities and differences in the strategies in Germany and Japan both with respect to the privatisation process as well as to international expansion strategies are examined and discussed. Special focus is placed on the activities of Japan Post and DHL in China and the Asia-Pacific region.

Pre-clusterization in emerging markets: the Toyota group's entry process in China
F. Hatani

Drawing on network analysis and informing the internationalization process of Japanese firms, this study introduces an ad hoc entry strategy, termed 'pre-clusterization'. Unlike conventional keiretsu firms, competitive suppliers in a well-integrated network can enter a new market and begin clustering in a location that the core firm targets before the full entry of the core firm. The process of pre-clusterization is illustrated using a case study of the Toyota Group in China. A number of testable propositions are presented. Findings reveal the importance of strategic collective actions when coping with intensive competition and uncertainty in emerging market contexts.

Product adoption and innovation diffusion: the case of Japanese marketing to China
S.A. Horn

Along with the growing prominence of China in corporate strategy and decision-taking, Japanese firms are increasingly aligning their activities to accommodate the shift towards a customer-led market environment and the advent of a major consumer market on Japan's doorstep. This study shows how Japanese firms adjust their marketing to changes in Chinese consumption patterns and address the impact of geographical and socioeconomic variables on innovation diffusion. By taking a fresh look at the marketing challenges amidst latent consumer ethnocentrism and cosmopolitanism, this study generates fresh insights into the reconfiguration of Japanese marketing and retailing activities in this emergent market.

Why Japanese multinationals failed in the Chinese mobile phone market: a comparative study of new product development in Japan and China
T. Marukawa

This industry case study examines the challenges experienced by Japanese MNEs as they transfer sources of competitive advantage to foreign markets. Despite holding certain technological advantages, Japanese mobile telephone manufacturers have performed poorly in the Chinese market. This is because the capabilities required differ between Japan and China: in Japan, handsets are sold as a part of a package that bundles together handsets and telephony services but in China they are sold as independent commodities. Japanese MNEs have the capability to develop sophisticated handsets according to the requirements of Japanese service operators, but such capability is not useful in China.

The impact of workgroup commitment on organizational citizenship behaviour, absenteeism and turnover intention: the case of Germany and China
J. Felfe and W.H. Yan

In Western cultures, high correlations have been found between commitment, turnover and performance. While most studies only consider organizational commitment, this study compares the influence of commitment to the workgroup on relevant outcomes (organizational citizenship behaviour, absenteeism, turnover intention) in different cultural contexts. Data were collected from German and Chinese employees. As expected, results indicate that workgroup commitment is more predictive in a collectivistic than in an individualistic context. Moreover, the relationships between components and foci of commitment were stronger in a collectivistic context. The results are discussed in the light of cross-cultural human resources management issues.

Competitiveness, localization and Japanese companies in China: realities and alternate approaches
H. Itagaki

Japanese multinational enterprises have traditionally been criticized for lagging behind Western companies in the localization of management practices, especially at managerial level. This has been ascribed to Japanese MNEs initiating offshore activities later than Western counterparts. Such reasoning cannot be applied to the case of China, where the 'starting line' was almost the same for all foreign firms. Drawing on case study evidence of Japanese firms in China, this study offers an alternate explanation for the lag in localization in respect of production methods and work style, and identifies a number of possible solutions for Japanese MNEs.

CONCLUSIONS AND IMPLICATIONS

The Changing role of China in the Transformation of Corporate Japan
Adam R. Cross and Sierk A. Horn

This conclusion to the volume examines how Japanese firms are responding to, and are affected by, increasing engagement with the Chinese economy. In addition to the three specific themes identified in the opening chapter to be of greatest concern to the transformation of corporate Japan (namely marketing and distribution, inter-corporate networks and human resources management) two additional themes can be discerned from the studies in this volume. These relate to institutional evolution and the challenges of localization. It is concluded that Japanese firms can be shown to have demonstrated flexibility in their engagement with China within this analytical framework.

Notes on contributors

Sierk A. Horn is Senior Lecturer in Japanese Studies at the University of Leeds. He was awarded a PhD in Japanese Studies and Habilitation from Freie Universitaet Berlin, Germany. He has published widely in the fields of consumer behaviour in East Asia as well as international knowledge transfer and strategic management of Japanese and European MNEs.

Adam R. Cross is Senior Lecturer in International Business, Centre for International Business, University of Leeds (CIBUL) and Director of the Centre for Chinese Business and Development (CCBD), also at the University of Leeds. He has published two edited books, and has contributed to more than forty scholarly papers and book chapters, mainly on cross-border licensing; intellectual property management; outward direct investment from emerging markets, and foreign market servicing strategies.

Dr Peter J. Buckley is Professor of International Business and Director of the Centre for International Business, University of Leeds (CIBUL), UK. He was President of the Academy of International Business from 2002 to 2004.

Andrew Delios is Associate Professor, Department of Business Policy, National University of Singapore. He earned his PhD in General Management at the Ivey Business School, University of Western Ontario.

Paul W. Beamish holds the Canada Research Chair in International Management at the Ivey Business School, University of Western Ontario.

Xuejuan Zhao is an MSc student at the NUS Business School, National University of Singapore.

Tim Goydke is Professor of Japanese Economy and Society at the School of International Business, University of Applied Sciences Bremen, Germany. Recent research includes institutional change in Japan and leadership and succession in Asia. He obtained his PhD from the University Duisburg-Essen, Germany, where he served as a research assistant following graduation.

Faith Hatani is Lecturer in International Business at Manchester Business School, the University of Manchester, UK. She holds a PhD in Land Economy from the University of Cambridge. Her research focuses on the impact of FDI in developing countries, power structures in global value chains, and the interface between manufacturing and transport in emerging markets.

Tomoo Marukawa is Professor of Chinese Economy at the Institute of Social Science, University of Tokyo. He is author of *Modern Chinese Industries*: *Strength and Weakness* of *the Chinese Firm* (Tokyo: Chuokoron-Shinsha) and other books.

Jörg Felfe is a Professor for Social and Organizational Psychology at the University of Siegen, Germany. He received his PhD from the Free University of Berlin. Major research fields are leadership, commitment and culture.

Wenhua Yan is Professor at the East China Normal University is Shanghai. Her research fields are occupational health, communication and cross cultural adaption.

Hiroshi Itagaki is Professor of Economics at the Department of Economics, Musashi University. His research focuses on the transfer of Japanese-style management and production systems abroad.

INTRODUCTION

Japanese management at a crossroads? The changing role of China in the transformation of corporate Japan

Sierk A. Horn[a] and Adam R. Cross[b]

[a]*Department of East Asian Studies, School of Modern Languages and Cultures, University of Leeds, Leeds LS2 9JT, UK;* [b]*Leeds University Business School, Maurice Keyworth Building, University of Leeds, Leeds LS2 9JT, UK*

Introduction

This study explores how the management practices and corporate strategies of Japanese multinational enterprises (MNEs) are being shaped by the growing importance of China to the East Asian region and the world economy as a whole. Three inter-related dynamics associated with the East Asian region – namely, Sino-Japanese political relations, deepening economic interdependency and the transformation of corporate Japan – provide the underlying rationale for our focus on this topic.

Broadly speaking, and especially from a Western perspective, political relations between China and Japan have long been seen as beset by seemingly intractable issues of rivalry, nationalism and conflict (Gurtov 2008). Political relations deteriorated steadily during Prime Minister Junichiro Koizumi's term of office (2001–2006), when Japan's ties with the US in particular were strengthened (Taniguchi 2005). By way of contrast, throughout the 1990s, and especially in the years following China's accession to the World Trade Organisation (WTO) in December 2001, bilateral trade and investment have expanded considerably and this has given rise to a high degree of economic interdependency between the two countries. This is due largely to China's economic growth policies and its associated policies towards, for example, state-owned sector reform, market liberalisation and market opening to foreign business, all of which has helped to engender one of the most sustained and rapid economic transformations the world has seen in the past 50 years (Herd and Dougherty 2005). China is now host to the fourth largest stock of Japanese foreign direct investment (FDI) by national economy (JETRO 2007a). It has also become Japan's second most important trading partner and the leading one on the basis of imports alone (Japan Ministry of Finance 2007). Intensification of business relations has been accompanied by a change of attitude towards China amongst the Japanese business community: it is no longer regarded mainly as a source of cheap labour and a threat to Japan's manufacturing base, but rather as a prime production location and key market (Taniguchi 2005). Discussions on current Sino-Japanese affairs that emphasise poor political relations and societal tensions often serve to discount the level of pragmatism demonstrated by many Japanese firms towards China and *de facto* prosperous economic relations – an ambivalence that has become encapsulated in the adage 'cold politics – hot economics'. Such an emphasis detracts from the key role that China now has in the current and future strategic development of Japanese MNEs.

In the 1980s, the rapid expansion of Japanese MNEs received considerable attention from scholars and practitioners alike (Aoki 1984, 1990, Abegglen and Stalk 1985, Buckley and Mirza 1985, Abo 1994). Many commentators argued for the superiority of the organisational structures and governance mechanisms of Japanese firms and of the range of management practices they employed, which collectively became known as the 'Japanese management system' (or 'J-system') (for an overview, see Chen 2004). However, the collapse of Japan's 'bubble economy' in the early 1990s and the ensuing sluggish performances of many of its MNEs meant that many of the 'secrets' of the Japanese management system subsequently became regarded more as shackles on future growth (Kishi 2003). This, arguably, led to a waning in the level of scholarly interest directed towards Aoki's (1990) 'miracle' economy and its MNEs, especially in mainstream international business literatures.

Since the late 1990s, however, many Japanese firms have sought performance gains through the implementation of widespread changes to governance mechanisms, corporate structures, labour relations and employment practices (Collinson and Rugman 2008). There is a growing literature to suggest that these changes are beginning to bear fruit (Kishi 2003, Yoshikawa *et al.* 2006, Jackson and Miyajima 2007). Recent research on Japanese MNEs has tended to concentrate on internationalisation motives and strategies (eg. Tejima 2000, Delios and Henisz 2003, Farrell *et al.* 2004, Makino *et al.* 2004, Delios and Beamish 2005, Pak and Park 2005, Siddharthan and Lakhera 2005, Tomiura 2005, Yoshida and Ito 2006, Kiyota and Urata 2007). Within this literature there is a burgeoning number of studies that specifically investigate the activities of Japanese firms in China: with most adopting the approach of estimating econometric models of sub-national location choice (Beamish and Jiang 2002, Belderbos and Carree 2002, Fung *et al.* 2003, Wakasugi 2005, Cassidy and Andreosso-O'Callaghan 2006, Cheng 2006, 2007, Ma and Delios 2007, but see, for example, Isobe *et al.* 2000, Haak and Hilpert 2003). To date, little attention has been given in this body of work to raising our understanding of how greater engagement with the Chinese economy is influencing the transformation of Japanese management practices. Rapid economic integration and increased economic linkages between China and the rest of Asia, including Japan, suggest the need for careful scrutiny of this issue (Yin and Choi 2005). It is at the juncture of the impact of the China-related activities of Japanese corporations on the transformation of Japanese management philosophies and practice that this book is situated.

The contributions are the outcome of an international workshop held at the University of Leeds in 2007 that was designed to shed new light on the activities of Japanese firms in China, and to assess the implications for corporate Japan of deepening integration of these two economic 'powerhouses'. Underpinning the event was the contention that an evaluation of how Japanese firms are (re)aligning and organising their activities in China could offer the potential for an alternative view of local competitive and operational conditions than is typically found in studies of Western investing firms.

In this introduction, we provide background and context for the book by characterising the evolution of China's position in the corporate strategies of Japanese MNEs over recent years. Three recurrent themes that emerged during the workshop are introduced and expanded upon. The contribution is in three parts. In the first, we chart the development of Japanese investments in China in the modern era by reviewing official aggregate FDI flow statistics reported at a national level and by seeking explanations for changes to investment level, activity, location and determinants through a review of extant literature. Our primary aim here is to highlight how institutional factors have exerted a strong effect on the investment behaviour of Japanese firms. We then describe how the position of China as an FDI host and Japan as an FDI source have changed over time from the perspective of each country and from this we draw inferences about the strategic intent of Japanese MNEs in the region. In the second part, we take three aspects of the Japanese management system, which we examine under the headings of marketing and distribution, intercorporate networks and human resource management (HRM), and reflect on some of the key challenges likely to confront Japanese firms in each area of practice as they look to extend their traditional sources of competitive advantage to their China operations. We then present an overview of the studies included in the book and show how each one relates to the themes we develop in this opening piece.

Key trends in Japanese FDI to China

Recent contributions to the international business strategy literature have attempted to relate the behaviour of investing firms to institutional change in host countries (eg. Meyer and Nguyen 2005, Wright *et al.* 2005). Underpinning the institutional theory approach is the assertion that institutions matter to businesses because they determine the 'rules of the game' (North 1990). China represents an ideal lens through which to examine relationships between institutions and the operations of Japanese MNEs. This is because the State Council and its agencies have strived over the last three decades to control the amount, geographic distribution and type of inbound FDI using a variety of policies and regulatory instruments in order to experiment with, and manage, the contribution of foreign business to the economic reform process. Arguably, an analysis of the character of Japanese FDI to a transition economy such as China is incomplete without due consideration of how both the political environment and policy uncertainty influence investing firm behaviour (Delios and Henisz 2003, Cheng 2007, Ma and Delios 2007). In Table 1, we identify five key phases to inward FDI policy development in China, following the approach of Buckley *et al.* (2005). This is mapped against the evolution of Japanese FDI in terms of annual aggregate FDI stocks and flows.

Before we do this, however, it is important to note at the outset that close Sino-Japanese economic ties are not a new phenomenon: indeed, trade and investment between the two countries have a long history. Even during Japan's seclusion period (1638–1858), trade between them flourished, albeit limited by shogunate directives. Trade concessions at the port of Nagasaki – the single point of access to Japan at this time – were granted only to Chinese and Dutch merchants, and numerous trade routes with coastal cities of China were established, all early manifestations of thriving economic links (Ôba 2000).

Table 1. China's FDI policy: motivation and developments (1979–2005).

Experimental period (1979–1983)
Policy motivation: To attract greater inward FDI, especially from overseas Chinese, as one of the 'four modernisations', and to learn from the experiences of the opened areas.

- A series of laws enacted on joint ventures (JVs) allowing FDI, defining equity JVs and setting out the fiscal arrangements for foreign invested enterprises (FIEs).
- Four Special Economic Zones (SEZs) established at Shenzen, Zhuhai, Shantou and Xiamen in Guangdong and Fujian provinces, and greater economic autonomy given to these two provinces.
- Inward foreign direct investment (FDI) controlled using approval procedures, performance requirements, local content requirements, limitations on investment location, and enforced joint venture formation. Access to domestic markets remained highly constrained for foreign investors.
- Investment incentives include land made available for commercial development, two year tax holiday on profits, fifty per cent reduction of the standard tax rate on profits earned in years three to five, simplification of approval procedures and reduction of duties on imports of capital equipment, machinery and intermediate inputs used in the production of exports.
- Ministry of Foreign Economic Relations and Trade (MOFERT) created (1982), responsible for FDI, trade and related economic affairs. Subsequently became the Ministry of Foreign Trade and Economic Cooperation (MOFTEC) (1993) and the Ministry of Commerce (MOFCOM) (2003).

Gradual development period (1984–1991)
Policy motivation: To build upon the success of the first SEZs and to divert FDI away from real-estate and into technology intensive, export-oriented and infrastructure-related sectors.

- Law for the Encouragement of Foreign Investment promulgated (1986) and implementing regulations announced (1987). Wholly-foreign owned subsidiaries were permitted.
- Investment restrictions gradually eased, mostly in sectors with few domestic firms (e.g. tourism and hotels) and where foreign capital and technology was sought (e.g. oil exploration).
- Hainan Island and 14 coastal cities across 10 provinces opened to FDI in 1984.
- Preferential income tax arrangements for FIEs granted in 1984.
- The Yangtze River (Changjiang) Delta, the Pearl River (Zhujiang) Delta and South Fujian area become Open Export Zones (OEZs) in 1985, followed in 1987 by Shandong and East Liaoning Peninsulars.
- Shanghai's Pudong New Area opened in 1989 as a flagship SEZ.

Peak period (1992–1993)
Policy motivation: To accelerate economic reform and to develop new export industries, under the encouragement of Deng Xiaoping.

- Foreign firms granted greater access to domestic markets.
- A number of sectoral and regional restrictions on FDI removed.
- Some FDI approvals conditional on achievement of certain policy goals. Special investment incentives available in preferred sectors.
- New sectors opened up experimentally to foreign investment (e.g. domestic retail trade, finance, tourism, shipping, resources development).
- FDI still tightly controlled by state policy, though approval procedures for smaller-scale projects were devolved to provincial and municipal government. Market entry remained tightly controlled through approval procedures, performance requirements, local sourcing requirements, location restrictions and enforced JV establishment.
- Further opening of 28 cities and 8 regions in the Yangtze River Delta area.

Adjustment period (1994–1999)
Policy motivation: To adjust the industrial structure of FDI and to provide national treatment for foreign investors.

- FDI are categorized as 'encouraged', 'permitted', 'restricted' or 'prohibited'. Encouraged sectors (typically export-oriented, technology intensive or import substituting investment) benefit from tariff exemptions and fiscal reductions. Wholly-foreign owned enterprises permitted in 'encouraged' sectors.
- Duties re-imposed in 1995 on imported machinery, equipment, parts and other materials by FIEs (but repealed in 1997 for FDI in 'encouraged' sectors).

Table 1 – *continued*

- Acquisitions by foreign firms permitted under the Provisional Regulations on the Use of Foreign Investment for the Asset Restructuring of State-Owned Enterprises (SOEs) (1998), followed by Regulations on the Merger and Division of Foreign Invested Enterprises (1999).
- Domestic market access continued to be constrained, to shelter inefficient and vulnerable state-owned enterprises from international competition, using similar policy instruments as before.
- Latterly, highly selective special investment regimes were gradually abandoned for more nationwide implementation of open policies.

Post-WTO period (2000 to date)
Policy motivation: To comply with China's WTO accession commitments and improve overall quality of FDI.

- Policies implemented to continue to encourage FDI, while improving the overall quality and industrial composition, especially in technology intensive and high value added sectors (especially environmentally friendly, energy-saving and resources exploiting technologies).
- MOFCOM published its Catalogue for Guidance of Foreign Investment Industries (2002, 2004 and 2007), which improved transparency and clarified 'encouraged', 'permitted', 'restricted' or 'prohibited' categories. The number of sectors in the 'encouraged' category increased, especially in relation to service industries, but FDI was still restricted in sectors deemed critical to the national economy.
- FDI in the central, western and northeastern provinces was promoted (to help balanced national economic development).
- Policy support for export-oriented FDI were curtailed and eliminated (to address China's trade surplus).
- Promulgation of Measures for Administration of the Takeover of Listed Companies (2002) provided greater transparency to the acquisition of SOEs.
- Fiscal incentives, tariff exemptions and other incentives were available to investments in 'encouraged' sectors and central, western and northeastern provinces, although many of the preferential tax arrangements enjoyed specifically by FIEs were eliminated (under the Corporate Income Tax Law of 2007) and tighter tax supervision imposed.

Source: Adapted from Office of the United States Trade Representative (2001), Buckley *et al.* (2005), OECD (2006), MOFCOM (various documents).

The advent of the Meiji period (1868–1911) triggered an unprecedented economic expansion that saw Japan gain ground on the industrialised nations and caused Japanese industrialists to seek expansion possibilities beyond the domestic market. To this young economy China offered an abundance of raw materials and markets, and within 30 years Japan had outpaced other foreign powers in terms of its economic engagement with China (Mizoguchi 1989). To illustrate, although by the turn of the twentieth century the bulk of FDI in China was from Britain, France, Germany and Russia, with Japan accounting for less than 4% of the total (Yoshino 1976, Zhou *et al.* 2002), over the next four decades growth in the nominal value of Japanese investment exceeded that for other nationalities to the extent that, by 1944, some 75% of FDI stock in China was Japanese-held, much of which was a consequence of military occupation (Zhou *et al.* 2002). In short, the pre-war period saw economic interdependence deepen, with the Chinese market quickly becoming an important source of growth for Japanese firms. Thus, for reasons of history, geographic proximity (Nagasaki is as close to Shanghai as it is to Tokyo) and aspects of a common cultural heritage, the Chinese economy has traditionally played an important role for corporate Japan. On this basis, it is plausible to argue that the recent intensification of trade and investment with China represents a return to 'business as usual' for corporate Japan, and that Japanese firms may thus view China as a less enticing prospect than do Western firms, many of which have '(re)discovered' China much more recently as an attractive investment location.

During 1949–1976, when China adopted a Soviet-style economic system and a strategy of self-reliance, FDI from all countries, including Japan, for the most part ceased. Doors to China's economy were formally re-opened to foreign investors with the implementation of the Sino-Foreign Equity Joint Venture Law in 1979 (Huang 2003). In the 'Experimental Period' (1979–1983), a number of preferential FDI policies were implemented, initially confined to the eastern coastal region. FDI was limited to four Special Economic Zones (SEZs) located on the coast at Shantou, Shenzen, Xiamen and Zhuhai, where a number of incentives to foreign investors were available (Zhou *et al.* 2002, Buckley *et al.* 2005, Cheng 2007). However, access to domestic markets remained highly restricted. The broad aim of these policies was to attract inward FDI, especially from the overseas Chinese, and to learn from the experiences of the opened areas (Buckley *et al.* 2005). Liberalisation of the investment regime led to an initial, albeit limited, wave of Japanese FDI in the early 1980s, mainly to the SEZs (Zhou *et al.* 2002). Although it might be presumed that this was cost-motivated (and related to the abundance of cheap labour), this is probably not the case. Xing (2004), for example, uses data from Japan's Ministry of Commerce to show that the bulk of Japanese investment at this time was in non-manufacturing related sectors, and these are generally less sensitive to labour cost issues than is manufacturing.

During the 'Gradual Development' period (1984–1991), the Chinese authorities looked to build on the success of the early SEZs and attract further FDI inflows, but with the aim of diverting this away from real-estate (which had attracted a lot of speculative investment) and towards infrastructure projects and technology intensive and export-oriented sectors in which few domestic firms competed. The Law for the Encouragement of Foreign Investment was promulgated in 1986, a number of investment restrictions were relaxed and preferential income tax arrangements were granted to foreign-invested enterprises (FIEs). Between 1984–1989 a series of cities and regions across 10 provinces were opened incrementally to FDI and a number of Open Export Zones (OEZs) were established, the majority based along the coast. At the same time, the appreciation of the Japanese Yen in the late 1980s caused many Japanese firms to strengthen and diversify their investment portfolios internationally in response to loss of competitiveness in export markets, and net Japanese FDI outflows rose steadily as a result (Cassidy and Andreosso-O'Callaghan 2006). However, despite improvements to the investment regime, China attracted very little Japanese FDI during this period – less than 0.5% of total outflows on average per annum during 1982–1984, and only around 3% by 1991 (JETRO 2007a). Nonetheless, from China's perspective, Japan was an important FDI source. MOFCOM data show that Japan was China's second largest investor, accounting for an annual average of 13.3% of total realised FDI inflow between 1988–1991, behind Hong Kong (58.4%) but ahead of the USA (9.1%), Western European countries (5.1% collectively) and Taiwan (2.8%) (MOFCOM 2006) (see Figure 1).[1]

Thus, whilst China was experimenting with FDI, this phase marked a learning period for Japanese firms in China. Investment disincentives included an opaque legislative framework, poor infrastructure, low labour productivity, bureaucratic obstacles and concerns about political stability following the Tiananmen Square incident in 1989 (Beamish and Jiang 2002). Rather, as with other Triad firms, Japanese MNEs directed the bulk of their investments towards the industrialised countries (mainly to develop new markets and to defend established positions from the threat of heightened barriers to extra-regional trade).

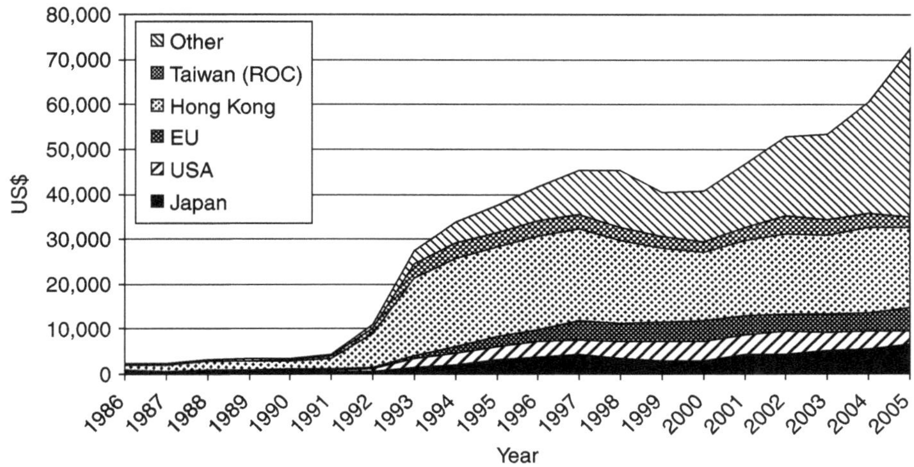

Figure 1. Source of inbound FDI to China (realized value) (US$1 mn).
Source: MOFCOM (2006).

Like that of other source countries, Japan's investment agenda for China was fuelled by the visit of Deng Xiaoping, the country's then paramount leader, to its southern region in 1992. This accelerated the economic reform process, especially the promotion of export-oriented industries, and paved the way for China's market orientation. During the 'Peak Period' (1992–1993), foreign firms were granted greater access to China's domestic market; fresh investment incentives were introduced for priority sectors, and new sectors and territories (including the capital cities of all inland provinces) were opened experimentally to FIEs. Although FDI continued to be tightly regulated, much of the decision-making on FDI-related matters was devolved to provincial and municipal governments, and numerous SEZs and industrial development zones sprang up as a result. During this period Japanese FDI to China rose sharply, especially in the Open Coastal Cities (OCC) (Zhou *et al.* 2002, Xing 2006). This was despite an overall contraction of total outbound FDI from Japan. It is clear that the early 1990s marked a resurgence of interest in China among Japanese firms and its increasingly liberal stance towards foreign business.

In the 'Adjustment Period' (1994–2000), the Chinese authorities sought to alter the industrial structure of FDI by promoting export-oriented, technology intensive and import substituting investment through tariff exemptions and fiscal benefits. Latterly, these selective special investment regimes were slowly abandoned in favour of nationwide implementation of a more open and non-preferential policy framework to FDI, in line with China's WTO accession commitments. Although greater domestic market access was granted to FIEs, limits were still in place, mostly to protect inefficient and vulnerable state-owned enterprises from international competition. Data suggest that Japanese MNEs were particularly quick to respond to the investment opportunities presented by policy liberalisation during the 'Peak Period' and the early years of the 'Adjustment Period'. Inflows of contracted Japanese FDI increased three-fold during 1992–1995 (MOFCOM 2006), much of which took place outside of the SEZs, notably in the OCCs (Zhou *et al.* 2002, Cassidy and Andreosso-O'Callaghan 2006). Over the same period, the share of Japan in total realised inbound FDI flows to China rose from 6.4% to 8.3%, revealing that Japanese firms collectively were investing at a faster rate than other nationality firms, while China's share of total Japanese outward FDI flow rose from 3.1% to 8.7%, which suggests that Japanese firms were now prioritising China as an investment location over other countries (see Table 2 and Figure 1) (MOFCOM 2006, JETRO 2007a). These trends can be explained by a combination of both push and pull factors, including stagnant growth in key markets and recessionary forces in Japan, and an increasingly attractive production location on Japan's doorstep.

The surge in Japanese FDI to China was relatively short-lived, however. Investment levels peaked early in the 'Adjustment Period'. According to JETRO statistics, this occurred in 1995 with an annual inflow of some US$4,478 million (an amount not matched again for almost a decade), although MOFCOM data on realised, as opposed to contractual, Japanese FDI suggest a somewhat later peak, in 1998. Japanese FDI to China declined thereafter in the second half of 1990s, both in absolute value terms and as a share of total outward flows from Japan, which stood at less than 2% by 1999 (JETRO 2007a, see Table 2). All this points to China being a key investment location for Japanese MNEs in the early to mid-1990s, but that its location attractiveness weakened subsequently relative to other host countries (especially in the industrialised world). Although this can be attributed to the Asian financial crisis, the start of the decline in fact preceded the events of 1997. Xing (2006), for example, argues that the prime stimulus was a sharp depreciation of the yen, which lowered the value of the financial assets of Japanese MNEs and raised production costs in China relative to other locations. However, there are at least two further plausible explanations. First, during the 1990s, firms of all nationalities were experiencing lower than expected returns on their Chinese operations (Beamish and Jiang 2002, Yin and Choi 2005) and poor profit expectations may have discouraged further investment by Japanese firms. Second, a significant number of Japanese MNEs by this time may have already established an appropriate investment 'beachhead', which allowed for the flexibility of further investment or divestment depending upon the direction and scale of economic progress in China. Such a strategy would also have avoided some of the problems of 'excessive internalisation' which Buckley (2004), among others, suggests was typical of some investments made by industrialised country firms in China during the 1990s.

In addition to the market potential that attracted consumer goods and service industries from Japan, Japanese MNEs also began to build manufacturing bases in China in substantial numbers during the 'Adjustment Period'. Xing (2006) estimates that as much as 79.9% of the value of Japanese FDI in China in 1995 was in manufacturing-related activities. Using a different data set, *Kaigai Shinshutsu Kigyô Sôran-Kuni Betsu* (Japanese overseas investments by country), Zhou *et al.* (2002) report that just under 75% of the 2933 Japanese-owned affiliates established in China by 1998 were involved in manufacturing-related activities and that these accounted for over 85% of total employment in China by Japanese firms. Unlike US and European investments in China, which were predominantly motivated by local market access considerations (Buckley and Meng 2005), Japanese investments at this time were mostly export-oriented (Xing 2004). In this respect, China was regarded by Japanese MNEs in much the same way as were other Asian countries: that is, as a low cost production base in which to conduct labour intensive, low value-added activities and from where to supply international markets (Cheng 2007). Off-shoring parts of the value chain to China allowed Japanese MNEs to: (i) improve the cost competitiveness of products in international markets (Fung *et al.* 2003, Pak and Park 2005, Cassidy and Andreosso-O'Callaghan 2006, Cheng 2007); (ii) broaden (and deepen) the geographic scope of regional production networks (Yoshida and Ito 2006); and (iii) mitigate some of the negative effects of yen appreciation (Xing 2006). The logic of the keiretsu production system meant that many Japanese supply firms also followed core firms to China in the 1990s. All these motivations are reflected in a survey

Table 2. Japan's outward FDI (based on reports and notifications) by country/region (US$ million and percentage of total).

	1979–1981	1982–1984	1985–1987	1988–1990	1991–1993	1994–1996	1997–1999	2000	2001	2002	2003	2004
Total (US$mn)	6207	8668	22,634	57,158	37,249	46,822	54,236	49,034	32,297	36,858	36,092	35,548
USA	28.3	33.4	44.6	46.7	41.6	44.0	32.3	25.2	20.0	22.3	29.3	13.2
Latin America	16.6	21.7	19.0	9.3	8.5	9.9	13.0	10.8	23.9	15.6	14.6	17.9
Asia	27.4	18.9	12.3	12.1	17.2	24.0	16.6	12.2	20.6	15.4	17.7	26.4
China	0.3	0.5	1.8	0.6	3.1	6.7	2.5	2.1	4.5	4.8	8.7	12.8
AsiaNIEs	9.5	10.4	6.8	6.7	5.9	6.9	5.2	5.6	7.4	5.3	3.2	7.5
ASEAN-5	21.1	10.4	5.4	6.6	9.6	11.7	9.9	5.1	11.5	6.2	6.3	7.5
Mid & Near East	2.3	2.1	0.3	0.2	1.0	0.5	0.5	0.0	0.1	0.1	0.0	0.0
Europe	10.4	14.2	17.0	22.1	21.8	15.7	31.2	49.9	32.8	41.9	35.0	36.5
Africa	4.2	4.7	1.2	1.1	1.3	0.8	0.8	0.1	0.7	0.5	0.3	0.3
Oceania	8.6	3.1	4.3	6.6	6.9	3.6	3.2	1.4	1.7	3.6	2.8	5.3

Notes: Percentages calculated as three year annual average of the ratio of annual country/region FDI to total FDI (1979 to 1999). AsiaNIEs (Hong Kong, Korea, Singapore, Taiwan), ASEAN-5 (Indonesia, Malaysia, Philippines, Singapore, Thailand).
Source: Authors' calculations based on JETRO (2007a) (dataset discontinued in 2004).

Table 3. Geographic distribution of the overseas affiliates of 600 Japanese MNEs (no. and percentage).

	China	NIEs3	ASEAN5	India, Vietnam and other Asia	North America	Latin America	EU15	Rest of the world	Total
Production bases	1750	498	1356	261	796	235	485	270	5651
	(31.0)	(8.8)	(24.0)	(4.6)	(14.1)	(4.2)	(8.6)	(4.8)	100.0
Sales bases	673	755	852	143	655	182	1056	405	4721
	(14.3)	(16.0)	(18.0)	(3.0)	(13.9)	(3.9)	(22.4)	(8.6)	100.0
R&D bases	56	12	45	7	83	3	55	11	272
	(20.6)	(4.4)	(16.5)	(2.6)	(30.5)	(1.1)	(20.2)	(4.0)	100.0
Others	119	62	154	29	254	49	152	53	872
	(13.6)	(7.1)	(17.7)	(3.3)	(29.1)	(5.6)	(17.4)	(6.1)	100.0
Total	2598	1327	2407	440	1788	469	1748	739	10,744
	(24.2)	(12.4)	(22.4)	(4.1)	(16.6)	(4.4)	(16.3)	(6.9)	

Note: NIEs-3 (Korea, Taiwan, Hong Kong), ASEAN-5 (Singapore, Thailand, Indonesia, Malaysia, Philippines).
Source: JBIC (2007).

of Japanese manufacturing MNEs conducted by Japan's Ministry of Economy, Trade and Industry in 1999. This found that, of the 2631 respondent firms with operations in China and Hong Kong, 22.2% had invested to take advantage of lower costs, 20.9% to expand market share, 8.9% to re-export to Japan and 7.7% to supply parts to established firms (Fung *et al.* 2003). Only 19 respondent firms (less than 0.7%) indicated that they had invested to undertake R&D activities.

At the beginning of the 'post-WTO accession' period (2000 to present), Japanese FDI once again gathered pace in terms of investment value and quickly accelerated thereafter. JETRO (2007a) report that China attracted US$4,567 million of annual Japanese FDI flows in 2004 (12.8% of the total), around the same amount (13.2%) that was directed to the USA (a share that has declined steadily from its peak of 45.8% in 1996) but less than that to Europe (36.5%). In 2005, Japanese firms accounted for 9.0% of realised FDI inflows (re-attaining investment levels last seen in the mid-1990s), an amount exceeded only by that from Hong Kong (MOFCOM 2006). Table 2 shows that this occurred at a time when net Japanese FDI outflows were falling. When viewed alongside the drop in Japanese FDI to the US in particular, a clear and growing trend towards regionalisation among Japanese MNEs is apparent, with China a key destination (Yin and Choi 2005, Collinson and Rugman 2008). However, more recent data on Japanese FDI flows to China (on a balance of payments basis) suggest a slowing trend. In 2007, China attracted 8.4% (US$6,218 million) of total outward investment from Japan, compared with 12.2% (US$6,169 million) in 2006 and 14.4% (US$6,575 million) in 2005 (JETRO 2007a). This was at a time when total Japanese FDI outflows were increasing (by around 10% from 2005 to 2006) but when annual world flows of FDI to China contracted (for the first time in seven years) by 4% on the previous year to stand at US$69 billion in 2006 (UNCTAD 2007). UNCTAD (2007) and JETRO (2007b) explain the decline in both global FDI to China and that from Japan in terms of rising labour costs, rising production costs, labour shortages and changes in government policy towards certain types of investment projects (in particular, export-oriented FDI, which is now less favoured than other types such as technology intensive activities). Nonetheless, a number of indicators point to the dominant position that China (and the Asian region more broadly) now has in the international activities of Japanese firms. China, for example, is now host to 6.7% of total outward Japanese FDI stock by country, a position only exceeded by the USA, the UK and the Netherlands (JETRO 2007a). Similarly, a recent survey of 600 Japanese manufacturing MNEs (defined as having three or more affiliates and at least one production operation abroad) conducted by the Japan Bank for International Cooperation (JBIC) in 2007 revealed that China and the ASEAN-5 countries are now host to around 43% of the overseas affiliates of participating firms (see Table 3). The same survey highlights the importance of China as a manufacturing location: just under one third (31%) of the respondents' overseas manufacturing operations are located in China, compared with 23.9% in the ASEAN-5, 14.1% in North America and 8.6% in the European Union. Moreover, compared with other regions captured by the survey, China is host to the largest number of R&D operations outside of the USA (JBIC 2007). A comparison with similar previous surveys reveals the evolving strategic priorities of Japanese investors in China. In particular, the percentage of Japanese firms that identify inexpensive labour costs and fiscal-based investment incentives as China's prime locational advantages is reported to have declined steadily each year since 2003, whereas the proportion of those that identify market attractiveness has increased (JBIC 2007). When viewed alongside historical trends, these findings provide further strong evidence for the growing regionalism of Japanese MNEs, as well as for a general shift away from labour-intensive assembly production towards more capital-intensive and knowledge-intensive production activities in China. They also point to a much stronger market-orientation among recent Japanese investors. All this is consistent with the view that Japanese affiliates in China are being positioned with the intention of using the country *both* as an export platform and as a target market (see Buckley and Meng 2004). In this respect, it can be argued that the strategic approach of Japanese MNEs in China is now converging towards models typically employed there by Western MNEs.

Scope and underlying themes

For reasons of history, geography and economic complementarity, Japanese MNEs appear particularly well placed to exploit the opportunities presented by market growth and institutional reform in China. The aforementioned evidence indeed suggests that Japanese firms are increasingly realigning and expanding the scope of their activities to accommodate China as both a manufacturing base and target market. Yet China has changed and is changing – and the question is whether Japanese firms can demonstrate sufficient flexibility and adaptability to fully exploit the business opportunities it presents (Yoshikawa *et al.* 2006). There is a body of literature to suggest that this might be problematic for Japanese firms. This literature asserts that the location-bound nature of the firm specific advantages (FSAs) of Japanese firms constrain their international competitiveness because these FSAs are not readily transferable to foreign markets (Delios and Beamish 2005, Siddharthan and Lakhera 2005). Indirectly, this standpoint is reflected in a recent survey on the sources of competitive advantage of Japanese MNEs. Of the 467 participating firms, a large proportion (62%) reported that the design of international business models could be improved (JETRO 2007b). Both internal and external constraints are identified in the literature (Collinson and Rugman 2008). The former relate to certain organisational and management practices of Japanese firms that are contingent upon the economic, social and cultural environments of Japan, and therefore apply to the internationalisation process in general. The latter relate to the operating conditions of the host country and, in the context of this book, are those constraints associated with the pace of change in China and its scale and heterogeneity. In this section, we speculate on a number of potential constraints to the successful transposal of FSAs from Japan to China. In so doing, we draw attention to the types of challenges that Japanese managers are likely to confront as they seek to further incorporate China into their sphere of operations.

Marketing and distribution

Although Japanese firms have become more international in recent years, research indicates that a large number continue to pursue primarily home country-focused strategies and generate the bulk of their sales in domestic and regional markets (Delios and Beamish 2005, Collinson and Rugman 2008). While Japanese manufacturers remain undisputed market leaders, in terms of both total and per capita retail sales, across a large number of industrial sectors in the Asia-Pacific region, economic downturn and deflationary pressures in Japan have led to sluggish domestic consumer spending in recent years, especially between 1999–2003 (The Economist 2007a). Falling birth rates and an ageing population are likely to further limit future growth in domestic consumer demand, while domestic competition levels are rising due to greater market penetration by foreign firms (Yoshikawa *et al.* 2006). Greater pressure is therefore being exerted on Japanese firms to internationalise in order to escape adverse conditions at home and to reduce dependency on home markets. A trend toward greater internationalisation is revealed in a recent survey of Japanese MNEs (JBIC 2007), which found that that two key indicators, the ratio of foreign to total production and the ratio of foreign to total sales, were forecast by respondents to rise between 2006–2007 (on average, from 30.5% and 33.2% to 31.6% and 34.6%, respectively) across most industrial sectors, especially in automobiles and general machinery. However, in order to expand existing market positions and establish new markets, especially in developing Asia, significant adjustments to the way that Japanese firms have traditionally devised and implemented their marketing strategy are likely to be needed (JETRO 2007b).

Japanese corporations, especially automobile and consumer goods manufacturers, have long been regarded as 'marketing champions'. Much of their competitive strength has derived from their ability to undertake customer-led new product development (Katahira 1998, Horn 2005) and to manufacture heavily branded, high value-added and technology intensive goods with effective design and performance qualities, using strong organisational knowledge creation capabilities (Nonaka and Takeuchi 1995, Fujimoto and Yasumoto 2005). For these reasons, Japanese firms have generally targeted high-income segments of developing country markets. However, it is the number and purchasing power of middle-income consumers that have risen rapidly across many developing countries in parallel with economic growth. To illustrate, the World Bank (2007) calculates that 56% of individuals that constitute the 'global middle class' (defined as households with annual income thresholds approximately equal to US$4000 and US$17000 in 2000 terms) now reside in developing countries, and that this figure will rise to 92% by 2030 on current projections (a growth rate that exceeds global population growth). The contribution of China to this global middle class is currently predicted to rise from 56 million people in 2000 to 361 million by 2030, with income levels becoming increasingly diffused within this group (World Bank 2007). If these projections are realised, it is probable that Chinese middle income consumers will increasingly take centre stage in the regional marketing strategies of MNEs, and that China will soon be viewed less as 'the workshop of the world' and more as 'the world's shop'. Such a trend may also see East Asian consumers increasingly shaping the marketing activities of MNEs, with the influence of industrialised country consumers becoming reduced over time (World Bank 2007). Numerous discussions about the rise of consumerism now gripping Chinese metropolises provide further evidence for this growing trend (Horn and Horn 2007).

Given their strong market-orientation and cultural heritage, Japanese firms are well placed to exploit the expanding and increasingly accessible mass consumer market in China, and many will be able to market products and services to a much larger audience in an extended 'home region' over the next two decades than they do today. However, the challenge – especially for latecomer firms and those that are relatively inexperienced at operating in emerging markets – will be to develop business models, brand strategies and competencies that are viable in this context, and that are appropriately sensitive to the demands of low and middle-income as well as high-income consumers, particularly those at the lower end of the income spectrum (in other words, to 'market to the poor') (Wright *et al.* 2005). A further challenge relates to the rate at which consumption patterns are evolving within China's expanding middle class. Although brand awareness and both individualistic and nationalistic purchasing behaviour are on the rise, this is taking place primarily in the more economically advanced regions of China, especially in the coastal provinces. The question is the degree to which the marketing strategies of Japanese firms need to take account of such nuances in order to be successful in China.

A further important dimension to be considered is geography. In the early 1980s, the pattern of Japanese FDI to China mimicked that of the early twentieth century in that it was concentrated mainly in Shanghai and the northern provinces, notably Dalian (the closest Chinese city to Japan) in Laioning Province. During the 1990s, Japanese FDI became distributed more widely but in terms of affiliate numbers the coastal regions still dominated, especially the Yangtze River Delta (Shanghai, Jiangsu and Zhejiang), which was host to around 40% of Japanese affiliates in China at the end of the 1990s, and the Bohai Bay region (Beijing, Tianjin, Hubei, Shandong and Liaoning) which was host to around 31% (Zhou *et al.* 2002, Yin and Choi 2005, Cassidy and Andreosso-O'Callaghan 2006). Less than 10% of Japanese FDI was located in the inland provinces. Wakasugi (2005) demonstrates the role of industry effects in this distribution, with electric machinery and electronics firms concentrated in Shanghai and Guangdong (in southern China); general machinery, chemicals and textiles firms in Shanghai and Jiangsu; transportation equipment firms in Sichuan and Tianjin; and food processing firms in Shandong. A number of studies show that this investment pattern was influenced by several locational advantages associated with these regions, relative to the rest of China. These sub-national locational advantages include: (i) the preponderance of OCCs and Economic and Technology Development Zones (ETDZs); (ii) higher levels of economic development; (iii) superior infrastructure; (iv) proximity to Japan (which facilitated intra-firm trade, especially for smaller, export-oriented Japanese firms); (v) superior human capital stocks; (vi) shared preferences for certain amenities (such as schools) and living standards; and (vii) agglomeration advantages (Belderbos and Carree 2002, Zhou *et al.* 2002, Fung *et al.* 2003, Wakasugi 2005, Cassidy and Andreosso-O'Callaghan 2006, Cheng 2006, 2007). Much of the spatial concentration of Japanese FDI in China is therefore explicable by a strong path dependency effect, with subsequent investment projects tending to follow prior investment by early entrants from the same industry or industrial group (typically the core firm of keiretsu networks). The benefits of agglomeration include greater opportunities for information sharing with early investors (important in regulatory settings that lack transparency), the fostering of close buyer-supplier arrangements, and the exploitation of technology and labour-related spillovers associated with prior investment (Belderbos and Carree 2002, Wakasugi 2005). Moreover, as Cheng (2007) reports, Japanese FDI has historically tended to avoid high concentrations of Chinese state-owned enterprises, because of low efficiency, bureaucratic management and corruption associated with these types of firms. However, the two main agglomerative regions, the Yangtze River Delta and Bohai Bay, together only account for around a quarter of the population of China. If Japanese firms are to exploit sub-national markets beyond traditional investment locations, it is likely that they will need to establish or extend their distribution and marketing operations into places with little or no prior Japanese investments (where experience effects and positive agglomeration externalities may therefore be much less in evidence); where state firms still dominate important aspects of the local economy, and where the general economic and business environment is generally less attractive (Cassidy and Andreosso-O'Callaghan 2006, Cheng 2007). It is important for research to understand how far Japanese firms are now expanding their operations in China beyond traditional business clusters, and, when they do, whether this process is accompanied by the development of new capabilities and competencies. Such research also needs to establish whether variations exist depending on, for example, the size, industry, strategic orientation (market-seeking or export-oriented) and network membership of firms (Belderbos and Carree 2002).

Inter-corporate networks

It is generally regarded that knowledge-creating interfirm networks, together with strong product and process innovation capability, have been fundamental to the success of Japanese firms, especially during the technological catch-up period of the post-war era (Ito 1993, Aoki 1994, Tejima 2000, Haak 2003). It is argued that the keiretsu structure – a backbone of Japanese industry – facilitated a fast and flexible reaction to demand fluctuations, while close supplier-assembler relations within this structure allowed for the efficient co-development of specialised components and intermediate products (Belderbos and Carree 2002). According to some, the poor recent performance of many Japanese firms indicates that the immanent logic of the keiretsu structure has come to an end (see Yoshikawa *et al.* 2006). A number of reasons for this poor performance have been given. One is the inherent absence of both shareholder activism and a market for corporate control. This is argued to have exerted a powerful inertial force for organisational change and has given rise to a somewhat 'isolationist', inward-looking perspective (manifested in a strong domestic market orientation) and a corporate mindset that prioritises growth over profit. A second concerns the tight links between network members, which have engendered dynamic inefficiencies and rigidities, and have prevented opportunities for cost reductions through standardisation and modularisation from being exploited fully. The latter point is illustrated by manufacturing labour productivity in Japan, which is reported to be 60% lower in Japanese-owned plants than in foreign-owned ones (The Economist 2007a). The thrust of these arguments is that the keiretsu structure has obstructed the ability of Japanese firms to tap the potentials of internationalisation (Katz 1998, Waldenberger 1999).

In order to address their competitive disadvantages, many Japanese firms are now reconfiguring organisational structures and implementing changes across a broad range of corporate functions (Park *et al.* 1999, Yoshikawa *et al.* 2006). It is difficult to generalise about the nature of the transformation of keiretsu structures because inter-firm relationships can be hard to discern and define, and often fluctuate considerably in strength over time. There is also much variation in the changes underway among individual firms. In the automobile industry, for example, firms such as Nissan are actively decentralising supplier networks away from established vertical keiretsu relationships in Japan to low cost manufacturing locations in Asia (which, in some instances, is accompanied by the divestment of group member firms). Other firms, such as Toyota, seem to be tightening established supplier links. Nonetheless, it is clear that China continues to offer the potential for further cost reductions for Japanese firms, especially in relation to labour and efficiency improvements, through the off-shoring of production of parts of the value chain to affiliates and independent firms. This option adds a further dimension to the reconfiguration of traditional keiretsu structures. As discussed before, historically off-shoring has tended to occur in agglomerations in China. But now a key driver is proximity between assemblers and suppliers, because this promotes the use of familiar J-system production methods such as just-in-time delivery, closely co-ordinated inventory control systems and product co-development, all of which are important sources of competitive advantage for Japanese firms (Belderbos and Carree 2002). Indeed, it has been argued that, by following leading firms, some Japanese firms that otherwise lacked competitiveness were only able to internationalise successfully because of the support of Japanese buyer networks in host countries (Delios and Beamish 2005). In other words, close buyer-supplier linkages in keiretsu networks mean that the FSAs of Japanese MNEs are often regionally-bound.

Although productivity levels are improving in the traditional sites for Japanese manufacturing in China, so too are labour costs (Beamish and Jiang 2002). Consequently, firms looking to offshore production to China are likely to come under increased pressure to locate activities to the interior regions, where labour costs are relatively lower. However, as discussed before, there are likely to be fewer agglomeration advantages in such locations until a critical mass of Japanese activity has been achieved. Moving production to the interior is also likely to raise transportation costs, both for intermediate products destined for final assembly in Japan and for the sale of final products to Japan and other international markets. Delivery times for certain types of goods may also become extended, which could become an issue for production processes or market-servicing strategies that are time sensitive. The decision to relocate production to China's interior therefore requires careful cost-benefit analysis vis-à-vis alternate location options in Asia.

An alternative approach for Japanese firms to exploit China's cost advantages is to outsource production to Chinese suppliers. However, those firm-specific advantages of Japanese MNEs that are associated with long-term, inter-firm relationships built on mutual trust and cooperation may become diluted when they are replaced by short-term outsourcing contracts with Chinese suppliers. Outsourcing arrangements raise transactions costs (Tejima 2000) and necessitate careful consideration of issues such as how best to protect intellectual property, knowledge and other types of proprietary assets, the types of quality control measures to be implemented, and how sub-contracting arrangements should be monitored to mitigate opportunism, amongst other things. Numerous recent press articles highlight some of the risks associated with relocating manufacturing to China using sub-contracting arrangements (e.g. *The Economist* 2007b, 2007c). These include the extent of counterfeiting and leakage of proprietary knowledge (which can become exacerbated when sub-contractors manufacture for a number of brand-owners), quality control problems and the problems of monitoring plants that sub-contract production themselves. A further risk factor to be considered relates to the position of China in world exports. It is possible that concerns surrounding trade imbalances between China and the leading industrialised countries may lead to protectionist measures and trade disputes which could ensnare Japanese-owned production in China and reduce its attractiveness as a production location relative to other countries (Yoshida and Ito 2006). Of course, these risks are not unique to Japanese investors and can be mitigated by a production strategy that incorporates other low cost manufacturing countries. Nonetheless, Japanese companies looking to expand production in China may be required to develop fresh competencies and capabilities that are not needed when working within familiar long-term supplier-assembler relationships. Decisions about, for example, which aspects of the value chain to transpose to China and which to retain elsewhere, how to maintain adequate control of proprietary assets and knowledge, and how to deal effectively with internalised and independent local suppliers are likely to become critical elements of a successful off-shoring strategy in China. Although many Japanese companies have successfully sourced from China, the recent recall of over 10 million lithium-ion batteries manufactured by Sony China (which led directly to losses estimated at US$429 million by the parent company in 2006, not to mention the damage done to the company's brand and image as a mainstay of consumer technology), provide some indication of the types of problems a company can experience when off-shoring manufacturing to China.

From these discussions, it can be seen that the challenge for research is to raise understanding of how the changing position of China as a manufacturing location is shaping the transformation of inter-corporate networks, global production networks and the internal management systems of Japanese MNEs.

Human resource management

Literature asserts that Japanese firms traditionally have had problems in adapting their employment practices to foreign markets (see Legewie 2002). Some authors argue (e.g Zhu and Warner 2000) that there are sufficient similarities between Japan's model of employment relations and the industrial and labour system of China (the development of which was influenced greatly by Japan in the last century), to suggest that Japanese firms may find it relatively easier to transpose management systems to their operations in China than to Western countries, for example. These similarities relate to the historic emphasis in both countries on secure employment, seniority, team work, common goals and targets, and loyalty and commitment to the company. However, the labour system is now in a considerable state of flux in both countries and for this reason the problems of localising employment practices in China may be magnified for Japanese companies.

In Japan, the leitmotif of long-term, stable employment and associated HRM practices (such as promotion by seniority, on-the-job training, job rotation systems, mentoring and so forth) and mutual trust between unions and management, for example, have long been regarded as important sources of location-bound FSAs for Japanese firms (Collinson and Rugman 2008). Such practices allow for the generation and promotion of consensus-based decision-taking, cross-functional capabilities, long-term relations and collaborative learning with key suppliers and customers, not to mention high levels of loyalty and obligation towards the organisation through social rather than financial contracts. Much of this is contingent on wider social and cultural influences in Japan, where commitment and obligation have long been seen as implicit components of the employment contract (Abegglen 1958). However, even though there is little radical change (such as mass lay-offs), the organisation and structure of the Japanese labour market have altered dramatically over the past decade (Holzhausen 1998): the role of internal labour markets has been slowly reduced, life-time employment is being eroded, and more flexible approaches to employment are being adopted, such as the use of part-time workers and short or fixed term employment contracts, especially for highly skilled workers.

In China, a homogenous employment system has yet to emerge. Instead we see what Zhu and Warner (2000) refer to as a tripartite system, in which vestiges of (i) a traditional industrial relations system (characterised by long-term employment, integration of management with political networks, flat reward structures, limited labour turnover, strong unionisation, and attractive welfare packages within state and collectively-owned enterprises) co-exists with (ii) an internationally-oriented (Anglo Saxon-type) HRM system (characterised by more market-driven imperatives, independent management, labour contracts, greater job mobility, performance and skills-related remuneration, and limited unionisation) and (iii) a transitional model between the old and the new forms.

Within this milieu, the design of appropriate HRM policies that suit local conditions is likely to become an increasingly important success factor for Japanese MNEs in China (Beamish and Jiang 2002). As Japanese firms strive to integrate cross-border regional networks in which China plays an increasing role, how far management practices such as strict quality control systems, flexible production runs, continuous improvements in production methods and so forth (all key elements of the success of the Japanese management system) are replicated in China will be a key issue for Japanese managers. Although a number of these methods have been practised in locally-owned firms and FIEs, several studies point to the difficulty in transposing such practices to China (Zhu and Warner 2000) or question the need to do so (Taylor 1999). One important additional dimension concerns the role of expatriates. Beamish and Inkpen (1998), for example, found that better performance of Japanese affiliates worldwide is associated with fewer expatriate employees, while Beamish and Jiang (2002) report a similar relation for Japanese affiliates in China. The use of expatriates adds to the cost of operations and reduces opportunities for tapping local knowledge and relationship-building, both of which are important in emerging market settings that are characterised by volatile policy and regulatory conditions (Isobe *et al.* 2000, Delios and Henisz 2003, Wright *et al.* 2005). At the same time, it is clear that labour markets in the more economically advanced regions of China present a number of difficulties to foreign firms in general, not least in relation to acute skills shortages, high staff turnover rates and low levels of employee loyalty (Malila 2007). Despite their high profile and strong reputation, many of these problems are magnified for Japanese investors. On the one hand, labour shortages and rising labour costs at home puts pressure on Japanese firm to localise the workforce as much as possible in China; while on the other, intense competition for skilled Chinese labour and the fact that Japanese employers are often seen as hierarchical and autocratic by Chinese workers can make staff recruitment and retention problematic. The challenge for research is to better understand the relationship between immanent changes to Chinese (and Japanese) labour markets and adjustments to familiar employment practices implemented in the Chinese affiliates of Japanese MNEs.

Contributions: contemporary challenges in the reality of East Asian economic integration

In the foregoing discussion, we have sought to establish how China might be acting as a catalyst for change in corporate Japan. However, it is clear that the situations in both China and Japan are complex and volatile, and a conclusive assessment of precisely how China will shape the global corporate activities of Japanese MNEs is not yet possible. With this in mind, we have assembled a number of studies for this book that shed light on various aspects of the core themes we identify above. Care was taken to prioritise studies that are informed by field-based case-study work (since this methodological approach is particularly good at generating meaningful insights in rapidly evolving research settings) and those with particular practitioner relevance.

The contribution by Peter Buckley sheds a comparative light on how Japanese management styles have evolved since his early work on the subject in the 1980s. It explores how the challenges of internationalisation are being addressed by Japanese firms today. Buckley describes how Japanese firms are now taking a lead role in the development of 'global factories' and elaborates on the difficulties associated with managing a geographically dispersed value chain. The main thrust of his argument is that, while Japanese firms are becoming more flexible in adapting to the volatilities of international business and are about to re-emerge as serious competitors in world markets, institutional and cultural factors mean that many remain distinctive from their Western counterparts in several important respects.

The study by Andrew Delios, Paul Beamish and Zhao Xue Juan examines Japanese investment strategies in China from an historical perspective. In their analysis of changes to the economic and regulatory framework of China, they reveal diverging investment patterns at a sub-national level and a regional 'bunching' in the destination of industry-specific investments at a national level. They argue that Japanese firms indeed exhibit a high degree of flexibility and are able to 'fine-slice' and fine-tune their activities to suit sub-national conditions in China. Their analysis is used to suggest how several international business research streams might be informed by greater understanding of the way that Japanese firms approach their activities in China.

Tim Goydke's comparative analysis of the privatisation process of Deutsche Post and Japan Post advances understanding of the transformation and overseas expansion processes of services MNEs. His examination of the internationalisation of these two logistical services providers illustrates the surge in the international activities of Japanese service firms, many of which are now targeting Asian growth markets – and especially China. While many similarities are identified between the privatisations of Japan Post and Deutsche Post, marked differences are found as well. In particular, Japan Post is shown to have adopted what might be described as a traditional 'introverted service supply' approach to internationalisation by following its Japanese customers to overseas markets.

In her study, Faith Hatani questions the relevance of aspects of conventional wisdom concerning the behaviour of Japanese conglomerate manufacturers when transplanting production networks to China. Using an in-depth, longitudinal analysis of the Chinese activities of the Toyota Group, she describes a network-based market entry strategy and highlights a number of challenges associated with translocation of Japanese organisational structures to emerging markets like China. In what she coins 'pre-clusterization', Hatani opens a new chapter on research on Japanese keiretsu through her analysis of Toyota's ability to coordinate a foreign market entry process in which supplier firms become first-movers prior to the full entry of the core firm. This is shown to be a response to, and a consequence of, incremental regulatory reform in China.

One of the most visible features of China's economic development is the advent of consumerism. Much recent Japanese investment in China is a consequence of the development of a large consumer market, where rising disposable incomes translate into growing demand for high quality consumer goods. In his study of innovation diffusion in China, Sierk Horn argues that Japanese firms are responding by adopting a more stringent market orientation in recent years. His study explores how Japanese firms are now tailoring their activities in reaction to an openness to, and rejection of, the influx of foreign brands to China.

The Japanese mobile telephony market is one of the most advanced in the world and in many respects serves as a trendsetter for other markets. At the same time, China has become the world's largest market for mobile phone diffusion. In his study of Japanese handset manufacturers, Tomoo Marukawa looks at the lessons that can be learned from the failure of Japanese manufacturers to secure market positions in China, in what would appear to be an optimum complementation of core competence and market scope. By contrasting the performances of Japanese manufacturers at home and in China, he shows how difficult it can be for Japanese manufacturers to transfer to emerging markets those business models and strategies that were designed primarily to meet demand conditions and the technology requirements of the home market.

The study by Joerg Felfe and W.H. Yan investigates key issues concerning HRM practice in China by foreign companies. The authors point to the Chinese labour environment being in a state of flux, with gratification, training and promotion serving as key change agents. In this milieu, motivational aspects of workgroup commitment in China are examined, particularly in relation to absenteeism and turnover intention. By comparing the influence of different types of work commitment in different cultural contexts (notably within the collectivism versus individualism paradigm), the study contributes to both an empirical and practical understanding of how commitment to the workgroup in China can be improved for the benefit of the organisation as a whole.

The localisation of HRM practices is often key to operating successfully in China. Hiroshi Itagaki sheds light on how Japanese firms implement recruitment and promotion policies in an environment where competition for talented personnel is high. He asserts that work-style and HRM practices differ greatly from Western models and underpin much of the competitiveness of Japanese firms. Cultural adhesiveness means that these idiosyncrasies are often not easily transferable abroad. HRM practices in three Chinese affiliates of Japanese MNEs are analysed and a number of recommendations for the recruitment and retention of 'key employees' are derived that may help Japanese firms to preserve aspects of human capital-related FSAs when operating in China.

In the concluding contribution we show how each one of these studies informs our understanding of the relationship between engagement with China and the transformation of corporate Japan in the broader context of the literature on industrialised country MNEs and emerging markets. In addition to the three themes identified *a priori* here, we discern two further common threads that run through each of the studies, which we discuss under the headings of 'corporate transformation' and 'institutional change'. We consider how the contributions both challenge and confirm aspects of conventional wisdom concerning Japanese MNEs and suggest further avenues for research on issues and developments concerning microeconomic dynamics in Sino-Japanese business relations.

Conclusions

Once much vaunted and acclaimed in academic and business circles, scholarly interest in the Japanese management system (or 'J-system') has diminished in recent times, not least because of the longest recession that Japan has experienced in its post-war economic history (with the 1990s commonly dubbed as the 'Lost Decade') and the concomitant prevalence of acquisitions, mass dismissals and lacklustre performances across much of corporate Japan. In response, traditionally-employed systems, business models and processes are now being transformed across a broad range of functional areas. Arguably, this has given rise to certain misconceptions, oversimplifications and misunderstandings about the realities of Japanese management as it is practiced today, especially in Western literature. We contend that it is therefore important for researchers to now question conventional wisdom concerning contemporary Japanese management practices.

With this in mind, our overarching objective in this introduction has been to draw particular attention to one dimension of 'J-system' reform that has been under-explored in prior international business literature, namely the extent to which Japanese firms are adjusting their business models and *modus operandi* to address the opportunities presented by large emerging markets such as China, and how. In particular, we have sought to establish in a more substantive way than hitherto achieved the theoretical relationship between greater engagement with the Chinese economy by Japanese firms and the on-going transformation of Japanese management practice. Arguably, the assumption that the rise of the Chinese economy as a dominant force in East Asia, combined with the decline of the world's second largest economy and Sino-Japanese complementarity of economic development, automatically equates to strong economic interdependence is short-sighted. Although geographic proximity means that Japanese firms will be important players in emergent East Asian markets, including China, this proximity does not necessarily translate into a sufficient understanding of local business conditions and the appropriateness of 'naturally held' firm specific advantages among Japanese MNEs. Nonetheless, Japanese firms have historically demonstrated an ability to adapt to adverse and changing business conditions. Thus, the resourcefulness of Japanese MNEs in China should not be under-estimated and needs careful analysis. Each of the studies included in this book sheds light on a number of key dimensions of Japanese corporate change and explores how the traditional 'J-system' is evolving vis-à-vis the extension of operations to China. In our concluding chapter, we further elaborate on the central themes identified above, and discuss the implications that arise for future research on the transformation of corporate Japan.

Acknowledgements

This book comprises a selection of studies presented at the workshop, *Cross-cultural management practices in East Asia: lessons for Japanese MNEs* held at the University of Leeds on 26 – 27 January 2007. The editors would like to thank the following organisations and individuals who helped to make the workshop such a success: Prof. Sung-Jo Park (Professor Emeritus, Freie Universität Berlin), the staff of the Embassy of Japan in the UK, especially Masato Takaoka (Minister for Economic Affairs) for his perceptive keynote speech; the British Academy, the Leeds Humanities Research Institute and the White Rose East Asia Centre (a collaboration between the Universities of Leeds and Sheffield, UK) for their generous financial assistance; and staff and doctoral students of Leeds University Business School, the Centre for International Business (CIBUL) and the Department of East Asian Studies, all at the University of Leeds, for their support of the event. We are also grateful to the conference attendees whose enthusiasm and insight helped spark suchstimulating debate, and especially Markus Thinnes (Technotrans East Asia), Miles Dodd (Asian Expertise), and Bill Reed (managing consultant on East Asian business), who shared their experiences in practitioner-focused sessions. We also wish to thank Sung-Jo Park, Tetsu Abo, John Cassidy, Keith Glaister, Frank McDonald, Masahiro Miyagawa, Vikki Hanlon and Natalie White (Taylor & Francis) and Chris Rowley and Malcolm Warner (editors of *Asia Pacific Business Review*), who each contributed to this special issue in various ways. Finally, Helen Ashworth, who provided administrative and operational support, is due special thanks.

Note

1. Based on MOFCOM FDI statistics. We note that data for Hong Kong include an indeterminate amount of investments routed through Hong Kong-based subsidiaries by parent companies whose ultimate ownership lies in other countries, including Japan.

References

Abegglen, J., 1958. *The Japanese factory: aspects of its social organization.* Salem, NH: Ayer Co.

Abegglen, J.C. and Stalk, G., 1985. *Kaisha, the Japanese corporation.* New York: Basic Books.

Abo, T., ed., 1994. *Hybrid factory: the Japanese production system in the United States.* New York: Oxford University Press.

Aoki, M., 1984. Aspects of the Japanese firm. *In*: M. Aoki, ed. *The economic analysis of the Japanese firm.* Dordrecht: North Holland.

Aoki, M., 1990. Towards an economic model of the Japanese firm. *Journal of economic literature*, 28 (1), 1–27.
Aoki, M., 1994. The Japanese firm as a system of attributes: a survey and research agenda. *In*: M. Aoki and R. Dore, eds. *The Japanese firm: the sources of competitive strength*. Oxford: Oxford University Press.
Beamish, P.W. and Inkpen, A., 1998. Japanese firms and the decline of the Japanese expatriate. *Journal of world business*, 33 (1), 35–50.
Beamish, P.W. and Jiang, R., 2002. Investing profitably in China: is it getting harder? *Long range planning*, 35 (2), 135–151.
Belderbos, R. and Carree, M., 2002. The location of Japanese investments in China: agglomeration effects, keiretsu, and firm heterogeneity. *Journal of the Japanese and international economies*, 16 (2), 194–211.
Buckley, P.J., 2004. The role of China in the global strategy of multinational enterprises. *Journal of Chinese economic and business studies*, 2 (1), 1–25.
Buckley, P.J. and Meng, C., 2005. The strategy of foreign-invested manufacturing enterprises in China: export-oriented and market-orientated revisited. *Journal of Chinese economic and business studies*, 3 (2), 111–131.
Buckley, P.J. and Mirza, H., 1985. The wit and wisdom of Japanese management: an iconoclastic analysis. *Management international review*, 25 (3), 16–32.
Buckley, P.J. *et al.*, 2005. China's inward foreign direct investment success: Southeast Asia in the shadow of the dragon. *Multinational business review*, 13 (1), 3–30.
Cassidy, J.F. and Andreosso-O'Callaghan, B., 2006. Spatial determinants of Japanese FDI in China. *Japan and the world economy*, 18 (4), 512–527.
Chen, M., 2004. *Asian management systems*. 2nd ed. London: Thomson Learning.
Cheng, S., 2006. The role of labour costs in the location choices of Japanese investors in China. *Papers in regional science*, 85 (1), 121–138.
Cheng, S., 2007. Structure of firm location choices: an examination of Japanese greenfield investment in China. *Asian economic journal*, 21 (1), 47–73.
Collinson, S. and Rugman, A.M., 2008. The regional nature of Japanese multinational business. *Journal of international business studies*, 39 (2), 215–230.
Delios, A. and Beamish, P.W., 2005. Regional and global strategies of Japanese firms. *Management international review*, 45 (Special Issue 2005/1), 19–36.
Delios, A. and Henisz, W.J., 2003. Policy uncertainty and the sequence of entry by Japanese firms 1980–1998. *Journal of international business studies*, 34 (3), 227–241.
Farrell, R., Gaston, N., and Sturm, J.-E., 2004. Determinants of Japan's foreign direct investment: an industry and country panel study, 1984–1998. *Journal of Japanese international economies*, 18 (2), 161–182.
Fujimoto, T. and Yasumoto, M., 2005. *Seikô suru seihin kaihatsu [Successful product development]*. Tokyo: Yuhikaku.
Fung, K.C., Iizaka, H., and Siu, A., 2003. Japanese direct investment in China. *China economic review*, 14 (3), 304–315.
Gurtov, M., 2008. Reconciling Japan and China. *Japan focus*. Available from: http://japanfocus.org/products/topdf/2627 [Accessed 15 February 2008].
Haak, R., 2003. Die japanische Unternehmung als lernende Organisation [The Japanese firm as learning organisation]. *In*: W. Dorow and H. Groenewald, eds. *Personalwirtschaftlicher Wandel in Japan [Changes in Japanese human resource management]*. Wiesbaden: Gabler, 133–155.
Haak, R. and Hilpert, H.G., 2003. *Focus China: the new challenge for Japanese management*. Munich: Iudicium Verlag.
Herd, R. and Dougherty, S., 2005. *China's economy: a remarkable transformation*. OECD Observer, 251, September, pp. 13–16.
Holzhausen, A., 1998. *Das japanische Beschäftigungssystem in der Krise [The Japanese employment system in crisis]*. Wiesbaden: Gabler.
Horn, S.A., 2005. *Interkulturelle Kompetenz im Zugang zu japanischen Maerkten [Intercultural competence in accessing Japanese markets]*. Wiesbaden: Deutscher Universitäts-Verlag.
Horn, S.A. and Horn, K., 2007. Retailing and consumption in China. *In*: M. Jovanovic *et al.* eds. *System transformation in comparative perspective*. Berlin: LIT Verlag, 333–363.

Huang, Y., 2003. One country, two systems: foreign-invested enterprises and domestic firms in China. *China economic review*, 14 (4), 404–416.
Isobe, T., Makino, S., and Montgomery, D.B., 2000. Resource commitment, entry timing and market performance of foreign direct investments in emerging economies: the case of Japanese international joint ventures in China. *The academy of management journal*, 43 (3), 468–484.
Ito, T., 1993. *The Japanese economy*. Cambridge, MA: MIT Press.
Jackson, G. and Miyajima, H., 2007. Introduction: the diversity and change of corporate governance in Japan. *In*: M. Aoki, G. Jackson, and H. Miyajima, eds. *Corporate governance in Japan: institutional change and organizational diversity*. Oxford: Oxford University Press, 1–47.
Japan Bank for International Cooperation, 2007. Survey report on overseas business operations by Japanese manufacturing companies: results of JBIC survey: outlook for foreign direct investment, 19th annual survey. Tokyo: Japan Bank for International Cooperation, November.
Japan External Trade Organisation, 2007a. *Japanese trade and investment statistics*. Available from: http://www.jetro.go.jp/en/stats/statistics/ [Accessed 4 January 2008].
Japan External Trade Organisation, 2007b. *White paper on international trade and foreign direct investment: increasing utilization of Asian FTAs and growth strategies for Japanese companies*. Tokyo: Japan External Trade Organisation.
Japan Ministry of Finance, 2007. *Trade statistics of Japan*. Available from: http://www.customs.go.jp/toukei/info/index_e.htm [Accessed 27 February 2008].
JBIC, *See* Japan Bank for International Cooperation.
JETRO, *See* Japan External Trade Organisation.
Katahira, H., 1998. *Pawâ burando no honhitsu [The essence of power brands]*. Tokyo: Daiyamondosha.
Katz, R., 1998. *Japan. The system that soured: the rise and fall of the Japanese economic miracle*. New York: M.E. Sharpe.
Kishi, M., 2003. Foreign direct investment by Japanese firms and corporate governance: in relation to the monetary policies of China, Korea and Japan. *Journal of Asian economics*, 13, 731–748.
Kiyota, K. and Urata, S., 2007. The role of multinational firms in international trade: the case of Japan. *Japan and the world economy*, Working paper 560, Research seminar in international economics, University of Michigan. Available from: http://ideas.repec.org/d/fbyokjp.html [Accessed 20 January 2008].
Legewie, J., 2002. Control and co-ordination of Japanese subsidiaries in China: problems of an expatriate-based management system. *International journal of human resource management*, 13 (6), 909–919.
Ma, X., and Delios, A., 2007. A new tale of two cities: Japanese FDIs in Shanghai and Beijing, 1979–2003. *International business review*, 16 (2), 207–228.
Makino, S., Beamish, P.W., and Zhao, N.B., 2004. The characteristics and performance of Japanese FDI in less developed and developed countries. *Journal of world business*, 39, 377–392.
Malila, J., 2007. The great look forward: China's HR evolution. *China business review*, July–August. Available from: http://www.chinabusinessreview.com/public/0707/malila.html [Accessed 1 March 2007].
Meyer, K.E. and Nguyen, H.V., 2005. Foreign investment strategies and sub-national institutions in emerging markets: evidence from Vietnam. *Journal of management studies*, 42 (1), 63–93.
Mizoguchi, T., 1989. The changing pattern of Sino-Japanese trade, 1884–1937. *In*: P. Duus, R.H. Myers, and M.R. Peattie, eds. *The Japanese informal empire in China, 1895–1937*. Princeton: Princeton University Press, 10–30.
MOFCOM, 2006. *Statistics of FDI to China: 2006*. Beijing: Ministry of Commerce.
Nonaka, I. and Takeuchi, H., 1995. *The knowledge-creating company: how Japanese companies create the dynamics of innovation*. Oxford: Oxford University Press.
North, D.C., 1990. *Institutions, institutional change and economic performance*. Cambridge: Cambridge University Press.
Ôba, O., 2000. Sino-Japanese relations in the Edo period, trans. J.A. Fogel. *Sino-Japanese studies*, 13 (1), 34–53.
OECD, *See* Organization for Economic Cooperation and Development.
Office of the United States Trade Representative, 2001. *Background information on China's accession to the World Trade Organization*. Available from: http://www.ustr.gov/Document_Library/Fact_Sheets/2001/Background_Information_on_China's_Accession_to_the_World_Trade_Organization_printer.html [Accessed 2 February 2008].

Organization for Economic Cooperation and Development, 2006. *OECD Investment policy reviews: China- Open policies towards mergers and acquisitions*. Paris: OECD.

Pak, Y.S. and Park, Y.-R., 2005. Characteristics of Japanese FDI in the East and the West: understanding the strategic motives of Japanese investment. *Journal of world business*, 40 (3), 254–266.

Park, S.-J. *et al.*, 1999. *Keiretsu am Ende? Die Neuordnung der Zulieferbeziehungen in der japanischen Automobilindustrie [The end of keiretsu? Reorganisation of supply chains in the Japanese automotive industry]*. Hagen: ISL-Verlag.

Siddharthan, N.S. and Lakhera, M.L., 2005. Foreign direct investment and location advantages: Japanese perceptions of India compared to China and ASEAN. *Journal of international and area studies*, 12 (1), 99–110.

Taniguchi, T., 2005. A cold peace: the changing security equation in Northeast Asia. *Orbis*, 49 (3), 445–457.

Taylor, B., 1999. Japanese manufacturing style in China? Production practices in Japanese manufacturing plants. *New technology, work and employment*, 14 (2), 129–142.

Tejima, S., 2000. Japanese FDI, the implications of 'hollowing out' on the technological development of host countries. *International business review*, 9, 555–570.

The Economist, 2007a. Gaijin at the gates. *The Economist*, 18 April, pp. 53–54.

The Economist, 2007b. China's toxic toymaker. *The Economist*, 18 April, pp. 57–58.

The Economist, 2007c. Counterfeit goods in China: Mind games. *The Economist*, 10 November, p. 102a.

Tomiura, E., 2005. Technological capability and FDI in Asia: firm-level relationships among Japanese manufacturers. *Asian economic journal*, 19 (3), 273–289.

UNCTAD, *See* United Nations Conference on Trade and Development.

United Nations Conference on Trade and Development, 2007. *World investment report: transnational corporations, extractive industries and development*. New York and Geneva: UNCTAD.

USTR, 2003. *Report to Congress on China's WTO compliance*, 11th December. Washington: Office of the United States Trade Representative.

Wakasugi, R., 2005. The effects of Chinese regional conditions on the location choices of Japanese affiliates. *The Japanese economic review*, 56 (4), 390–407.

Waldenberger, F., 1999. *Organisation und Evolution arbeitsteiliger Systeme [Organisation and evolution of labour systems]*. München: Iudicium-Verlag.

World Bank, 2007. *Global economic prospects: managing the next wave of globalization*. International Bank for Reconstruction and Development. Washington: The World Bank.

Wright, M. *et al.*, 2005. Strategy research in emerging markets: challenging the conventional wisdom. *Journal of management studies*, 42 (1), 1–33.

Xing, Y., 2004. Japanese FDI in China: trend, structure and the role of exchange rates. *In*: K.H. Zhang, ed. *China as a world workshop*. Armonk, NY: M.E. Sharp.

Xing, Y., 2006. Why is China so attractive for FDI: the role of exchange rates. *China economic review*, 17, 198–209.

Yin, E. and Choi, C.J., 2005. The globalization myth: the case of China. *Management international review*, 45, 103–120.

Yoshida, Y. and Ito, H., 2006. How do the Asian economies compete with Japan in the US market? Is China exceptional? A triangular trade approach. *Asia pacific business review*, 12 (3), 285–307.

Yoshikawa, T. *et al.*, 2006. Financial and product market integration: responses of Japanese firms. *Management international review*, 46 (5), 529–555.

Yoshino, M., 1976. *Japan's multinational enterprises*. Cambridge, MA: Harvard University Press.

Zhou, C., Delios, A., and Yang, J.Y., 2002. Locational determinants of Japanese foreign direct investment in China. *Asia pacific journal of management*, 19 (1), 63–86.

Zhu, Y. and Warner, M., 2000. An emerging model of employment relations in China: a divergent path from the Japanese? *International business review*, 9, 345–361.

The rise of the Japanese multinational enterprise: then and now

P.J. Buckley

Leeds University Business School, Maurice Keyworth Building, Leeds LS2 9JT, UK

Introduction

This examination of Japanese multinational enterprises (MNEs) compares 'then' and 'now'. 'Now' is easily defined – 2008. 'Then' is a concept that tries to pin down the heyday of Japanese firms and therefore of the Japanese economy – or rather the point at which critics and commentators felt that the Japanese economy was at its height. An arbitrary date of 1985 might be used. During the craze for 'Japanese management', Japanese MNEs were felt to hold the answers to many of the key problems of Western economies – harmony (between capital and labour); efficiency in the use of resources; a widely networked economy (Gerlach and Lincoln 2004) based on long-term relationships (Liker *et al.* 1995, Dyer 2000); adaptability of the firm to changing economic locations and of products to local needs and, of course, constant innovation (Aoki 1984, 1990, Imai 1986). 'Now' (2008) looks different. The Japanese economy has an ageing population, rigidities in its domestic structure (very few mergers and acquisitions for instance) and inefficient services, including the vital area of financial services (Hoshi and Kashyap 2004). Japanese management no longer seems the panacea many once thought it to be and Japanese MNEs no longer seem so dominant, even so prevalent and certainly they are less salient.

This study sets out to show that the record of Japanese firms and Japanese management was never so good as it was claimed to be in its heyday, and that Japanese MNEs and their associated management styles are not so irrelevant as they are currently thought to be.

Literature review

Japanese style management and the Japanese economy

In 1985, the author co-wrote a paper on 'The Wit and Wisdom of Japanese Management' that set out to show that too much was being claimed for Japanese management and that no one unified style of management existed in Japanese firms (Buckley and Mirza 1985).

Further, much of the success of Japanese management was due to long-standing factors in the Japanese economy. Overnight success it was not! The then paradigmatic elements of 'Japanese management' were: lifetime employment, the seniority system and the enterprise union (Chen 2004). This was to conveniently ignore the fact that these elements applied only in a small subset of the Japanese economy. Non-core employees were not subject to these elements and there were key deficiencies in the management of intellectual property and in innovation. *The Economist* reports that although Japan:

> spends far above the OECD average on research and development (R&D) as a share of GDP, this money is not always put to good use. The Science Council of Japan estimates that Japan's R&D is only about half as efficient as Europe's and America's. Entrepreneurial start-ups account for only around 4 percent of firms in Japan, compared with 10 percent in Europe and over 14 percent in America, and Japan comes bottom in several rankings of entrepreneurship. (*The Economist* 2007, p. 3)

The Japanese economy

Then (in the 1980s) Japanese firms enjoyed high growth and market share, had high bank borrowing levels and achieved high levels of investments (the capital efficiency of this was largely ignored) (Abegglen and Stalk 1985, Imai 1986). Following high asset inflation and the subsequent bursting of the bubble, direct financing through bonds and equity is replacing bank financing, there is a focus on cash flow and the redesign of the Kaisha (Japanese corporations) is underway (Abegglen 2006).

However, there is continuity. Despite the increasing attention to corporate governance in Japan, Japanese firms still do not give excessive attention to the share price (protected as they are from predators by cultural and institutional barriers) (Kishi 2003, Chen 2004).

Has the world passed Japanese multinationals by? First, we must explore the modern (Western) multinational firm – the global factory – and then ask how far Japanese firms fit the model and how far Japanese exceptionalism exists. The 'global factory' is an ideal type of modern flexible multinational firms. It has been applied to Western multinational firms (Buckley 2007) and contrasted with older vertically and horizontally integrated multinationals. The analysis has not, so far, been applied to Japanese firms and there is a great opportunity to do so.

The global factory

Elements of the global factory

The notion of the global factory was introduced in Buckley (2004) and developed in Buckley and Ghauri (2004). The key idea is that MNEs are becoming much more like differentiated networks. They choose location and ownership policies so as to maximize profits but this does not necessarily involve internalizing their activities. Indeed, they have set a trend by outsourcing or offshoring their activities. Outsourcing involves utilizing 'buy' rather than 'make' in the Coasean 'externalize or internalize' decision (Coase 1937). Offshoring involves both the externalization option together with the 'make abroad' location decision (Buckley and Casson 1976). MNEs have developed the ability to 'fine slice' their activities on an even more precise calculus, and are increasingly able to alter location and internalization decisions for activities that were previously locationally bound by being tied to other activities and which could only be controlled by internal management fiat (Buckley 2004, 2007, Buckley and Ghauri 2004).

The opening up of the global factory has provided new opportunities for new locations to enter international business. Emerging countries such as India and China are subcontracting production and service activities from the brand-owning MNEs (Sturgeon and Lester 2003). The use of the market by MNEs enables new firms to compete for business against the internalized activities of the MNE. This not only subjects every internalized activity to 'the market test', it also results in a differentiated network (Figure 1), which we term 'the global factory'.

Components of the global factory

The global supply chain is divided into three parts. The Original Equipment Manufacturers (OEMs) control the brand and undertake design, engineering and R&D for the product (Shenkar 2005), although these may be outsourced (see Figure 1). They are customers for contract manufacturers (CMs) who perform manufacturing (and perhaps logistics) services for OEMs. In this so-called modular production network, CMs need to possess capabilities such as mix, product and new product flexibilities, while at the same time carrying out manufacturing activities at low costs with mass production processes (Sturgeon and Lester 2003). Flexibility is necessary to fulfil consumers' product differentiation needs (local requirements) and low cost for global efficiency imperatives (Wilson and Guzman 2005). The third part of the chain is warehousing, distribution and adaptation carried out on a 'hub and spoke' principle, in order to achieve local market adaptation through a mix of ownership and location policies. As Figure 2 shows, ownership strategies are used to involve local firms with marketing skills and local market intelligence in international joint ventures (IJVs), whilst location strategies are used to differentiate the wholly owned 'hub' (centrally located) from the jointly owned 'spokes'.

The information structure of the global factory

Casson (1997) highlights the importance of information costs in the structure of business organisation. He sees the brand owner as essentially a specialist in the search and specification functions (for customers and products respectively). 'The brand owner, by intermediating

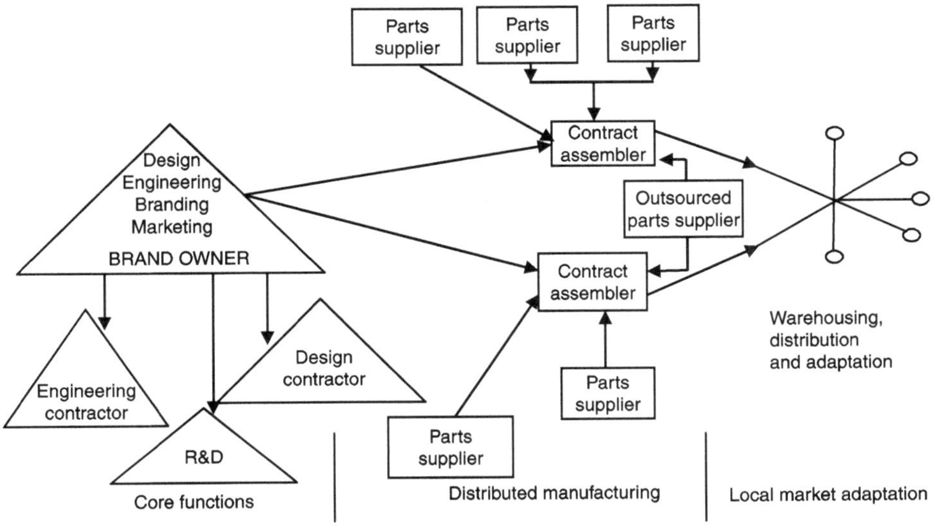

Figure 1. Globally distributed production: 'the global factory'.
Source: Buckley (2004).

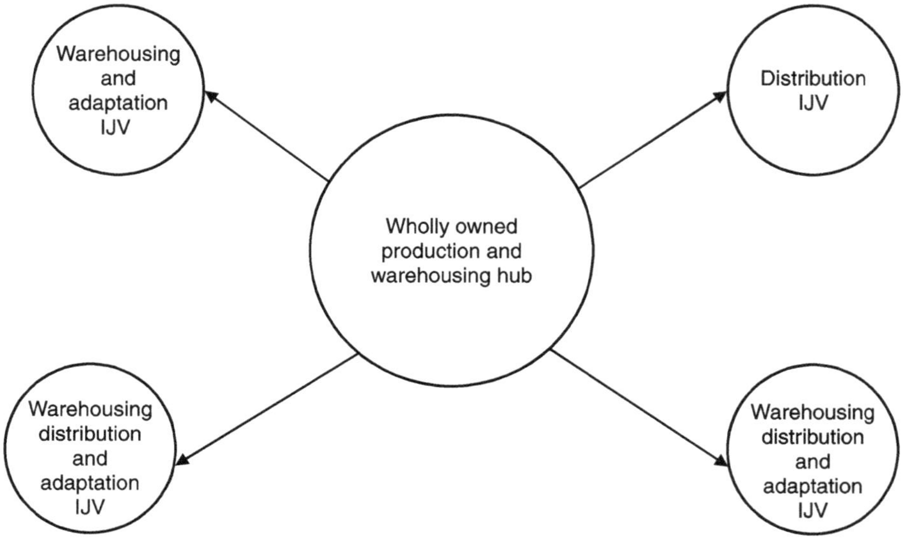

Figure 2. 'Hub and spoke' strategies: an example.
Source: Buckley and Ghauri (2004).

between the producer and the retailer, coordinates the entire distribution channel linking the worker to the final customer' (Casson 1997, p. 159). This intermediation by the brand owner/market maker is intermediation of information, not production. The information structure of the global factory is shown schematically in Figure 3. This shows that the brand owner is the information hub of the global factory. The brand owner organizes the market process itself. The organisation of production is conventionally within firms but the organisation of the whole production and trade sequence is intermediated by the market making global factory. In many industries, particularly service industries, such as banking and insurance, the essence of competitiveness is the processing of information (Casson 1997, Buckley and Carter 2002).

Quasi-internalisation

The global factory structure means that the operational boundaries and the accounting boundaries of the MNE do not coincide. The move to being a global supply chain coordinator means that influence, not ownership, is the global factory's ruling principle.

Research questions: ownership, location and the coordination of activities

Although complex in detail, the key analytical decisions in the global factory are very simple – control and location. The manager of the global factory has to ask two very straightforward questions of each activity in the global network. Where should this activity be located? How should this activity be controlled?

The first question of the optimum location for each activity is of course complicated by managing the interrelationships between activities. The relocation of one piece of the global network will have profound effects on many others (as the links in Figure 1 illustrate) but the principles of least cost location are paramount.

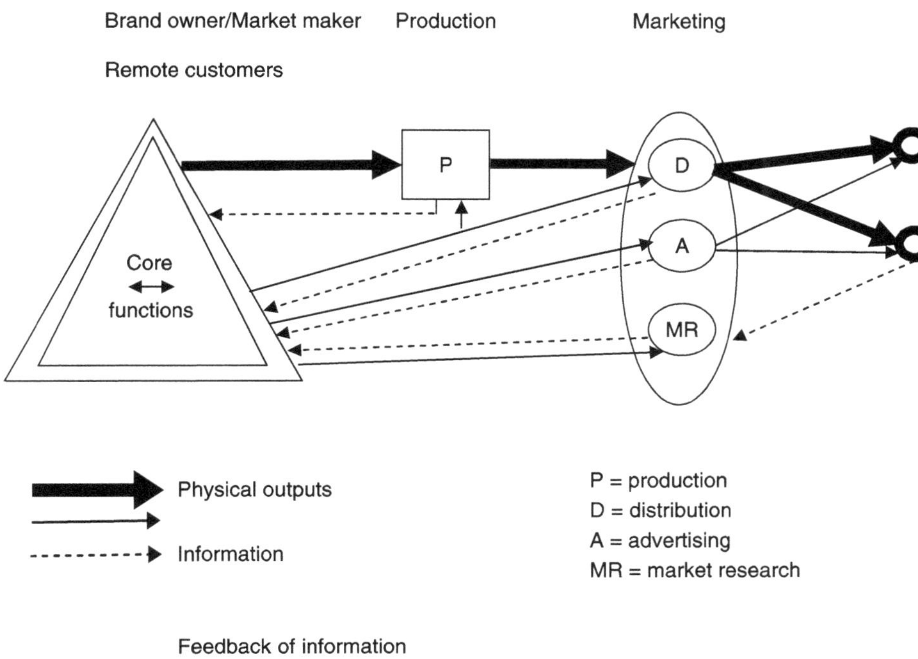

Information flow	into production - techniques, product specification
	from production - improvements in quality
Information flow	into distribution - adaptation, logistics
	from distribution - refinements of adaptation and logistics
Information flow	into advertising - production description associations
	from advertising - effectiveness, need for production change and new products
Information flow	into market research - targeting
	from market research - product intelligence
Information flow	direct to consumers - brand targeting
	from consumer - wants

Figure 3. The information structure of the global factory.
Source: Buckley (2007).

The second question concerns the means of control. Should the activity be managed by the market via a contract and price relationship, or should it be internalized and controlled by management? There are of course important mixed methods, such as joint ventures, which have elements of market relationships and elements of management fiat (Rangan 1998).

It is of course essential to realize that these decisions are taken in a volatile, risky and dynamic situation, that the decision making process is information intensive and the environment and competitive pressures are constantly changing. These decisions have to be revisited on a continuing basis. However, the principles should never be overwhelmed by detail. The need for flexibility, for judicious collection and use of information and for a knowledge management strategy are complements to the key decisions of location and control (Capel 1992, Kogut and Kulatilaka 1994, Allen and Pantzalis 1996).

The role of MNEs has always been to combine internationally mobile resources (such as knowledge), with locationally fixed ones (labour, natural resources, markets). The notion of the MNE as a network, moving around intangibles whilst locationally anchored at given fixed points by key inputs has been around for a long time (Buckley and Casson 1976). What has changed within the global factory is the degree to which management has the ability to 'fine slice' activities, to locate these in their optimal positions globally and to combine these dispersed activities through coordinating mechanisms that rely decreasingly on ownership. The global factory has perfected control, even at a huge distance, without ownership.

The key problems of the global factory are external. They arise from the existence of unpriced external effects and from the remoteness of much value adding activity from shareholders (and from customers) (Khanna and Palepu 1999). The first set of effects include environmental effects (including pollution), social effects and negative impacts on local firms. The second means that it is difficult for the owners to control the dispersed and disparate activities of the global factory. These two effects can interact making it difficult for shareholders to oversee, and to correct, negative externalities (Nolan *et al.* 2002).

The management effects of this can be serious. Expatriate managers can be absent from their own peer groups for extended periods of time and can be very exposed unless properly supported. Local managers may not manage facilities in the way that (foreign) shareholders might wish. The operation of manufacturing and service facilities in outsourced, offshore locations often do not conform to the standards of the headquarters (HQ) of the global factory. Accusations of running 'sweat shops' and poor conditions within call centres may be diffused by distance ('out of sight, out of mind'). However, it is no longer acceptable for HQ of global factories to pronounce that 'they are not our factories because we do not own them'. Global factories have to recognize that they are responsible for the whole of their supply chains and take social responsibility for their operations. Compliance to standards can be enforced internally (conference calls, video-conferencing, inspections, reports) or can itself be outsourced to specialist companies and non-governmental organisations (NGOs) that monitor social and environmental conditions in low-cost labour conditions.

There remain, however, clashes between local cultures and the world culture of the global factory. At the limit, were global factories to pay advanced country wages in cheap labour countries, this would negate their locational cost advantage and would deter global factories from placing facilities there. It is generally the case that work in global factories is better paid than outside them, particularly when the alternative is low productivity agriculture. Criticism of exploitation of cheap labour is a major cause for concern for global factories. The rise of the 'ethical consumer' and 'Fair trade' products are a sign that at least a segment of consumers are willing to pay higher prices for products made under more humane conditions with better ethical and environmental outcomes.

The extent to which factories and service facilities in cheap labour countries can be upgraded over time is a key issue in examining the impact of the global factory on development. It is also critical that spillovers should be positive in terms of upgrading the workforce through training and education, encouraging local entrepreneurship and fostering indigenous suppliers. Negative spillovers, such as pollution and harmful serial effects, need to be monitored and eliminated if the global factory is to achieve global legitimacy.

Findings: Japanese multinationals – hybrids in two senses

Then, as now, Japanese firms remain a special case in organization, philosophy and structure. However, we should note that the industry structure of Japanese firms is peculiar. Table 1 shows that the nine Japanese firms in the world's top 100 non-financial firms in 2004 were three motor vehicles firms, three trading firms and three electronics firms. The transnationality index of these firms is 52.2 – exactly the same as Germany, but less than France and far less than the UK (Table 2). This is partly a very large economy effect because the USA is lower at 48.8. The role of the financial market in Japan is highlighted by Table 3, which shows that only three Japanese firms figure in the 50 largest financial transnational corporations in 2004 and that they had a relatively low spread index, illustrating their domestic bias (a range of 25.7 to 27.8 against GE Capital Services' index of 64.7). The relative domestic focus of financial services in Japan is reflected in the internationalization of its MNEs which, being more reliant on the domestic capital market, are thus more insular (Kishi 2003). Hoshi and Kashyap (2004) show that Japanese firms are provided with insurance via domestic banks. This contrasts with more entrepreneurial risk taking firms. Ahearne and Shinada (2005) claim that many 'zombie' firms exist in the non-traded goods sector of Japan. The highly inefficient, debt ridden zombie firms are supported by finance from the banks exacerbating a declining productivity performance. It is against this unpromising domestic background that we must evaluate Japanese multinational firms.

Today, a growing number of Japanese firms are alleged to be 'hybrids' between Western and stereotypically 'Japanese' firms (see *The Economist* 2007). *The Economist* sees Japan developing 'a new hybrid model of capitalism that brings together aspects of the old Japanese model, which ran into trouble in the early 1990s, with carefully chosen

Table 1. Japanese multinationals in world's top 100 non-financial transnational corporations 2004.

			Rank by		
			Foreign assets	TNI	II
1	Toyota Motor Corporation	Motor vehicles	(8)	62	91
2	Honda Motor Co. Ltd	Motor vehicles	21	(29)	87
3	Nissan Motor Co. Ltd	Motor vehicles	28	41	90
4	Mitsubishi Corporation	Wholesale trade	32	87	68
5	Sony Corporation	Electrical and electronic equipment	41	47	(17)
6	Mitsui & Co. Ltd	Wholesale trade	42	71	69
7	Matsushita Electric Industrial Co. Ltd	Electrical and electronic equipment	68	64	27
8	Hitachi Ltd	Electrical and electronic equipment	81	96	77
9	Marubeni Corporation	Wholesale trade	83	91	76

Notes: TNI: Transnationality index – average of foreign assets to total assets, foreign sales to total sales, foreign employment to total employment. II: Internationalisation index – number of foreign majority-owned affiliates to total majority-owned affiliates. The top Japanese firm in each category is bracketed.
Source: UNCTAD (2006), pp. 280–282.

Table 2. Japanese non-financial transnational corporations 2004.

	TNI	No. of entries
Top 100 largest TNCs	56.8	100
USA	48.2	25
France	59.5	15
Germany	52.2	13
UK	69.2	11
Japan	52.2	9

Note: Observe the comparison with Germany (Kudo 2006).
Source: UNCTAD (2006), p. 33.

elements of the more dynamic American or Anglo-Saxon variety of capitalism'. We may query the 'carefully chosen' element of this – again it implies top-down planning and great foresight on the part of unidentified powers in the Japanese economy – but 'hybridity' (or, more accurately, business culture borrowings) seems to be a reasonable description of modern Japanese business (Abo 1994). However, there is a second sense in which they can be said to be hybrids. If we examine Table 4, three distinct types of MNE can be outlined.

The first is an 'international' firm where the source country headquarters are dominant and where foreign affiliates are treated as merely subcontractors or sales units. The firm

Table 3. Japanese firms in top 50 financial transnational corporations 2004.

	Rank	Spread index
Mitsubishi Tokyo Financial Group	33	27.8
Mizuho Financial Group	36	26.0
Sunutomo Mitsui Financial Group	37	25.7
[NB G.E. Capital Services	1	64.7]

Note: The Spread Index is the square root of the Internationalisation Index (II) multiplied by the number of host countries. The II is the number of foreign majority-owned affiliates divided by the total number of foreign owned affiliates.
Source: UNCTAD (2006), p. 287.

Table 4. Models of multinational firms.

1. '*International*'
- Headquarters (HQ) dominant
- Subsidiaries treated as (preferential?) subcontractors
- Increase in internalization for control
- Often support for exports from source country

2. '*Multinational*'
- HQ delegates functions to subsidiaries
- 'Clone' model as extreme case
- Finance, branding (research & development) retained in centre
- Core functions internalized

3. '*Global factory*' (network model)
- HQ retains branding and associated functions
- All activities located in optimum locations
- Shift to externalization of functions (offshoring, outsourcing)

Table 5. The global factory and the hybrid Japanese ideal type.

	Global factory and Japanese hybrid	
	Similar	Different
Information system	√	
Supply chain	√	
Team working	√	
Labour market		?
Innovation system		?
Hierarchy		?
Openness to foreigners [at top level]		X
Capital market relationships		X

uses internalization rather than contracting, outsourcing or licensing and this reinforces control, centralization and hierarchy. The key focus of the international structure is to support exports from the source country.

The second archetype is the 'multinational' firm in which functions are delegated to foreign affiliates and the extreme case is the 'clone' model where 'miniature replicas' of the parent firm are located in key markets. Production and marketing are separated and located in the locations most suitable for these operations. Finance, branding and other core functions such as R&D are retained in the source country HQ and core functions are internalized.

The third form is the 'global factory', as described above, where HQ retains only branding and its associated functions (including financing). All the firm's activities are 'fine-sliced' and are located in the places that give optimum cost conditions for the supply chain as a whole. There is a major and profound shift to the externalization of functions through outsourcing and offshoring.

Japanese firms may be said to be hybrids of types 1 and 3. There has been a long-standing externalization of functions within large (and medium-sized) Japanese companies with a definite strategy of the relocation of activities (particularly production) to low-cost locations, largely in Asia (Makino *et al.* 2004). Indeed, Japanese firms were leaders in the offshoring movement and led the opening up of China as a low-cost production source. However, this is combined with a dominant HQ and the philosophy that the foreign units of the 'hybrid Japanese global factory' are more akin to subcontractors than to network partners.

This can be summarized in Table 5, which compares 'the global factory' with 'the hybrid Japanese ideal type'. Both use global information systems, sophisticated, integrated supply chain management and team working. However, the innovation systems in Japanese firms are less open than in true global factories, the internal labour markets of Japanese firms are less permeable to outside market forces and there remains more hierarchy in Japanese firms (Chen 2004). A good example that links the last two points is that far fewer non-Japanese rise to senior management and board-level positions in Japanese companies, than non-nationals do in European or American companies. The capital market relationships of Japanese companies are also less open than in the normal case of the global factory (Aulakh and Mudambi 2005). There remain close links between individual companies and banks, and Japanese companies are less open to receiving foreign finance (equity and debt) than other MNEs (Kishi 2003).

Some of this has an evolutionary explanation. For instance, Ozawa (2002) posited four stages of Japanese FDI:

(1) Labour – intensive industrialization and 'elementary stage' of overseas investment.
(2) Heavy and chemical industrialization and the 'resource seeking' stage of multinationalism.
(3) Subcontracting – dependent, assembly based industrialization and the 'assembly transplant' stage of multinationalism.
(4) Flexible manufacturing and the 'strategic localisation' stage of global operations.

It is possible to argue that these stages also describe the past development of US and European investment and that a time-dependent model is far more appropriate than a nationality of ownership explanation. What Ozawa (2002) has described is the changing patterns of relative location costs as the source country develops and its interaction with types of external markets that are most easily internalized (markets in cheap labour and low technology intermediate goods, in relatively unprocessed inputs in a vertically integrated operation, in market-seeking operations and finally, in high technology inputs, sophisticated labour and information). None of this requires specifically 'Japanese' explanatory variables. The retreat of internalization and the shift to outsourcing and offshoring has been the most recent stage in the development of MNEs as we have seen. Again, this has been the policy of both 'Western' and Japanese multinationals and it is even being utilized by the 'new' emerging country multinationals. In many ways, Japanese MNEs were ahead of the trend in offshoring as the literature on hollowing-out shows (see Tejima 2000).

Discussion

The rise and continued success of Japanese MNEs is not a conventional or uniform story. It is important to contrast Japan's most internationalized companies versus the rest, and Japanese small and medium enterprises (SMEs) have suffered more than proportionately from the impact of hollowing-out, the credit crunch and the aforementioned lack of entrepreneurial start-ups (Kikkawa 2006). Japanese MNEs, like all MNEs, vary by sector, by firm and by their administrative heritage (history). The principles governing their operations are the same as for 'Western MNEs' and their evolution and strategy has much in common with their Western counterparts.

There are special issues, however, in examining Japanese MNEs. Their financial integration with world capital markets still remains less than 'normal' MNEs and their insularity in financing reflects this, although financing remains available at attractive rates (Suzuki 1987). Knowledge management policies seem to differ between Japanese and Western MNEs. Japanese firms are less open and their innovation systems are less internationally networked. Japanese MNEs are facing demands to increase their flexibility and openness – hence the 'hybrid' state frequently alluded to in the financial press.

As always, internationalization issues are closely linked to the structure and institutions of the domestic economy. Japanese MNEs reflect the capital market, the innovation system and the business culture of the home economy (Buckley and Casson 1976, Collinson and Rugman 2008). These institutional and cultural factors have led to 'capitalism with Japanese characteristics' and therefore to MNEs that reflect this. Japan has always retained local competition rather than encouraging the creation of a single 'national champion'. This has had the benefit of several Japanese MNEs being able to run foreign experiments and to use different global strategies. However, Japanese MNEs have persisted with licensing rather than foreign investment (Okimoto 1989, Anchordoguy 1990) and the consequent loss of control of the global platform has not served them well. In addition, 'catching-up' has proved easier than taking global leadership (Murtha *et al.* 2001, Hoetker 2006). Globalisation requires new strategies. It also requires new domestic policies and structures to support Japanese global firms and the global factory system. Although the Japanese government has taken steps to promote corporate change, the full impact of these policies on firm performance is as yet unclear. Japan has not yet fully adapted to the new system of global competition in which the head office orchestrates a global factory based on a flexible and resilient international network (Buckley 2009).

Conclusions

From 'then' to 'now', the world has changed. The rise of India and China make global competition much more aggressive. There are far more suitable locations for cost-based competition. The integration of markets and the wider pool of economies drawn in to a modern globalization process means that the world economy is far more volatile (Buckley and Casson 1998). A key response of MNEs to volatility is to be increasingly flexible. Japanese firms have responded to this by developing 'global factory' like strategies in outsourcing, offshoring, relocating and fine-slicing their global activities, especially to locations in East and Southeast Asia and Eastern Europe. However, they have not yet fully responded in opening up their internal capital markets to external influences and their top-level labour markets to foreign executives. Headquarters control and high levels of internal integration of activities that leading Western MNEs have outsourced has led to the idea that Japanese MNEs remain 'hybrids' between 'international' firms and fully global firms in their strategies. An implication to be drawn from this conclusion is that deeper understanding is needed of whether this 'hybridity' represents a new *status quo* or merely reflects a stage of transition to new organizational forms.

References

Abegglen, J.C., 2006. *21st century Japanese management*. Basingstoke: Palgrave.

Abegglen, J.C. and Stalk, G., 1985. *Kaisha, the Japanese corporation*. New York: Basic Books.

Abo, T., ed., 1994. *Hybrid factory: the Japanese production system in the United States*. New York: Oxford University Press.

Ahearne, A.G. and Shinada, N., 2005. Zombie firms and economic stagnation in Japan. *International economics and economic policy*, 2 (4), 363–381.

Allen, L. and Pantzalis, C., 1996. Valuation of the operating flexibility of multinational corporations. *Journal of international business studies*, 27 (4), 633–653.

Anchordoguy, M., 1990. *Computers Inc*. Cambridge, MA: Harvard University Press.

Aoki, M., 1984. Aspects of the Japanese firm. *In*: M. Aoki, ed. *The economic analysis of the Japanese firm*. Dordrecht: North Holland, 3–43.

Aoki, M., 1990. Towards an economic model of the Japanese firm. *Journal of economic literature*, 28 (1), 1–27.

Aulakh, P.S. and Mudambi, R., 2005. Financial resource flows in multinational enterprises: the role of external capital markets. *Management international review*, 45 (3), 307–326.

Buckley, P.J., 2004. The role of China in the global strategy of multinational enterprises. *Journal of Chinese economic and business studies*, 2 (1), 1–25.

Buckley, P.J., 2007. *The global factory: manufacturing and services in the new global economy*. Vienna: UNIDO.
Buckley, P.J., 2009. The role of headquarters in the global factory. *In*: V. Holm and V. Andersson, eds. *Headquarters role in the contemporary MNE*. Cheltenham: Edward Elgar.
Buckley, P.J. and Carter, M., 2002. Process and structure in knowledge management practices of British and US multinational enterprises. *Journal of international management*, 8 (1), 29–48.
Buckley, P.J. and Casson, M., 1976. *The future of the multinational enterprise*. Basingstoke: Macmillan.
Buckley, P.J. and Casson, M., 1998. Models of the multinational enterprise. *Journal of international business studies*, 29 (1), 21–44.
Buckley, P.J. and Ghauri, P.N., 2004. Globalisation, economic geography and the strategy of multinational enterprises. *Journal of international business studies*, 35 (2), 81–98.
Buckley, P.J. and Mirza, H., 1985. The wit and wisdom of Japanese management: an iconoclastic analysis. *Management international review*, 25 (3), 16–32.
Capel, J., 1992. How to service a foreign market under uncertainty: a real option approach. *European journal of political economy*, 8 (3), 455–475.
Casson, M., 1997. *Information and organisation: a new perspective on the theory of the firm*. Oxford: Clarendon Press.
Chen, M., 2004. *Asian management systems*. London: Thomson Learning.
Coase, R.H., 1937. The nature of the firm. *Economica*, 4 (n.s), 386–405.
Collinson, S. and Rugman, A.M., 2008. The regional nature of Japanese multinational business. *Journal of international business studies*, 39 (2), 215–230.
Dyer, J., 2000. *Collaborative advantage: winning through extended enterprise networks*. Oxford: Oxford University Press.
Gerlach, M. and Lincoln, J., 2004. *Japan's network economy*. Cambridge: Cambridge University Press.
Hoetker, G., 2006. Do modular products lead to modular organization? *Strategic management journal*, 27 (6), 501–518.
Hoshi, T. and Kashyap, A., 2004. *Corporate financing and governance in Japan: the road to the future*. Cambridge, MA: MIT Press.
Imai, M., 1986. *The key to Japan's competitive success*. New York: McGraw Hill.
Khanna, T. and Palepu, K., 1999. Policy shocks, market intermediaries, and corporate strategy: evidence from Chile and India. *Journal of economics and management strategy*, 8 (2), 271–310.
Kikkawa, T., 2006. Reorganisation of enterprises in Japan: the response of Keiretsu and small companies. *In*: G.D. Hook and H. Hasegawa, eds. *Japanese responses to globalization*. Basingstoke: Palgrave, 184–202.
Kishi, M., 2003. Foreign direct investment by Japanese firms and corporate governance: in relation to the monetary policies of China, Korea and Japan. *Journal of Asian economies*, 13 (6), 731–748.
Kogut, B. and Kulatilaka, N., 1994. Operating flexibility, global manufacturing and the option value of a multinational network. *Management science*, 40 (1), 123–139.
Kudo, A., 2006. The response of Japanese capitalism to globalization: a comparison with the German case. *In*: G.D. Hook and H. Hasegawa, eds. *Japanese responses to globalization*. Basingstoke: Palgrave, 131–150.
Liker, J.K., Ettie, J.K., and Campbell, J.C., 1995. *Engineered in Japan: Japanese technology – management practices*. Oxford: Oxford University Press.
Makino, S., Beamish, P.W., and Zhao, N.B., 2004. The characteristics and performance of Japanese FDI in less developed and developed countries. *Journal of world business*, 39, 377–392.
Murtha, T.P., Hart, J.A., and Lenway, S.A., 2001. *Managing new industry creation: global knowledge formation and entrepreneurship in high technology*. Stanford, CA: Stanford University Press.
Nolan, P., Sutherland, D., and Zhang, J., 2002. The challenge of the global business revolution. *Contributions to political economy*, 21 (1), 91–110.
Okimoto, D.I., 1989. *Between MITI and the Morbeet*. Stanford, CA: Stanford University Press.
Ozawa, T., 2002. *Pax-Americana led macro-clustering and flying-geese style catch-up in East Asia: mechanisms of regionalised endogenous growth*. Columbia University Centre on Japanese Economy and Business working paper series.

Rangan, S., 1998. Do multinationals operate flexibly? Theory and evidence. *Journal of international business studies*, 29, 217–237.
Shenkar, O., 2005. *The Chinese century*. Upper Saddle River, NJ: Wharton School Publishing.
Sturgeon, T.J. and Lester, R.K., 2003. The new global supply-base: new challenges for local suppliers in East Asia. Industrial Performance Centre (IPC) working paper, MIT-IPC-03-006. Cambridge, MA: Massachusetts Institute of Technology.
Suzuki, Y., 1987. *The Japanese financial system*. Oxford: Clarendon Press.
Tejima, S., 2000. Japanese FDI, the implications of 'hollowing out' on the technological development of host countries. *International business review*, 9 (5), 555–570.
The Economist, 2007. Going hybrid. *The Economist*, 1 December, p. 3.
UNCTAD, 2006. *World investment report 2006*. Geneva: UNCTAD.
Wilson, J. and Guzman, G.A.C., 2005. Organisational knowledge transfer in modular production networks: the case of Brazil. *Proceedings of the Academy of International Business annual conference*, July, Quebec.

The evolution of Japanese investment in China: from toys to textiles to business process outsourcing

A. Delios[a], P.W. Beamish[b] and X. Zhao[a]

[a]*NUS Business School, National University of Singapore, 1 Business Link, 117592, Singapore;*
[b]*Richard Ivey School of Business, University of Western Ontario, London ON, N6A 3K7, Canada*

Introduction

Foreign investors have long been urged to consider the merits of the Chinese market. Investment in the early 1980s in the People's Republic of China (henceforth China) by American companies, and those from other nations, was driven as much by a 'group think' about not wanting to be left out of the China market, and the prestige of having been to China, as by a logic that was driven by bottom line considerations (Pye 1986). Although it has been almost 30 years since the first wave of investments struck China's eastern coast, pressures persist on companies to not miss out on the opportunities in China. Growing Chinese exports in the 1990s, and outward foreign direct investment (FDI) in the 2000s, to the West have only increased this pressure to be in China (Buckley *et al.* 2007). This pressure is much the same as that faced by American business to increase their presence in Japan in the 1980s, when Japanese companies were at their competitive peak.

Japanese companies have not only been among the leading investors in Western economies, they have been among the largest investors in China. By 2006, more than 40% of Japan's 5000 multinational companies had established at least one foreign subsidiary in China (UNCTAD 2001, Toyo Keizai 2007). During the 1990s, China was absorbing around 40% of Japan's annual FDI outflows. The rapid growth of the presence of Japanese companies in China has occurred hand-in-hand with tremendous growth in FDI from other nations. Nonetheless, Japanese companies have been among the most aggressive in placing foreign subsidiaries in China. Japanese firms have developed extensive production networks in China, and by the early 2000s, China had superseded a number of other Asian nations to hold the second largest stock of Japanese FDI, behind only the US. As leaders in the China market, the experience of Japanese investors can help us understand how FDI in China has developed, and how it will develop.

The changing nature and evolution of Japanese international activity in China has created substantial opportunities and challenges to scholars and practitioners alike. The challenge comes from trying to develop a nuanced understanding of subnational variations in Japanese firms' strategies in China. The opportunities come from the chance to deepen research in three particular areas of scholarly endeavour, which this study identifies. In specific, we address three research questions:

(1) What are the subsidiary development and multinational firm strategy implications of the developments in China?
(2) What are the corresponding implications for our understanding of institutions and international business?
(3) What are the related developments for offshoring, outsourcing and international business theory?

In terms of structure, after reviewing the main trends in Japanese FDI in China and, in particular, changing patterns of regionalism by Japanese investing firms, this study examines each of these three areas of research opportunity in turn. Our purpose is to identify fruitful directions for further research that will raise understanding of the strategies Japanese multinational enterprises (MNEs) are using to approach business opportunities presented by China.

Literature review

Japanese foreign direct investment in China

Japanese investment in China is currently in a state of rebound. Japanese companies began to experience sub-satisfactory levels of performance in their China-based subsidiaries from the middle of the 1990s. The sub-standard levels of performance, coupled with a persistent lack of economic growth in Japan through the 1990s and into the years following 2000, made China's future as one of the foremost recipients of Japan's foreign investment in the early 2000s uncertain.

The establishment of new plants by foreign companies helped to create employment for large numbers of people in China, many of whom were laid off from failing state-owned enterprises. The inflow of capital of foreign companies helped to establish new cities such as Shenzhen, and helped the renaissance of other cities such as Shanghai. The production of the goods and services of foreign companies helped to bring new technology to China, and revamp its manufacturing sector, while developing a strong domestic market for well-trained and educated middle and senior management staff (UNCTAD 2001, p. 26). These benefits to China's economy have been pronounced but have also created pressures for multinational firms to alter their China entry strategies, as much as the same levels of economic growth did for firms that had invested in Taiwan and Hong Kong in the 1970s and 1980s.

Japanese firms are responding to these changes in China's investment environment. The story of Japan's investment in China can be told in three chapters (Appendix and Figure 1). The first chapter would be one of reacquaintance, where, after a 40 year hiatus, Japanese companies began again to invest slowly in China, following its opening with the institution of the Joint Venture Act in 1978, and continuing until the onset of the 1990s. Chapter two recounts the period of explosive growth of Japanese FDI in China, in which

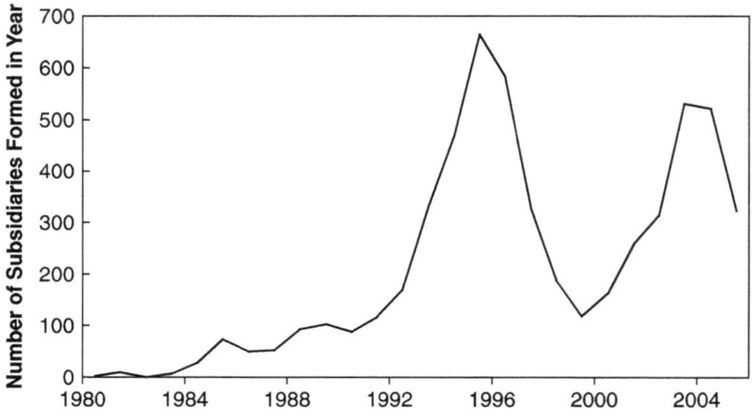

Figure 1. Annual formation of Japanese foreign subsidiaries in China (1979–2006).
Source: *Japanese overseas investments* (Toyo Keizai), various years.

China at its peak (1994–1995) consumed more than 40% of all Japanese outbound FDI in a given year. Chapter three has yet to be completed, but it starts with a slowdown in Japanese foreign investment in China at the start of the 2000s, and then a quick recovery in the mid-2000s. That said, it is not clear that Japanese foreign investment levels will ever recover to the levels observed in the mid-1990s, at least in terms of volume, and perhaps in terms of industries and regions for investment.

Figure 1 displays annual flow of Japanese foreign subsidiaries (joint ventures, wholly owned subsidiaries and acquisitions) in China. The explosive growth in Japanese foreign investment in China in the first half of the 1990s is very evident in Figure 1. From an average of somewhat less than 100 subsidiaries formed per year in the second half of the 1980s, Japanese companies formed an average of more than 300 subsidiaries per year in the first six years of the 1990s. This rapid growth in subsidiary establishments peaked in 1995, with the formation of 665 subsidiaries. Just as rapid as the growth in Japanese investment flows was its decline. From its peak, Japanese investment had fallen to late-1980s levels by 1999, with the aforementioned recovery in the mid-2000s (see Table 1).

Japanese investment tendencies and FDI in China

To move beyond the present to the future status of Japanese FDI in China, we can look to the past, to the history of foreign investment by Japanese companies in other parts of the world. Just as China was the hotspot for Japanese foreign investment in the late 1990s, other parts of the world have been the dominant sites for Japanese foreign investment at different junctures in the history of outbound Japanese foreign investment.

In the 1960s and 1970s, during Japan's post-1940s resumption of foreign investment activity, nations in South America were among the most popular spots for their foreign investment. Two of the most notable among these nations were Brazil and Argentina. In the 1972–1976 period, they received 10% of all Japanese foreign investments, which was five times greater than the 2.1% average as a destination for Japanese investment in the 1960–2000 period. Thirty-six percent of all Japanese foreign investments in Brazil and Argentina until 2001 were made during this 1972–1976 period. Furthermore, of all the foreign investment made by Japanese companies in Brazil to 2001, 36% were made in the 1972–1976 period, and more than half in the 1970s.

Table 1. Japanese entries into China: number and size by year of entry.

Year	Number of entries	Employment	Capitalisation (US$ million)	Sales (US$ million)
pre-1984	18	1,367	10.00	12.29
1984	28	198	3.97	326.60
1985	74	257	15.61	15.97
1986	49	322	11.52	20.05
1987	53	177	3.79	194.42
1988	94	308	12.75	48.33
1989	103	309	11.08	23.13
1990	87	236	20.28	20.35
1991	116	200	10.79	32.45
1992	169	250	29.64	27.09
1993	333	299	18.91	44.54
1994	469	196	25.87	12.41
1995	665	214	20.71	10.77
1996	584	184	7.34	9.78
1997	326	143	10.07	7.63
1998	188	95	10.61	9.72
1999	120	352	8.08	23.66
2000	165	134	5.84	5.12
2001	260	109	6.32	4.47
2002	314	89	14.08	4.09
2003	532	286	9.17	7.74
2004	521	76	9.34	3.69
2005	323	91	36.27	4.32
2006	14	38	7.47	n.a.

Note: Employment, capitalisation and sales are mean values for subsidiaries formed in the corresponding year or period.
Source: *Japanese overseas investments* (Toyo Keizai), various years.

This characteristic of bunching in foreign investment is not restricted to Brazil and Argentina. Indeed, bunching in foreign investment, in which Japanese companies follow one another in entering a country, is more the rule than the exception (Delios *et al.* 2008). This bunching occurs first among competing companies, in a form of oligopolistic reaction (Knickerbocker 1973), in which competing companies tend to enter a country within proximate times of one another. As examples, in 1962, as Japanese companies began to take up foreign investment positions across the world, Nissan established its first automotive manufacturing plant in Thailand. Two months after Nissan's plant opened, Toyota's manufacturing subsidiary in Thailand began operations. Two years later, Mitsubishi established its own manufacturing facility and Honda set up a sales subsidiary. Another three years later, Honda constructed a manufacturing plant in Thailand.

Meanwhile, across the Pacific, the same Japanese companies were developing operations in Canada. In 1964, Toyota established its first sales subsidiary in Canada. Less than a year later, this was followed by Nissan's entry. Mazda's entry came in 1968 and Honda's in 1969. Further, in the mid-1980s, this round of subsidiary formation was followed by another series of grouped entries, this time for the manufacture of automobiles.

This bunching occurs again as secondary companies in production networks follow lead companies into a market (Martin *et al.* 1998). To continue with the example above, concurrently or shortly after major Japanese automotive assemblers established automotive production plants in Canada, other major part suppliers followed, to retain business with their existing Japanese client companies. With inter-firm competitive rivalry, and the desire to replicate domestic production networks abroad as motivations, concentrated periods of foreign investment in a host nation are common.

It is these firm-level dynamics that yield the concentration in investments in a given market, in a given time period. In this sense, the recent experience of Japanese companies in China is not without direct analogies in the past. For example, South Korea received 35% of all its Japanese foreign investments in the 1987–1990 period. Canada and the United States likewise received a high concentration of investments in the same period. In the Japanese build-up of FDI prior to the establishment of the European Union in 1992, several European nations, such as the Netherlands and France, saw high percentages of total FDI inflows from Japan made during the 1988–1991 period.

In the 1990s, several countries in Asia saw concentrated instances of Japanese investment. These included Malaysia in 1989–1992, China in 1993–1996 and India in 1995–1998. Although the concentration of investment in a short period is similar across these examples, the magnitude of the investment, particularly at its peak, has been much greater in China than for that in any other country in the world, with the exception of the United States.

That the magnitudes are different across nations is not that surprising when one considers such basic facts as the size and potential of a host market economy. The United States has been the largest economy in the world for decades. China has been recognised as the one with the largest market potential, at least since the 1980s. Investment flows have been consistent with the size and potential for growth. Investment flows also respond to advantages that can accrue to a company from locating production in a particular country. In a country like the United States, these advantages can be access to technology and close access to a large consumer market. In a country like China, these advantages can be close access to a potentially large consumer market, and access to low-cost factors of production such as an inexpensive labour force, low tax and tariff rates in economic zones designated for export-oriented production, and low costs for land and the construction of plants. It is the evolution in these factors of production that might be causing a change in the investment strategy of Japanese firms in China such as the industries and regions in which Japanese companies invest. In addition, from the beginning of 1980s, the Chinese government has gradually deepened the openness of the Chinese market and issued a series of favourable policies to attract FDI as an important means for economic development and technology upgrade.

Theory

Advantages

A variety of explanations have been advocated as to why companies have invested in China. These explanations revolve around the market potential of China and the cost advantages of producing in China. China's cost advantages were initially stark in comparison to the rest of the world. With a workforce whose size was without parallel versus any other nation (with the exception of perhaps India, whose workforce numbered nearly 800 million in 2006), and with a shift in workforce participation from state-owned enterprises to domestic and foreign-owned enterprises, great potential existed for a foreign company to reduce labour costs when producing in China.

Two features of the Chinese economy have worked to mitigate this advantage in the 1990s and 2000s. The first is the strong growth of China's economy, and the second is the decline in performance in other economies in Asia in the post-1997 period. For the first, strong growth has led to rising incomes and a rising cost of living in China. This growth is most strongly reflected in the eastern coastal provinces of China, but it is also evident in other provinces.

Table 2 depicts changes in the consumer price index (CPI) in the municipalities and provinces of China. The growth in prices has been strong in this 1992–2001 period, with price levels increasing by as much as 2.3 times in Beijing, and 2.2 times in Shanghai. Several other provinces had a CPI that more than doubled in this period, with the slowest growth in CPI, an increase of 1.75 times, occurring in Hebei. To put such price increases in context, the CPI in the United States increased by only 1.27 times in the same period.

Growth in mean wage rates by province show a similar trend, although more pronounced on a nominal basis. Table 3 displays increases in the nominal wage index from a level of 1.00 in Beijing, for example, to a level of 4.22. This more than four-fold increase in mean wage rates in the 1991–2000 period can also be found in the eastern coastal provinces of Fujian and Zhejiang. Growth in wage rates was somewhat slower in the

Table 2. Consumer price index (CPI) by city/province in China 1992–2004.

Region	1992	1995	1998	2001	2004
Anhui	100	153	195	192	202
Beijing	100	158	218	232	231
Chongqing	100	171	208	193	200
Fujian	100	149	185	187	195
Gansu	100	153	207	199	206
Guangdong	100	152	189	185	189
Guangxi	100	157	199	188	197
Guizhou	100	151	207	205	214
Hainan	100	171	204	197	205
Hebei	100	143	182	175	185
Heilongjiang	100	152	197	188	196
Henan	100	142	189	177	190
Hubei	100	154	209	199	213
Hunan	100	158	208	212	227
Inner Mongolia	100	148	195	196	207
Jiangsu	100	149	192	188	196
Jiangxi	100	149	192	192	201
Jilin	100	144	184	176	184
Liaoning	100	150	193	189	197
Ningxia	100	149	194	190	199
Qinghai	100	146	200	199	214
Shaanxi	100	156	213	204	211
Shandong	100	145	192	190	198
Shanghai	100	160	213	221	227
Shanxi	100	151	196	200	209
Sichuan	100	151	206	202	215
Tianjin	100	155	201	197	203
Tibet	N/A	N/A	N/A	100	104
Xinjiang	100	154	212	205	210
Yunnan	100	153	210	208	223
Zhejiang	100	155	201	200	210
Mean (all regions)	100	153	200	193	202

Note: CPI in 1992 for each city/province set to 100, except for Tibet where earliest observation was in 2000, which was set to 100.
Source: China Statistics Bureau various years.

Table 3. Nominal wage rate index by city/province in China 1992–2003.

Region	1991	1994	1997	2000	2003
Anhui	100	254	278	282	426
Beijing	100	180	328	422	653
Chongqing	100	199	348	264	409
Fujian	100	202	323	425	575
Gansu	100	337	245	249	358
Guangdong	100	197	329	377	545
Guangxi	100	490	273	291	454
Guizhou	100	534	243	269	398
Hainan	100	377	247	234	328
Hebei	100	176	269	287	413
Heilongjiang	100	167	225	248	349
Henan	100	237	312	333	517
Hubei	100	190	267	281	397
Hunan	100	203	261	285	429
Inner Mongolia	100	311	249	246	399
Jiangsu	100	178	309	341	520
Jiangxi	100	309	263	283	424
Jilin	100	153	264	249	348
Liaoning	100	153	233	222	328
Ningxia	100	353	248	278	420
Qinghai	100	529	228	247	377
Shaanxi	100	261	238	281	413
Shandong	100	194	321	367	526
Shanghai	100	197	309	346	510
Shanxi	100	258	244	230	357
Sichuan	100	199	348	271	406
Tianjin	100	168	291	306	457
Tibet	100	723	359	373	671
Xinjiang	100	447	255	271	412
Yunnan	100	603	295	346	483
Zhejiang	100	203	333	405	661
Mean (all regions)	100	290	282	300	450

Note: Wage index in 1991 for each city/province set to 100.
Source: China Statistics Bureau various years.

interior provinces, with the largest, Sichuan, and its former municipality, Chongqing, showing increases in wage rates of 'just' 2.7 (2.6) times. These differences in wage rate growth suggest the declining price competitiveness of China overall, but particularly the eastern coastal provinces.

This decline in cost competitiveness is exacerbated by another trend, the climb in the value of the Chinese Yuan relative to other major Asian currencies in the latter part of the 1990s (Table 4). Although the Chinese Yuan (and Hong Kong dollar) has been more or less fixed against the US dollar (US$) since 1994, other currencies in Asia float against the US$. Sharp increases in the value of these currencies, coupled with the devaluation of the Chinese Yuan in 1994, against the US$ increased the cost competitiveness of production based in China in the first half of the 1990s. In fact, the revaluation of the Chinese Yuan in 1994, to just two-thirds (0.58%) of its 1993 value against the US$ (and Japanese Yen), coincided with the Japanese FDI explosion in China in the mid-1990s.

This relationship between a revaluation of a major currency and a striking growth in FDI flows is not without precedent (Kojima 1973). The revaluation of the Yen against the US$ as part of the Plaza Accord in 1985 sparked the large Japanese wave of FDI into the

Table 4. Chinese Yuan (RMB) to one unit of Asian and US currencies.

Year	US Dollar	Japanese Yen	Thai Baht	Hong Kong Dollar	Singapore Dollar	Malaysian Ringgit	Philippine Peso	Taiwan New $	South Korean Won	Indonesian Rupiah	Vietnamese Dong
1990	4.72	0.032	0.18	0.60	2.50	1.75	0.22	0.18	0.0070	0.0026	–
1991	5.23	0.039	0.21	0.67	2.98	1.92	0.19	0.20	0.0073	0.0028	–
1992	5.40	0.043	0.21	0.70	3.30	1.99	0.21	0.21	0.0071	0.0027	–
1993	5.84	0.046	0.23	0.75	3.52	2.25	0.24	0.23	0.0074	0.0028	–
1994	8.70	0.078	0.34	1.13	5.41	3.18	0.32	0.33	0.0107	0.0041	–
1995	8.44	0.086	0.34	1.09	5.80	3.30	0.34	0.32	0.0106	0.0038	–
1996	8.29	0.079	0.33	1.07	5.83	3.23	0.32	0.30	0.0105	0.0036	–
1997	8.33	0.071	0.32	1.08	5.93	3.37	0.32	0.30	0.0098	0.0035	–
1998	8.31	0.063	0.15	1.07	4.69	1.81	0.19	0.24	0.0047	0.0010	–
1999	8.28	0.073	0.22	1.07	4.91	2.17	0.21	0.26	0.0071	0.0010	0.00060
2000	8.28	0.078	0.22	1.06	4.96	2.18	0.20	0.27	0.0073	0.0011	0.00059
2001	8.28	0.070	0.19	1.06	4.78	2.18	0.16	0.25	0.0065	0.0009	0.00057
2002	8.28	0.070	0.19	1.06	4.77	2.18	0.15	0.24	0.0070	0.0009	0.00054
2003	8.28	0.077	0.21	1.07	4.87	2.18	0.15	0.24	0.0069	0.0010	0.00053
2004	8.28	0.081	0.21	1.06	5.07	2.18	0.15	0.26	0.0080	0.0009	0.00052
2005	8.07	0.068	0.20	1.06	4.85	2.14	0.15	0.25	0.0080	0.0008	0.00051
2006	7.81	0.066	0.22	1.06	5.08	2.21	0.16	0.24	0.0084	0.0009	0.00049

Source: Datastream.

US that followed in the remainder of the 1980s. Similarly, the stimulus to FDI in China provided by the devaluation of the Chinese Yuan relative to the US$, the Japanese Yen, and the appreciating currencies of other Asian nations, provided a sharp drop in the comparative cost of operations in China in the first half of the 1990s.

Since the onset of the Asian financial crisis in 1997, and the continued peg of the Chinese Yuan to the US$, the currency situation has been in reverse. The Chinese Yuan has been appreciating relative to other Asian currencies. Since 1997, the Chinese Yuan has appreciated by nearly a factor of 4 against the Indonesian Rupiah. It has doubled in value against the Philippine Peso, and increased in value by at least 1.5 times against the South Korean Won, the Malaysian Ringgit and the Thai Baht. These increases in the value of the Chinese Yuan have in most cases returned exchange rates to around their 1990 values. The worry for policy makers in China is that FDI flows into China from Japan and other nations will also return to 1990 levels. This concern is not without substance, especially as domestic price and cost levels have increased at the same time as the Chinese Yuan has appreciated, hence raising the costs of production in China much above their 1990 values.

Regionalism in Japanese FDI in China

The changes we have detailed in the economic conditions underlying the investment environment in China are but part of the set of factors influencing the strategies of Japanese firms in China. That said, these changes can induce a substantive change in how Japanese firms have been approaching the market in China, and how they will approach it.

The changes in how Japanese firms have approached investments in China largely relate to the ways in which they have constructed their FDIs, as well as where they have situated their FDIs. For the latter, there has been a consistent expansion in the provinces and municipalities that have received foreign subsidiaries. This expansion is shown in Figure 2 which tracks investment flows (annual number of subsidiaries set up by Japanese firms) to six regions in China. These regions are:

(1) North: Beijing, Tianjin, Hebei, Shanxi, Inner Mongolia.
(2) Northeast: Liaoning, Jilin, Heilongjiang.
(3) East: Shanghai, Jiangsu, Zhejiang, Anhui, Fujian, Jiangxi, Shandong.
(4) Mid-South: Henan, Hubei, Hunan, Guangdong, Guangxi, Hainan.
(5) Southwest: Chongqing, Sichuan, Guizhou, Yunnan, Tibet.
(6) Northwest: Shaanxi, Gansu, Qinghai, Ningxia, Xinjiang.

As can be seen in Figure 2, the East has been the dominant recipient of FDI, with Shanghai receiving the bulk of FDI by Japanese firms (in terms of numbers of subsidiaries formed), followed by Jiangsu province. The strength of Shanghai as an investment destination for Japanese firms has been consistent since the early 1990s, leading it to be the host for 30% of Japanese firms stock of subsidiaries in China.

A second dominant region for Japanese FDI has been the North, at least until the end of the 1990s. Beijing and Tianjin have been the major FDI recipients in the North, with Beijing consuming 9.3% of all Japanese FDIs made into China and Tianjin having 5%. The second place standing of the North was surpassed by the mid-South region in the year 2000. The strength of the mid-South is driven principally by investments in the province of Guangdong, which has received 14.3% of all Japanese FDI. Other provinces such as Henan, Hubei and Hainan, even though the latter is a Special Economic Zone (SEZ), have not received much more than a 1% share of Japanese FDI in terms of subsidiary numbers (Japanese Overseas Investments (Toyo Keizai), various years).

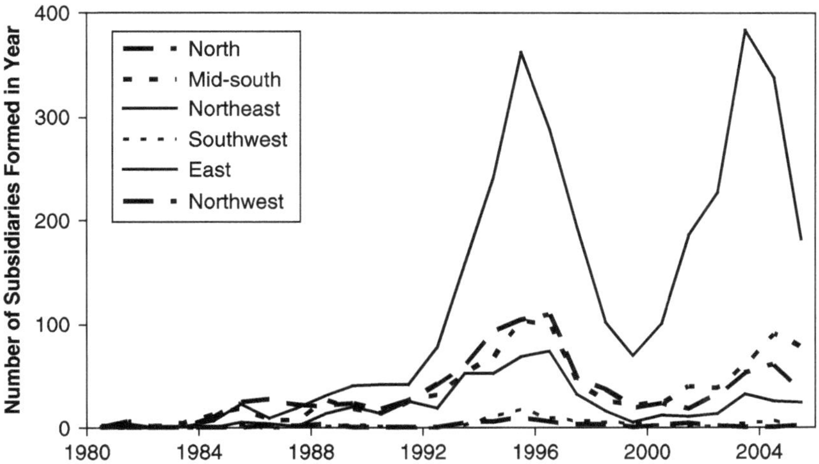

Figure 2. Annual formation of Japanese foreign subsidiaries by region in China (1979–2006).
Note: North = Beijing, Tianjin, Hebei, Shanxi, Inner Mongolia; Northeast = Liaoning, Jilin, Heilongjiang; East = Shanghai, Jiangsu, Zhejiang, Anhui, Fujian, Jiangxi, Shandong; Mid-south = Henan, Hubei, Hunan, Guangdong, Guangxi, Hainan; Southwest = Chongqing, Sichuan, Guizhou, Yunnan, Tibet; Northwest = Shaanxi, Gansu, Qinghai, Ningxia, Xinjiang.
Source: *Japanese overseas investments* (Toyo Keizai), various years.

The other three regions remain as the secondary sites of Japanese FDI, although their prominence has been growing slowly but not substantively. There are an increasing number of investments being made in the hinterland regions of China, but this growth of investments in new regions of China is not as strong as the growth of FDI in the East coast area during the 1990s.

An important trend, aside from the slow shift away from the East and North in Japanese FDI in China, has been that of the province-industry mix. This mix is displayed in Tables 5 and 6. In these tables, we show the stock of Japanese FDI in a region by industry for four given points in time (1990, 1995, 2000, 2006). The mix is indicated by the identification of the dominant manufacturing industry in the region, and its associated concentration (number of FDIs in that industry divided by the overall number of manufacturing FDIs in the province). In Beijing, for example, we can see a shift from low-value-added industries such as food products (1990) and apparel (1995) to high-value-added industries such as electronic equipment (2006). Shanghai has also shown a similar shift from the dominance of the apparel industry in the 1990s, to a stronger presence for electronics (2006).

Again, although the shifts in industry by province (municipality) are not tremendously strong, they are evident. FDIs by Japanese firms in the East Coast seem to be shifting from low-wage, technologically less sophisticated industries, to higher technology, higher value-added industries. This shift is not surprising given the changes in cost conditions that have been occurring in major metropolises and other regions of China, as we have indicated in our earlier discussion.

The consequence is that we now see lower value-added industries either migrating inland, or perhaps even being shifted out of China, to countries such as Vietnam. Also, the regionalism of investment emerges with a strong focus on electronics in the East, Northeast, North and South (2006), and transportation equipment in the Southwest (Table 6). This emerging regionalism stands somewhat in contrast with the situation in the mid-1990s,

Table 5. Japanese FDI industry concentration by province (municipality) in China (1990, 1995, 2000, 2006).

Region	Industry (1990)	Conc. (%)	Industry (1995)	Conc. (%)	Industry (2000)	Conc. (%)	Industry (2006)	Conc. (%)
Beijing	Food products	12	Apparel	18	Industrial machinery	19	Electronic equipment	21%
Tianjin	Industrial machinery	23	Chemicals	15	Transportation Equipment	22	Transportation Equipment	21%
Hebei	–	0	Industrial machinery	19	Industrial machinery	31	Industrial machinery	28%
Shanxi	Industrial machinery	100	Chemicals	50	Chemicals	25	Chemicals	25%
Inner Mongolia	Apparel	100	Apparel	44	Apparel	57	Apparel	43%
Liaoning	Apparel	22	Apparel	20	Electronic equipment	19	Electronic equipment	21%
Jilin	Electronic equipment	100	Food products	25	Transportation Equipment	38	Transportation Equipment	33%
Heilongjiang	Food products	50	Food products	36	Food products	27	Food products	40%
Shanghai	Apparel	27	Apparel	24	Apparel	19	Electronic equipment	18%
Jiangsu	Apparel	32	Apparel	20	Industrial machinery	17	Electronic equipment	23%
Zhejiang	Apparel	38	Apparel	18	Electronic equipment	17	Electronic equipment	19%
Anhui	–	0	Fabricated metal Products	33	Industrial machinery	33	Industrial machinery	29%
Fujian	Food products	27	Electronic equipment	31	Electronic equipment	29	Electronic equipment	27%
Jiangxi	–	0	Transportation Equipment	100	Transportation Equipment	67	Transportation Equipment	50%
Shandong	Food products	35	Food products	30	Food products	21	Food products	22%
Henan	Food products	100	Food products	46	Food products	21	Transportation Equipment	20%
Hubei	–	0	Apparel	33	Apparel	31	Electronic equipment	38%
Hunan	Apparel	100	Apparel	40	Transportation Equipment	45	Transportation Equipment	36%
Guangdong	Electronic equipment	28	Electronic equipment	29	Electronic equipment	31	Electronic equipment	31%
Guangxi	–	0	–	0	Electronic equipment	67	Chemicals	50%
Hainan	Food products	100	Food products	50	Food products	50	Food products	40%
Chongqing	Food products	67	Transportation Equipment	59	Transportation Equipment	54	Transportation Equipment	55%

Table 5 – *continued*

Region	Industry (1990)	Conc. (%)	Industry (1995)	Conc. (%)	Industry (2000)	Conc. (%)	Industry (2006)	Conc. (%)
Sichuan	Primary metal industy	100	Transportation Equipment	29	Transportation Equipment	44	Transportation Equipment	39%
Guizhou	Industrial machinery	50	Transportation Equipment	100	Transportation Equipment	100	Transportation Equipment	100%
Yunnan	–	0%	Chemicals	100%	Chemicals	100%	Chemicals	67%
Shaanxi	–	0%	Industrial machinery	42%	Industrial machinery	50%	Industrial machinery	43%
Ningxia	–	0%	Fabricated metal products	100%	Primary metal industries	50%	Primary metal industries	25%
Xinjiang	Food products	50%	Food products	50%	Chemicals	100%	Chemicals	100%

Table 6. Industry concentration by region in China (1990, 1995, 2000, 2006).

Region	Industry (1990)	Conc. (%)	Industry (1995)	Conc. (%)	Industry (2000)	Conc. (%)	Industry (2006)	Conc. (%)
North	Industrial machinery	16%	Industrial machinery	15%	Industrial machinery	17%	Electronic equipment	17%
Northeast	Apparel	20%	Apparel	18%	Industrial machinery	17%	Electronic equipment	19%
East	Apparel	27%	Apparel	20%	Apparel	16%	Electronic equipment	19%
Mid-south	Electronic equipment	26%	Electronic equipment	27%	Electronic equipment	28%	Electronic equipment	30%
Southwest	Food products	50%	Transportation equipment	50%	Transportation equipment	49%	Transportation equipment	47%
Northwest	Food products	25%	Industrial machinery	33%	Industrial machinery	41%	Industrial machinery	32%

Note: North = Beijing, Tianjin, Hebei, Shanxi, Inner Mongolia; Northeast = Liaoning, Jilin, Heilongjiang; East = Shanghai, Jiangsu, Zhejiang, Anhui, Fujian, Jiangxi, Shandong; Mid-south = Henan, Hubei, Hunan, Guangdong, Guangxi, Hainan; Southwest = Chongqing, Sichuan, Guizhou, Yunnan, Tibet; Northwest = Shaanxi, Gansu, Qinghai, Ningxia, Xinjiang.

Source: *Japanese overseas investments* (Toyo Keizai), various years.

where apparel was a major industry in the Northeast and East, not electronic equipment. Hence, we have some evidence pointing to a change in the perceptions of Japanese firms on the value of setting-up a subsidiary operation in a particular industry, in a particular province/municipality of China.

Research questions

As a consequence of these developments, we believe it is important for future research to consider, and to perhaps pursue, three critical research questions in its evaluation and understanding of the strategies Japanese MNEs are using to approach the market in China. As we have earlier stated, these research questions, which we explore in the next section, are:

(1) What are the subsidiary development and multinational firm strategy implications of the developments in China?
(2) What are the corresponding implications for our understanding of institutions and international business?
(3) What are the related developments for offshoring, outsourcing and international business theory?

Data analysis

Growth of foreign activity in China – subsidiary evolution

A dynamic aspect of FDI is the evolution of investment strategies over time, on a host country basis, as well as the evolution of a subsidiary's role in a multinational firm over time. Historically, there have been two routes to a subsidiary's evolution. The first route is one led by the headquarters of a multinational firm. This route is one in which a subsidiary receives its schedule and scope of activities as an assignment from headquarters. The second route is one led by a subsidiary itself. In this route, managers in a foreign subsidiary take responsibility for leading the development of the subsidiary, through their own initiative and lobbying efforts in the multinational firm (White and Poynter 1984, Bartlett and Ghoshal 1986, Jarillo and Martinez 1990, Gupta and Govindarajan 1991).

A central concern in FDI strategy is how a subsidiary's role in a multinational firm evolves over time. To understand the evolution of a subsidiary's role, we need to be aware of the external environment in which a subsidiary operates. The characteristics of the external environment influence the strength of the value-added activities of a subsidiary. A foreign subsidiary performs an activity, or activities, that augment the value of the products and services produced by the multinational firm. In its value-added activities, a subsidiary can augment a multinational firm's competitiveness (Birkinshaw and Hood 1998).

A subsidiary can fulfil this role in a multinational firm either by conducting a single activity, such as manufacturing, or a full range of value-added activities – research and product design, input sourcing, manufacturing, distribution and marketing. A subsidiary carries out an activity or a set of operations in a host country, and it may operate in any one of a number of industries. These activities add value to the multinational firm at various points in the firm's value-chain.

The types of value-added activities a subsidiary performs can be called its role in the multinational firm, or more formally, we can call a subsidiary's set of activities its mandate or charter. The businesses in which a subsidiary operates, and its responsibilities in the multinational firm, can also be thought of as its charter (Birkinshaw and Hood 1998).

Essentially, a subsidiary's charter captures the products it produces, the technology it houses, the markets it serves and the functional areas included in its operations.

A subsidiary's role, or its mandate or charter, can and does change over time. It changes over time because the host country environment is a dynamic one. A multinational firm itself is in constant development as it seeks lower cost of production, new product and new geographic market opportunities. A subsidiary evolves in response to environmental dynamism.

This evolution can lead to a declining importance of a subsidiary in a multinational firm, and perhaps its eventual closure, or it can lead to an augmentation of the role of a subsidiary. The external environment is important in this development, and the type of role a subsidiary assumes in a multinational firm. For subsidiaries situated in the East, mid-South and North regions of China, the external development in the environment, particularly as it relates to increases in costs of production, is creating pressures for subsidiaries to either close (because they become unprofitable) or increase the scope and depth of value-added activities.

These developments in China's economic environment hence create opportunities to better understand issues of subsidiary development and evolution in multinational firm strategy, particularly as Japanese firms have established extensive production networks in China. In addition, this opportunity is one of the first provided in the context of a large country, thus allowing the possibility for a subsidiary to relocate in the same country, relocate to another country, develop or close. This research opportunity was not present for the study of subsidiary development in smaller economies, such as Malaysia or Canada.

Research on subsidiary evolution would also be useful when the emphasis is moved from the individual subsidiary to a group of subsidiaries, either those that are affiliated with a single MNE or with multiple different MNEs. Japanese MNEs are well known for having numerous subsidiaries overseas, among which peer-networking activities have been quite popular in these countries. We need to better understand how this network of subsidiaries should be best constructed to improve their individual performance and contribute to their parents' success. Being one of the largest hosts of Japanese FDI, China provides an ideal setting to investigate this research question.

Growth of foreign activity in China – institutions and international business

Foreign investment and foreign trade have been important to the growth of many developed and developing economies in the 1990s (UNCTAD 2001). China, in particular, has placed a high priority on seeking investment from foreign companies. Investment from foreign companies has brought managerial skills and technology to China (Anand and Delios 1996), and it has brought needed employment to China. The need for privately owned enterprises, domestic or foreign in ownership, to provide employment is particularly pronounced in China, as state-owned enterprises (SOEs) have been reduced in number and size.

The 200 million people previously employed in SOEs would have fallen into the ranks of the unemployed and underemployed unless they were picked up by domestic-owned private enterprises, new foreign-invested companies, or growth from already-invested foreign companies in China. In the future, policy makers in China concerned with domestic employment levels must consider whether foreign investors, such as those from Japan, will continue to enter the country. Policy makers should also consider the likelihood of new, non-Japanese investors entering China, if competitive Japanese companies are exiting due to a lack of profitability in operations there.

Japanese companies and many foreign companies have had difficulty in making a reasonable, not excessive, level of profits from China-based operations. Steps taken to date to facilitate foreign investment in China to reduce the difficulty of operations include substantial improvements in the transportation, financing and communications infrastructure, as well as the development of economic zones that provide tax and tariff-based cost concessions to foreign investors. Since China's accession to the World Trade Organization (WTO) in 2001, there have been substantial improvements in tariff rates, in equalising tax treatments (a potential investment disincentive), and in the further opening of service industries to foreign firms. That said, intellectual property protection remains a concern, even with the Chinese government's efforts to implement legal reforms in accordance with the WTO Agreement on Trade-Related Aspects of Intellectual Property Rights (TRIPS Agreement). Adequate monitoring and enforcement of these new regulations remains a serious concern.

Through steps such as these, policy makers have created four distinct regimes of FDI in China (Fu 2000). The early regime, 1979–1983, began with the establishment of the Joint Venture Law in 1979 and the creation of four SEZs in 1980. The next regime, 1984–1991, saw 14 coastal cities and the island of Hainan opened to FDI, with foreign investment further encouraged by the passing of the Law on wholly foreign-owned enterprises in 1986. The third regime, 1992–1994, was in many ways the peak of foreign investment to China, as our data show. Local municipal governments increased incentives to FDI, new industries such as finance, real estate, tourism and shipping were opened to FDI, and the message from Deng Xiaoping's early 1990s' tour of the southern provinces was to aggressively pursue market opportunities. The most recent regime, 1995 to the present, has seen increased competition for FDI arise from other countries in Asia, South America, and the transition economies of Eastern Europe. The State Council in China has continued to refine its definitions of which sectors can receive investment, while re-imposing duties on imported machinery, equipment parts and other materials used in foreign-invested joint ventures, but has avoided making substantial changes in areas that can significantly facilitate and protect the operations of foreign firms.

Without substantial changes in the institutions for investment, the results in the most recent regime of FDI have been lacklustre. The policy steps in each regime have provided part, but not all, of what needs to be done to attract and retain FDI. Fiscal incentives, for example, reduce costs so that the baseline for achieving profitable operations is lower. However, such fiscal incentives only camouflage systemic problems and can easily be revoked. Infrastructure improvements also do not provide an advantage that is translatable to the bottom line, especially on a comparative basis across nations. The improvements made to date at best ameliorate the significant disadvantages of operating a subsidiary in China.

Foreign investors establishing operations in China increasingly look beyond these simple improvements to signs that substantive steps, not increased rhetoric, are being taken to enhance the possibility for achieving a reasonable level of profitable operations in China. A foreign investor considering setting up export-oriented or market-seeking operations in China looks for more positive and progressive signs of change. Fundamental institutional change would be one of these signs. Until 2006, the institutions in China for governing competition have not been well established. While exceptions exist, such as the creation of a number of National Accounting Institutes, much remains to be done. However, since Hu Jintao assumed the reins of the national government, the Communist Party of China has shown resolution to fight against corruption, in particular, with a firm hand.

Foreign companies continue to face significant knowledge and operating disadvantages compared to domestic companies. Late entering foreign companies to China's market are likely to face even more substantive disadvantages because the best potential domestic allies for facilitating investment are often already tied-up in alliances with the early entrants to China (Beamish and Jiang 2002). Late entrants to China also face a substantially altered geography of investment in China. In the early days of investment, the best opportunities for investment were in the eastern cities, in the coastal band extending from Bohai Bay to the Pearl River Delta. By 2006, the costs and competitive environments of operating in this eastern coastal band had increased considerably. The cost advantages that had prompted investments in the 1980s and early 1990s had been eroded by the late 1990s. To stem an overall erosion of FDI into China, the seeds of investment in the interior provinces, which have seen less substantive increases in factor costs than the eastern coastal provinces, must be sown and fertilised by improvements in the institutional environment.

With the creation of new policy zones in the interior provinces, the policy-created advantages of investing in Shenzhen, Zhuhai and Xiamen are not as great. The new policy zones do not have the same policy incentive structures as the well-known SEZ created in the early and mid-1980s. Instead, the new policy zones are more specialised. The zones include types such as the New and High Technology Development Zones created in 1991 and 1992, Economic/Technology Development Zones created from the mid-1990s, and Free Trade or Tax Protection Zones (Zhou *et al.* 2002). The creation of these zones has resulted in more than 180 cities in China having some sort of policy initiative to stimulate foreign investment.

Although these new policy zones have reduced the policy advantage of the eastern coastal provinces, the level of infrastructure development and the lack of density of competitive domestic industry in the interior regions mean that the investment environment is still nascent. When thinking of investing in China, the relevant comparison point for a foreign investor, such as a Japanese firm, might not be China versus another country. Neither would it necessarily be between the eastern coastal areas and the interior of China. Instead, the appropriate comparison might be between the interior Chinese provinces and other nations such as Vietnam. Sichuan province, for example, has a population comparable to Vietnam but a per capita GDP greater than Vietnam. Although Sichuan enjoys cost advantages relative to the eastern parts of China, it is at a disadvantage relative to Vietnam. The interior areas of China have been aggressively opened up to FDI but new, potential sites for investment such as Vietnam, represent a competitive alternative, and Japanese firms have already begun to site a growing amount of FDI in Vietnam in recent years.

Growth of foreign activity in China: offshoring, outsourcing and international business theory

An internalisation theory framework is a pervasive theoretical frame in international business (Buckley and Casson 1976, Rugman 1981, Hennart 1982). Market failure related to the exchange of intermediate products is a crucial point in internalisation theory. Five elements can be differentiated in terms of the market failure for the intermediate knowledge products (Buckley and Casson 1976, 1991): (1) the absence of a futures market for knowledge production, requiring both the planning of knowledge development and its exploitation by a firm; (2) the inability of external markets to allow optimal price discrimination when selling proprietary knowledge; (3) the frequent occurrence of bilateral bargaining problems between monopolistic suppliers and monopolistic buyers of knowledge; (4) buyer uncertainty; and (5) various difficulties associated with pricing knowledge.

The above five elements are manifested in '... vertically integrated process industries, knowledge-intensive industries, quality assurance-dependent products and communication-intensive industries' (Buckley 1988, p. 182). A key question to be considered when applying an internalisation theory framework to internationalisation issues for high value-added activities is whether the intermediate products of knowledge that are endemic to high value-added activities are costly when being exchanged in external markets, or valuable when being exchanged in internal markets (Buckley and Casson 1991). The international business literature has distinguished between two kinds of intermediate products. The first kind refers to the output of specific privileged assets that grant ownership advantages to the possessors. The greater the imperfections in the market exchange for these assets, the more likely the possessors choose FDI to utilise their advantages across national boundaries. Advantages come from the internalisation of those products, compared to the high transaction costs in external market transactions for these types of assets.

The second kind of intermediate products refers to those whose value is increased if they are used or traded with other intermediate products, although the transaction costs for external market transactions may not be unusually high. In other words, there exist economies of scope or scale for these kind of products. The internalisation of this kind of product can internalise some of the external benefits associated with market transactions (Dunning and Kundu 1995). The internalisation of these products creates opportunities for economies of scope and scale.

An internalisation theory framework has been applied to manufacturing and service firms alike. Included in this profile of industries that have been studied is the banking industry. Banks are active agents that can gather, process and utilise specialised information about their clients, including lenders and borrowers. As the main function of a bank is financial mediation, the core element of a bank's activity is dealing with that type of information. This type of information constitutes a valued set of knowledge specific to the bank. The failure of the market for knowledge in banking operations is a key factor in the internalisation decision and the internalisation of information is the principal advantage of a multinational bank (MNB). The process of generating bank-specific knowledge and information advantages in response to imperfect markets is the essence of internalisation in terms of MNBs (Rugman 1981). Consequently, an internalisation theory framework can not only capture the specific characteristics of MNBs as one part of the service industry, but also provide some consistent understandings of an MNB's decision to enter a foreign market (Qian and Delios 2008).

MNBs are also among the types of high-knowledge firms that have been leading the recent waves of offshoring and outsourcing activities. Offshoring involves the movement of co-located activities to different locations abroad that typically are low-wage sites. Meanwhile, outsourcing is the procurement of products and services from sources that are external to the organisation. Both offshoring and outsourcing conceptually represent a movement of the productive activities of a firm outside of the immediate organisational and geographic boundaries of the firm. This conception has a similarity to core decisions in internationalisation – licensing, franchising, technology transfer, alliances and FDI.

The conception of outsourcing and offshoring involves consideration of whether the activities are done within a firm's boundary and, thereby, remain linked to the firm, and whether the activities remain in the same location as other activities. Where the activity remains in the firm (it has full ownership of the process), but if it is done in a new location, this is considered offshoring, by writers in the offshoring literature. Yet, this same activity is not dissimilar to the formation of a foreign subsidiary. If that same process is undertaken by another firm in an overseas location, it is both offshored and outsourced, which conceptually resembles a licensing agreement.

These developments in offshoring and outsourcing, as well as the emergence of FDI from nations such as China and India, offer an opportunity to reinvigorate international business research. International business research is driven by phenomenon, which often places it at the forefront of emerging managerial, organizational and strategic issues. To the extent that we have new emergent trends in the international business environment, particularly in large emerging economies such as India or China, we have the opportunity to add steam to the international business research agenda (Buckley 2002).

For example, a starting point for an IB focused agenda on firm boundaries and internalisation might rest in the key differences between the traditional international business conceptions of offshoring and outsourcing. These differences rest in how one views the levels of integration between the various processes or activities in a firm. Integration in the firm is greater in the case of offshoring and outsourcing than for a licensing, franchising, alliance or wholly owned subsidiary. Hence, the issues of knowledge and coordination are more prominent in outsourcing and offshoring than for traditional modes of internationalisation. This difference creates opportunities to extend key theories in international business, such as the internationalisation theory, which has already been shown to be robust to explaining both services and manufacturing FDI.

The importance of this extension is provided by the recent experiences of Japanese firms in China. Although not reflected in the data on FDI, offshoring and outsourcing is becoming an increasingly important activity of Japanese firms in China. These high value-added activities are taking place in Liaoning province, principally in Dalian. The growth of these activities is consistent with the overall shift in FDI from low to high value-added activities in this region.

As an example[1] of this new trend in the international business activities of Japanese firms in China, according to the China Software Industry Association, China has already become the largest overseas software outsourcing manufacturing base for Japan. Beijing exported US$0.15 billion of software development towards Japan in 2004. This trade value is expected to increase by 50% per year. As another example of growth in this sector, China will need around 3750 more Japanese language software engineers annually, and the number is expected to increase by 150% per year. Finding and retaining qualified and affordable staff in China, where labour turnover is common (Beamish 2006) has become an even greater challenge.

As mentioned earlier, Dalian has become a major destination for outsourcing and offshoring activities. Since the early 1990s, companies such as Dalian Hi-Think have started to do business with Japanese firms, as vendors for those firms. Since 2000, the software and information service industry in Dalian has maintained its high growth momentum with an annual increase rate of sales income of 60% and exports of 78%. In 2005, the total sales in this sector was RMB 10 billion, with exports of US$300 million.

In 2005, there were 510 software and information service enterprises in Dalian. The scale is small, with only seven enterprises having more than 1000 employees and just 50 enterprises with more than 100 employees. Two hundred and eighty enterprises have taken residence in Dalian Software Park. Japanese companies co-exist with these firms, with a large number of major Japanese firms such as Sony Corp. and Toshiba Inc., having set up operations in the city.

Even given the importance of these trends, a major challenge to research is the availability of data. Outsourcing and offshoring data are simply not readily available. The US$2.8 billion figure for China's software exports in 2004 from China's Ministry of Commerce includes, for example, not just offshoring and outsourcing for foreign customers but also embedded software products produced in China for mobile phones, home appliances and other export-oriented consumer electronics. For software outsourcing, the total revenue in China includes both offshore outsourcing and the very large domestic, or onshore, component of outsourcing. According to CCID (a Beijing-based market research firm), Japan accounted for 64% of China's offshore outsourcing market in 2004. Most of Japan's outsourcing demand is for embedded software: in cameras, cars, medical equipment, machine tools, and so on, according to Liu Jiren, founder and chairman of Neusoft. Liu also suggests that more outsourcing will be done in China as more manufacturing is done here because customers find that the supply chain is already in place in China, and that software costs are lower.

The software export to Japan and IT outsourcing business have 10 years experience in Dalian, which ranks first in China regarding the history of export business with Japan and the export volume. One observer has suggested that Dalian has become for Japan what Bangalore has become for America and other English-speaking countries: an outsourcing centre.

Concluding remarks

Japanese international activity in China in the second half of the 2000s has been in a modest period of recovery. The mid-2000s have seen a resumption of FDI at a moderate level, compared with earlier years, and the FDI has begun to assume different characteristics from the previous generation of FDI.

Japanese FDI has become more widespread in its regional coverage across China, with substantially more investments being made in the hinterland region (interior provinces) of China. Notably, the investment in the East, mid-South and North is still strong but of a changing nature. With the declining cost-competitiveness of the operating environment in the East, mid-South and North, and the developing highly skilled labour market, Japanese MNEs have begun to place a greater emphasis on high value-added activities, including offshoring and outsourcing in Eastern seaboard provinces and municipalities in China. Meanwhile, low value-added, high labour component activities are shifting out of the East, mid-South and North, to the interior of China or to other regions in Asia.

These empirical trends create substantial opportunities for understanding FDI, subsidiary strategy, MNE strategy and the influence of the institutional environment on the decisions multinational firms make. Specifically, the changes in Japanese investment in China have created opportunities for research in three areas:

(1) Subsidiary development and multinational firm strategy.
(2) Institutions and international business.
(3) Offshoring, outsourcing and international business theory.

Research is not limited to exploring these areas but given that these three topical areas are vibrant and active ones in current international business research, the setting of Japanese FDI in China provides a good opportunity to provide a deeper understanding of these core areas of international business research.

Acknowledgements

This research was generously supported by an academic research grant from the National University of Singapore (NUS Academic Research Grant R-313-000-095-112) and by a Social Sciences and Humanities Research Council of Canada Grant (#410-2001-0143).

Notes

1. Material in the remainder of this section draws on various sources, including: China Software Industry Association website, industry news: http://www.csia.org.cn/chinese_en/index/news html [Accessed 3 October 2006].
   Jing Guowei, Software and information service industry in Dalian. Dalian Bureau of Information Industry. Available from: http://www.asocio.org/file/The%20Software%20and%20Information%20Service%20Industry%20in%20Dalian.pdf [Accessed 17 November 2006].
   China rivals India in services-software outsourcing in Asia's billion-dollar-plus giants bears distinctly different fruit. The business of technology 2005. San Mateo, CA: Red Herring Inc. Available from: http://www.redherring.com/Home/13618 [Accessed 17 November 2006].

References

Anand, J. and Delios, A., 1996. Competing globally: how Japanese MNCs have matched goals and strategies in India and China. *Columbia journal of world business*, 31 (3), 60–74.

Bartlett, C.A. and Ghoshal, S., 1986. Tap your subsidiaries for global reach. *Harvard business review*, 64 (6), 87–94.

Beamish, P.W., 2006. The high cost of cheap Chinese labor. *Harvard business review*, 84 (6), 23.

Beamish, P.W., Delios, A., and Lecraw, D.J., 1997. *Japanese multinationals in the global economy*. Basingstoke: Edward Elgar Publishing Limited.

Beamish, P.W. and Jiang, R., 2002. Investing profitably in China. Is it getting harder? *Long range planning*, 35, 135–151.

Birkinshaw, J.M. and Hood, N., 1998. Multinational subsidiary evolution: capability and charter change in foreign-owned subsidiary companies. *Academy of management review*, 23 (4), 773–795.

Buckley, P.J., 1988. The limits of explanation, testing the internalization theory of the multinational enterprise. *Journal of international business studies*, 19, 181–193.

Buckley, P.J., 2002. Is the international business research agenda running out of steam? *Journal of international business studies*, 33, 365–373.

Buckley, P.J. and Casson, M., 1976. *The future of the multinational enterprise*. 1st ed. London: MacMillan Publishing.

Buckley, P.J. and Casson, M., 1991. *The future of the multinational enterprise*. 2nd ed. London: MacMillan Publishing.

Buckley, P.J. *et al.*, 2007. The determinants of Chinese outward foreign direct investment. *Journal of international business studies*, 38, 499–518.

China Statistics Bureau, various years (1991–2004). *China statistical yearbook* [ZhongGuo TongJi NianJian]. Beijing: China Statistics Press.

Delios, A., Gaur, A.S., and Makino, S., 2008. The timing of international expansion: information, rivalry and imitation among Japanese firms, 1980–2002. *Journal of management studies*, 45 (1), 169–195.

Dunning, J. and Kundu, S., 1995. The internationalization of the hotel industry-some findings from a field study. *Management international review*, 35 (2), 101–133.

Fu, J., 2000. *Institutions and investment: foreign direct investment in China during an era of reforms*. Ann Arbor, MI: University of Michigan Press.

Gupta, A.K. and Govindarajan, V., 1991. Knowledge flows and the structure of control within multinational corporations. *Academy of management review*, 16, 768–792.

Henisz, W.J. and Delios, A., 2001. Uncertainty, imitation and plant location: Japanese multinational corporations, 1990–1996. *Administrative science quarterly*, 46, 443–475.

Hennart, J.-F., 1982. *A theory of multinational enterprise*. Ann Arbor, MI: University of Michegan Press.

Jarillo, J.C. and Martinez, J.I., 1990. Different roles for subsidiaries: the case of multinational corporations in Spain. *Strategic management journal*, 11 (1), 501–512.

Knickerbocker, F., 1973. *Oligopolistic reaction and multinational enterprise*. Cambridge, MA: Harvard University Press.

Kojima, K., 1973. Macroeconomic approach to foreign direct investment. *Hitotsubashi journal of economics*, 14, 1–21.

Martin, X., Swaminathan, A., and Mitchell, W., 1998. Organizational evolution in the interorganizational environment: incentives and constraints on international expansion strategy. *Administrative science quarterly*, 43, 566–601.

Pye, L.W., 1986. The China trade: making the deal. *Harvard business review*, July, 74–79.

Qian, L.H. and Delios, A., 2008. Internalization and experience: Japanese banks' international expansion, 1980–1998. *Journal of international business studies*, 39 (2), 231–248.

Rugman, A.M., 1981. *Inside the multinationals*. London: Croom Helm.

Sachwald, F., ed., 1995. *Japanese firms in Europe*. Luxembourg: Harwood Academic Publishers.

Toyo Keizai, *Kaigai Shinshutsu Kigyô Sôran*. 2007. Tokyo: Toyo Keizai.

UNCTAD, 2001. *World investment report 2001: promoting linkages*. New York and Geneva: United Nations.

White, R.E. and Poynter, T., 1984. Strategies for foreign-owned subsidiaries in Canada. *Business quarterly*, 49 (2), 59–69.

Zhou, C., Delios, A., and Yang, J.Y., 2002. The location of Japanese foreign direct investment in China. *Asia Pacific journal of management*, 19 (1), 63–86.

Appendix

Data source for analysis of Japanese foreign direct investment in China

We use a single data source for our account of the history and 2006 status of Japanese foreign investment in China. The single source is the Japanese language version of Toyo Keizai's annual publication entitled *Japanese overseas investment* (Kaigai Shinshutsu Kigyô Sôran). This publication has been published annually since the 1970s. To construct the sample and data used for the analyses in this study, we consulted each annual edition from 1979, when China first reopened its doors to foreign participation in the economy, to 2006. By consulting each annual edition, we were able to construct a complete investment history of subsidiary establishments.

Although *Japanese overseas investment* is a reputable data source that is created by a company with a more than 100 years history of compiling and reporting statistical information and company demographics (Beamish *et al.* 1997), a single source can have its limitations. The major limitation with which we were concerned was the extent of coverage of Japanese overseas investment. The data reported in *Japanese overseas investment* were compiled by Toyo Keizai as part of annual surveys of public and private companies with foreign investment activity. In 1997, for example, 55% of the companies responded to the survey. Where responses were not received, staff at Toyo Keizai used the previous year's data and, in some cases, information was updated using additional sources such as securities reports, telephone interviews and other accounts reported in the media (such as newspapers).

The earlier editions of *Japanese overseas investment* did not include all companies that have made foreign direct investments; however, the coverage has been improving over time. Our assessment of the coverage of parent firms found that in 1999, all but 33 firms (about 1.5%) of the more than 3000 Japanese public firms that had foreign subsidiaries were listed in *Japanese overseas investments* (Henisz and Delios 2001). Further, the 33 firms that were not listed had just 70 foreign subsidiaries, which was less than 0.5% of the foreign subsidiaries listed in the 1999 edition of *Japanese overseas investments*. This is corroborated by UNCTAD (2001), which reported that there were 4334 Japanese multinational firms in the year 2000, a number very close to that recorded in Toyo Keizai. The one discrepancy between the sources was the number of foreign affiliates of Japanese firms, which was stated to be more than 60,000 in UNCTAD but 19,000 in Toyo Keizai. This large discrepancy might be definitional in nature, as *Japanese overseas investment* does not count branch offices, representative offices and the like, even if wholly owned, in its primary listing of foreign subsidiaries.

Aside from *Japanese overseas investment*, other possible sources include Ministry of Finance data on the dollar flows of FDI, the data compiled by the surveys of the Japanese External Trade Organization (JETRO) or those of MITI. However, these surveys tend to have lower response rates than Toyo Keizai's survey, and the resultant information is more incomplete (Sachwald 1995).

The transformation of Japan Post into a global player

T. Goydke

Bremen University of Applied Sciences, Germany

Introduction

The former Japanese Prime Minister Koizumi Jun'ichirô regarded the privatisation of the country's postal administration, the Postal Services Agency, as the centrepiece of his premiership. Against heavy resistance, this reform project was put firmly on track before he left office in September 2006.

The reform of Japan's postal administration received much attention in the media and in scholarly publications. However, attention was focused primarily on the effects of privatisation on the Postal Savings Bank (*yûbin chokin*, or briefly: *yûcho*) and on Postal Life Insurance (*kan'i hoken*, or briefly: *kampo*). The reason for this interest lies mainly in the immense assets and the sheer size of these two financial institutions. However, little academic attention has been paid to the reform and expansion of Japan Post into new business areas, a process which began even before privatisation was completed. The aim of this study, therefore, is to evaluate the process by which Japan Post was privatised, and how this has influenced the internationalisation of the organisation, both generally, and in the specific context of the East Asian region. With both the privatisation process, as well as the move into new markets, showing obvious similarities with the transformation of Deutsche Post into the global player DHL, this will be achieved by comparing the privatisations of the Japanese and German postal systems, and an assessment is made as to what extent the Japanese government used the German case as a model. The expansion of Japan Post into new international business fields to 2007 is also compared with the expansion strategy of the German firm.

The study is organised as follows. In the next section, literature is reviewed on postal privatisation from a corporate governance perspective, in order to provide a theoretical rationale for the study. An overview of the privatisation efforts of postal services in Japan is then presented, followed by a comparison of these efforts with postal privatisation in Germany. The move of Japan Post into new international markets during the course of privatisation and afterwards is then assessed, and a comparison is made of the internationalisation strategies of Deutsche Post and Japan Post. Conclusions are then drawn and some implications for policy are discussed.

Literature review

The transformation of state monopolies

That a free market order promotes the highest economic efficiency is no longer seriously challenged, since it has been clearly proven by various empirical and theoretical studies. Various incentive and sanction mechanisms that result from the interaction of property rights and the application of the principles of competition form the basis of this efficiency. Governments have often justified their intervention in a free market economy either with the market failure argument or with the argument that a natural monopoly exists (Knorr 1993).

The theory of natural monopoly is considered as the classical reason for the justification of state intervention in the postal service sector, especially in letter post services (Knorr 1993, p. 9ff). Proponents argue that postal services require high investments in delivery infrastructure. The existence of economies of scope and scale are seen as further justifications. Furthermore, it is argued that private companies lack the incentive to provide a universal postal service covering all regions of a country (see for instance, Sharkey 1982). However, these arguments lack a strong theoretical and empirical foundation.[1] It was not the lack of theoretical or empirical justification but the continuous financial losses of many national postal administrations, as a direct consequence of absent competitive pressure, which has led to deregulation in several countries since the late 1980s. While these measures were welcomed by opponents of the former postal monopolies, the process of deregulation raised other concerns as well. In many cases, postal administrations could maintain a monopolistic position in some or all of their core markets, or market access for private competitors became heavily regulated. These measures were generally justified for social reasons (like security of supply, employment status of former public servants, and so forth) and because the necessary protection would be provided to assure a smooth transformation from a state-owned to a private enterprise.

However, critics have argued that postal administrations often use their monopoly gains to finance aggressive expansion into new businesses, squeezing private competitors out of their markets. This criticism has been particularly pronounced for the activities of Deutsche Post (formerly Deutsche Bundespost), which has gained a leading position in the global mail and express market through a worldwide acquisition strategy (see Sappington and Sidak 2003, Cohen 2004).

Although it has been criticised for its partly uncompetitive behaviour, Deutsche Post has proved rather successful in its transformation into a global player. It is, therefore, not surprising that the Japanese government took the case of Deutsche Post as a model when privatisation efforts for the Japanese postal service administration began in the late 1990s.[2] Or, as Cohen puts it: 'The new business model they [the Japan Post] discovered was the one that Deutsche Post adopted. The centrepiece of this model was entry into new markets at home and abroad' (Cohen 2006, p. 35).

For a better understanding of the discussion that follows, it is necessary to give some further explanation of what is meant by postal services.

The postal service sector

Postal services are generally comprised of delivery services, regardless of whether this concerns letters, parcels, newspapers or courier mail items. The items pass through five organisationally separated stages (Knorr 1993): (1) collection of items at the place of origin; (2) (rough) pre-sorting according to target areas; (3) transportation; (4) final (fine) sorting in the target; and (5) delivery of the items to the place of destination. These stages can be either combined into one vertically integrated enterprise or they can be performed by separated but cooperating single service providers (Knorr 1993).

Among postal service providers it is common to distinguish postal services horizontally according to product groups. This distinction reflects the special characteristics of these groups, as well as the needs and preferences of respective customers (Knorr 1993, DPWN 2005). Product groups include: (i) written notes and correspondence; (ii) mail items or catalogues with identical content; (iii) express delivery; (iv) packages and parcels; and (v) newspapers and magazines. This distinction has generally been used when, in the course of privatisation, postal administrations were split into separate units or enterprises.

The internationalisation of service suppliers

The reasons for the internationalisation of Japanese companies and their strategies have been widely discussed. Haak (2001) argues that the basic motives for internationalisation are either the search for resources or for markets. The exploitation of resources (in the sense of key supplies such as energy, natural resources or labour) is the driving force for industries with a competitive advantage derived from access to resources. The exploitation of markets, on the other hand, motivates mass-producing industries in which competitive advantage is based on cost reduction derived from economies of scale. While the main motivation for Japanese companies to expand their activities in the East and Southeast Asian region have historically been resource-seeking (mainly cheap labour), it has changed in recent years to become more seeking markets (Haak 2001, Yamazawa 2003).

Literature on the internationalisation of Japanese firms generally focuses on manufacturing companies (Aoki 1984, 1990). Relatively little attention has been paid to service firms, especially those in transportation and logistics sectors. Lemoine and Daguæs (2002) provide four reasons why service firms expand their activities on an international scale:

(1) to generate greater economies of scale and scope;
(2) in response to the internationalisation of competitors;
(3) in response to the internationalisation of customers who require service suppliers to follow and to build-up global networks;
(4) in response to improvements in communication and transportation technologies that enable service firms to set-up and manage complex global networks.

Increasing global competition has forced manufacturing firms in recent years to apply business concepts such as just-in-time, outsourcing, offshoring and other cost-minimising strategies. These developments have also changed the perception of transportation and logistics which are now recognised as integral parts of a firm's production strategy (Lemoine and Daguæs 2002). More specifically, Dodgson *et al.* (2004) distinguish five business strategies that postal operators have adopted in recent years:

(1) 'Vertical integration' through the inclusion of activities that do not belong to the traditional postal value chain, such as logistics.
(2) 'Horizontal integration' in order to use synergies between express, mail and logistics.
(3) 'Internationalization' driven by customers' demands or to seek new markets (because express post and logistics markets are traditionally more international, global expansion often results from vertical or horizontal integrations, or both).
(4) 'Cost efficiency measures' motivated by increased competition, regulation of tariffs or financial difficulties.
(5) 'Development of new products' such as priority and non-priority mail, hybrid mail (email messages sent to postal services providers for conventional on-forwarding) or sales channel innovations.

While these developments are observable on a global scale and are not unique to Japanese service providers, there are some specific aspects that require further discussion. Ström (2004) argues that a key characteristic of Japanese manufacturing firms is 'introvert service supply'. Firms tend to use inhouse service suppliers or suppliers affiliated to one of the large company groups (*keiretsu*), or in more general terms, to a network. From his observations of Japanese business service suppliers in the UK, Ström (2004) concluded that the choice of a service supplier is driven largely by loyalty, personal ties and the affiliation of firms to a specific network. Given this observation, the internationalisation of Japanese service firms tends to be driven by customers demand and is, to a lesser extent, a proactive market-seeking strategy.

Privatisation and corporate governance

The term corporate governance describes the relationship between a company and its stakeholders (Ahmadjian and Song 2004). From an institutional theory viewpoint, it refers to factors which change the expected returns of transactions and transfers control to delegated actors. The basic idea is thus to reduce transaction costs by improving information flows and avoiding false or misguided expectations. Moreover, effective governance institutions increase the accountability of agents as principles can replace agents or withdraw their investments (Dyck 2000). Corporate governance is part of a country's socioeconomic system, and is directly linked to the financial and employment system, as well as to growth and innovation patterns (Aoki 2001, Hall and Soskice 2001).

Since the 1990s, there has been a growing awareness worldwide of inefficiencies in government regulations which can give rise to increasing transaction costs, a waste of resources, corruption and market distortion. For example, Cornett *et al.* (2003), found in 16 East Asian countries that private banks tended to have higher profit and efficiency levels than state-owned banks, while La Porta *et al.* (2002) show that a strong correlation exists between levels of state-bank ownership and lower per capita income and productivity growth as well as underdeveloped financial systems.

Governments have therefore implemented various reforms aimed at enhancing efficiency, reducing corruption and saving resources through the privatisation of state-controlled assets. In order to pursue these goals it is important to build confidence among participants that this will lead to many competitors being engaged in fair competition. Modern corporate governance is also based on sound legal and bankruptcy systems which effectively uphold the rights of shareholders and creditors. In order to monitor the privatised entity, reliable accounting and auditing standards need to be implemented (Wiwattanakantang 2006).

In Japan, the bursting of the asset price bubble in the early 1990s and the banking crisis that ensued has underlined certain deficiencies in Japan's corporate governance system. The Japanese government reacted with a number of reforms. In order to increase accountability and transparency, the Commercial Code was revised in 1993, 1997 and 2002. Revision of accounting regulations began in 1996 with the announcement of the 'Big Bang', which sought to introduce global standards to Japan's financial markets (Ahmadjian and Song 2004). The privatisation of Japan Post is one amongst several major privatisations since the 1980s when the Nippon Telegraph and Telephone Public Corporation (NTT), Japan Tobacco and Salt Public Corporation (JTSPC) and Japan National Railroad (JNR) were transformed into private companies. The objectives behind Japan's privatisation efforts have been articulated in several government reports: namely, enhanced transparency, increased profitability and the intensification of competition levels to prepare Japan's economy for increasing globalisation of world markets (Tamamura 2002).

Research questions

Given this backdrop, the present study considers the following questions:

- How does the strategy of Japan Post compare to the privatisations of the German postal services?
- To what extent did the Japanese government use the German case as a model?
- How does the privatisation of Japan Post fit into the overall picture of corporate governance reform in Japan?

Data analysis: the privatisation of postal services in Japan

Overview of Japan Post

Japan Post comprises the original mail delivery business, Postal Service, and two other divisions, Postal Savings and Postal Life Insurance Welfare Corp. The company as a whole has 271,000 employees (making it the country's largest employer) and has 25,000 branches throughout the country. It delivers 24.7 billion letters every year (fiscal year 2006). In the market for parcels, Japan Post only has a share of 10%, with approximately 30% held by the market leader Yamato Transport with its *kuroneko* (black cat) and *takkyûbin* (home express post) services.[3] The Japanese Postal Savings Bank has deposits of 227 trillion Yen (approx. US$2 billion), and accounts for around 30% of all private savings deposits in Japan. It is the world's largest financial institution, and is about twice the size of the world's next two largest banks, Mitsubishi UFJ Financial Group and Citigroup (with around one billion US deposits each). Similarly, the postal life insurance business constitutes around 40% of all assets held in life insurance products in Japan (122 billion Yen) and is, therefore, larger than the four largest private life insurers in Japan combined (Figure 1). Around 25% of all privately held assets – including securities, stocks and bonds – in Japan are held by the Postal Savings Bank and Postal Life Insurance (Porges and Leong 2005).

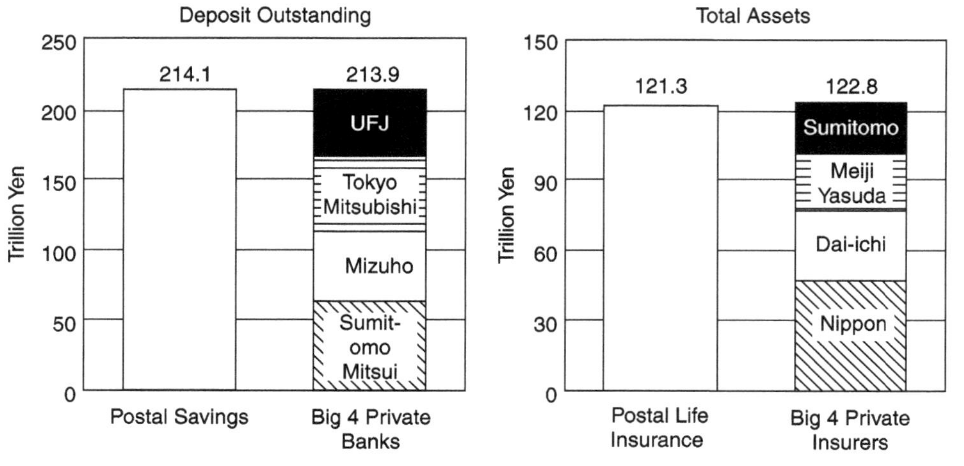

Figure 1. Japanese postal savings and life insurance and its private competitors.
Note: Data refers to fiscal year 2005 (01 April 2004–31 March 2005).
Source: Japan Center for Economic Research (2005).

Reasons for privatisation

A first wave of privatisation efforts occurred in Japan in the 1980s, primarily as a consequence of the high state deficit, which had grown following the oil crises of the 1970s (Walke 2004). Again, Japan developed immense national debt as a consequence of failed economic stimulation programmes in the recessionary and low growth phases of the 1990s. Therefore, the obvious conclusion to draw is that a reduction of state deficit was a key motive for the privatisation of the Japanese postal administration in the 1990s. Indeed, the Japanese government provided three reasons for its reform:

(1) a reduction of state expenditures and thus a contribution to the reduction of national debt;
(2) an increase in the efficiency of capital markets and thus greater attractiveness for foreign investors;
(3) an expansion of the service spectrum of the post and its competitiveness in global markets.

In contrast to privatisation projects in Europe, postal reform in Japan was not directed primarily towards more competition in the postal delivery sector, but at a diversification of the considerable assets of the Postal Savings Bank and the Postal Life Insurance businesses (Porges and Leong 2005, Cohen 2006).

Outline of the privatisation process

In the mid-1990s, Junichiro Koizumi put the topic of a postal reform high on the agenda in his bid for the Liberal Democratic Party (LDP) presidency against Hashimoto Ryûtarô. He was eventually defeated by Hashimoto but, as a member of the Hashimoto cabinet, Koizumi developed the first plan for the privatisation of the country's postal administration. In 1997 a plan was submitted, which recommended the transfer of post offices, Postal Savings Bank and Postal Life Insurance into one single public enterprise. As a first measure, the Japanese postal administration was converted into a governmental agency, the Postal Services Agency (*yûseichô*) in 2001. Thus, the business activities of the postal system remained part of the state budget. It was not subject to taxation, and deposits with the Postal Savings Bank and the Postal Life Insurance remained guaranteed by the government (Maclachlan 2004, Porges and Leong 2005).

Koizumi made further postal reform one of the government's most important goals as he took the office of prime minister in April 2001. In 2002, a bill was submitted that authorised the transfer of the postal agency into a public enterprise and allowed private competitors to enter the postal delivery business. In April 2003, Japan Post (*nihon yûsei kôsha*) was established as a public enterprise through the reorganisation of the Postal Services Agency (under the Japan Post Corporation Law) into three divisions: mail services; postal savings; and postal life insurance. After his re-election as LDP chairman in 2003, Koizumi assigned his most important advisory committee, the Council on Economic and Fiscal Policy (CEFP), to further develop the reform plans. In April 2004, the committee recommended that Japan Post be split into four individual enterprises (Walke 2004, Cargill and Scott 2006).

The Japanese cabinet accepted the plan on 10 September 2004. According to the cabinet's decision:

(1) The three existing divisions plus a newly created division (to provide counter services for the other three businesses) should be gradually transferred into four private enterprises under the umbrella of a holding company from April 2007 onwards.
(2) Two-thirds of the shares of the holding company should be in private hands by March 2017.
(3) The government would reserve the right to buy back the shares.
(4) The Postal Savings Bank and the Postal Life Insurance businesses should be denationalised first and be treated according to bank and insurance laws as appropriate.
(5) For the postal delivery service, the letter monopoly should be left unchanged at first and prices should remain under government control.

Among other elements of the deregulation process, the cabinet's decision also envisioned the development of new domestic and international business fields by the postal service (Walke 2004).

The cabinet's decision was submitted as a bill to the two chambers of the Japanese parliament in July and August 2005. While the bill passed the Lower House (or the House of Representatives, *shugiin*) with a small majority (with many LDP members defecting from the ruling coalition); it was rejected in the Upper House (or the House of Councillors, *sangiin*), although Koizumi had threatened the dissolution of the Lower House (as the Upper House cannot be dissolved). Koizumi thereupon dissolved the Lower House and new elections were set for 11 September 2005. Postal reform was the dominant topic in the election campaign such that the election effectively became a referendum on postal privatisation. The new elections brought the LDP and Koizumi a fulminant victory and a mandate for reform. The LDP and its coalition partner increased their share of seats in the Lower House from 54% to 67%. After this victory, Koizumi's reform package was accepted in September 2005 by both chambers with only minor changes (Porges and Leong 2005, Cargill and Scott 2006).

According to the law passed, after privatisation the branch network was to remain unchanged and, in the branches, products of the Postal Savings Bank and the Postal Life Insurance should be sold. In addition, branches could now sell the services of other private suppliers. Only existing savings accounts and/or insurance policies remain guaranteed by the government. Employees were to lose their special status as government officials, and the Postal Savings Bank and Postal Life Insurance businesses could expand into new business fields abroad (Cargill and Scott 2006). A timeline for the privatisation of the Japanese postal administration is provided in Figure 2.

The outcome of the privatisation process had been criticised particularly by representatives of the private banking sector, who feared that the enterprises that were previously state monopolists would become omnipotent competitors. A further criticism is that the Postal Savings Bank and the life insurance businesses might advance into new business fields before the privatisation process was completed. Regional banks in Japan,

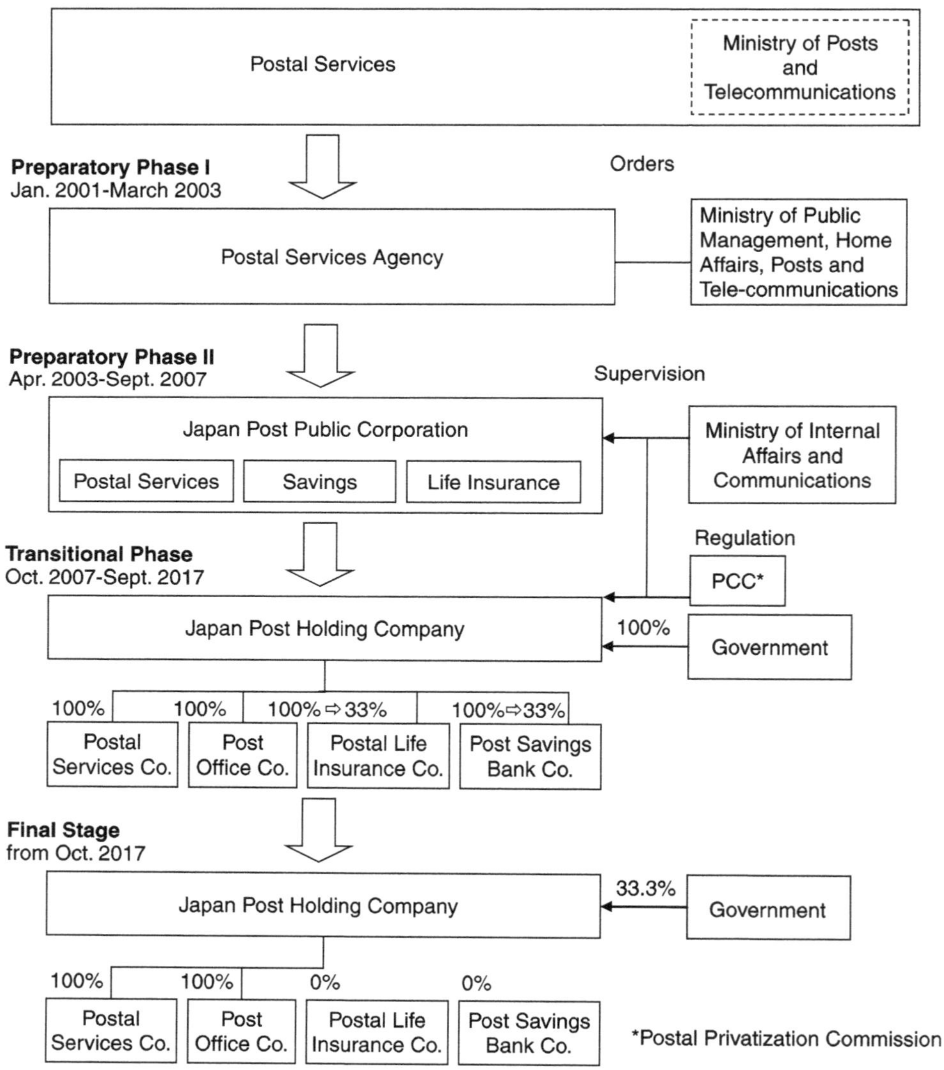

Figure 2. Phases of the transformation of the Japanese post.
Source: Author, after Cohen 2006 (p. 6), MIC 2006 (p. 4), Watanabe 2006 (pp. 65–67).

in particular, see the potential for unfair competition, since the Postal Savings Bank can utilise the branch network of the post and threaten their core business by expanding into the loan business (Bastian 2006). In principle, more competition in the mail delivery business is envisaged. However, market entrance regulations for new competitors are formulated so vaguely that critics assume that the Ministry of Internal Affairs and Communications (MIC) (established in 2001 through the integration of the Ministry of Posts and Telecommunications, the Ministry of Home Affairs and the Management and Coordination Agency) will use its discretionary scope, as permitting authority, to prevent potential competitors from market entry.[4] Although direct subsidies for the post are omitted under the new system the post will still enjoy certain privileges. Thus, until 2017, special tax treatments will be granted and vehicles of the post will be excluded from strict traffic regulations and may stop in places in which competitors may face penalties. In addition, the post remains excluded from strict customs regulations and does not have to go through expensive and time-consuming customs clearance procedures. Furthermore, the post is not subject to certain strict safety regulations, which have applied since 11 September 2001 to other courier and logistics enterprises (Japan Center for Economic Research 2005, Cohen 2006).

Discussion: a comparison of the privatisations of Deutsche Bundespost and Japan Post

Postal administration in Germany and Japan

There are many similarities between the Japanese postal administration prior to privatisation and the former state monopolist in Germany, Bundespost. It comes as little surprise that the privatisation process of both agencies show several similarities too.

Deutsche Post traces its roots back to the fifteenth century when the first regular mail delivery service was set up by the Taxis family following orders by Emperor Maximilian I. The 'real' history of Deutsche Post goes back to 1876 when the existing post and telegraph administrations were unified in the German Reich. In 1924, Deutsche Reichspost was founded as an independent enterprise. In 1950, the Allied Powers in Germany established Deutsche Bundespost as a state monopoly to provide uniform postal and communication services (DPWN 2006).

In Japan a modern, Western-style postal administration was established in 1871 as part of the government's efforts to overcome Japan's 'backwardness', which resulted from more than 200 years of isolation. The government undertook immense efforts to provide uniform services for all citizens. By the 1880s, geographic coverage was at almost 100% (Hunter 2005). Although Japan, like Germany, was occupied after its surrender in 1945, the Allied forces did not intervene in the postal sector and the postal administration remained basically unchanged.

Postal administrations in both countries combined mail service and postal savings. Postal savings were introduced in Germany in 1939 while they were established in Japan in 1875, only four years after the establishment of the Japanese postal administration. In Japan, the post began in 1916 to offer life insurances, a business in which the Bundespost was never active. In contrast to Japan, telecommunications services were provided by the Bundespost as well (Scher 2004).

In Japan, as well as in Germany, postal savings were meant as a 'savings bank for ordinary people'. One main difference between the two countries lies in the volume of savings deposits, which amount in Japan to around 30% of all savings, while in Germany only approximately 7% are held in the savings accounts of the postal bank (Figure 3).

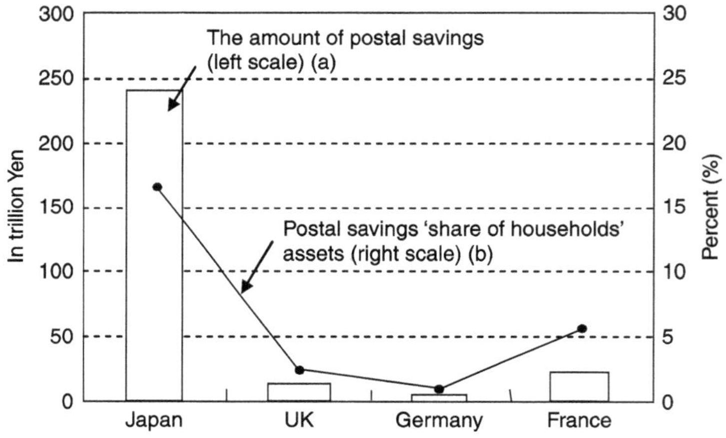

Figure 3. Comparison between Japanese and European postal savings.
Note: Data for Japan refers to fiscal year 2001, for other countries fiscal year: (a) 2000; (b) 1999.
Source: Adapted from Watanabe (2006).

Only in Japan did the Postal Savings Bank play an important role as an instrument for economic development in the post-war period (Scher 2004). Since the 1950s, the assets of postal savings and postal life insurance businesses in Japan have been channelled by the Trust Fund Bureau of the Ministry of Finance into the Fiscal Investment and Loan Program (FILP), a special budget of the government to finance infrastructure projects and industrial policy measures.[5] Considerable criticism of the non-transparent distribution of funds led to a reform of the FILP in 2001, with substantial implications for postal savings and life insurance. Postal savings and life insurance funds are no longer channelled into the FILP but can be invested into government bonds (FILP bonds). Public enterprises can no longer finance their activities through state-guaranteed FILP credits but are now forced to emit FILP Agency bonds. However, postal savings and life insurance are, with a share of 76% (2001), the largest investors in FILP bonds and therefore still play a considerable role in the financing of the FILP (Scher 2004, Amyx *et al.* 2005, Porges and Leong 2005, Watanabe 2006).

Postal privatisation in Germany

From the 1960s onwards the Bundespost was constantly making losses, which reached 800 billion Deutschmark in the late 1980s. Mounting losses motivated the German federal government to consider a deregulation of the postal administration. With the postal reform of 1989 (Postreform I), the Bundespost was fundamentally reformed by dividing it into three independent enterprises: Deutsche Bundespost Telekom (telecommunications), Deutsche Bundespost Postdienst (postal services) and Deutsche Bundespost Postbank (postal savings bank). In a second step in 1995, these enterprises were converted into stock corporations with the German federal government initially as the exclusive shareholder (Postreform II). In November 1996, the initial public offering of the Deutsche Telekom AG took place. In 1997 the Federal Ministry for Post and Telecommunications was dissolved and, since 1998, the Regulatory Authority for Telecommunications and Posts (*Regulierungsbehörde für Telekommunikation und Post*, or 'RegTP') supervises the markets for post and telecommunications (Postreform III). The RegTP has three basic functions: (i) to issue licenses necessary for activities in postal services; (ii) to review rates for postal services; and (iii) to have overall responsibility that a universal postal service is ensured (Campbell 1995). Deutsche Post AG took over Deutsche Postbank AG from the government in 1999. On 20 November 2000, Deutsche Post AG was listed on the stock exchange and renamed as Deutsche Post World Net (DPWN). However, the federal government sold only 29% of shares and remained the majority shareholder. In 2004, DPWN sold 33.2% of its share in Deutsche Postbank AG. In recent years the federal government has transferred most of its shares in DPWN to the government-owned development bank, KfW Bankengruppe. KfW sold a tranche of 72.8 billion DPWN shares in 2004, leaving 7% in the government's possession and 49% in the hands of KfW (BMWT 2002, Sommer 2005).

In 2000, the Swiss company Danzas, at the time the world's leader in air freight and second in ocean freight, was acquired by Deutsche Post World Net. In 2001, DPWN bought Air Express International, America's largest air freight provider and integrated the company into the Danzas group (DHL 2006). In 2002, it acquired DHL, an air express company founded in 1969 by Adrian Dalsey, Larry Hillblom and Robert Lynn. DHL was the first company to use aircraft for the rapid delivery of documents and shipments. In 2003, DPWN consolidated all of its express and logistics activities into the single brand DHL. The network of DHL was further expanded when in 2005 the British transport and logistics provider Exel was bought. Cohen (2004) estimates that Deutsche Post spent 10 billion Euro on acquisitions between 1996 and 2003.

The German Postal Law of 1998 clearly stated that after a transitional phase all postal services should be opened up to private competition. The delivery of letter post items and catalogues weighing less than 200g and mass mailing would remain exclusively reserved to Deutsche Post until 2002 at first. Decisions taken by the European Commission in 2003 and 2006 reduced the monopoly to letters under 100g and 50g respectively. However, following heavy political pressure the monopoly was extended until 2007. Almost 70% of the income of the mail division in 2002 came from this protected area. DPWN itself stated that the European Union decisions led to additional losses in market shares of 4.0% (2003 decision) and to 4.7% (2006 decision) (BMWT 2002, Cohen 2004, DPWN 2005).

Comparisons

In both countries the initial motivation for the privatisation of postal services was the fact that the postal administrations were consuming large parts of the government budget. Due to the immense deficit of Deutsche Bundespost this argument was most likely more pressing in Germany. In Japan, the privatisation debate concentrated to a larger extent on the postal savings and postal life insurance businesses. That the potential returns from a sale of these two units would help Japan's government to reduce the mounting budget deficit was therefore another important factor.

In Japan, privatisation started with the transformation of the postal administration into a governmental agency in 2001. In 2003, Japan Post became a public enterprise. At the end of 2007, Japan Post was divided into four separate enterprises under the umbrella of a holding company. During a transitional phase of 10 years the government will sell its share in postal savings and life insurance, while its share in the remaining two enterprises shall be reduced to 30%. The German efforts started in 1989 with the transformation of Deutsche Bundespost into three independent but 100% state-owned enterprises. These enterprises were transformed into stock companies in 1995 with the government as sole shareholder at first. Subsequently, the government's share was reduced to 56% (in 2004).

The German government moved fast in the initial stage of transforming Bundespost into enterprises, while in Japan it took several intermediate steps to achieve this goal. However, even 15 years after the start of the privatisation process the German government still held 56% of Deutsche Post's shares. If Japan's privatisation continues as planned, the government's share will be much smaller in 2017.

Both Japan Post and Deutsche Post still enjoy preferential treatments. For Germany the post can maintain its monopoly for letter post and for mass mailing until the end of 2007 (at the time of writing). Japan Post no longer has a legal monopoly but regulations for entry in the postal delivery sector are set in a way that it is *de facto* very difficult, if not impossible, for competitors to enter into this field. Also, in Germany, competitors need a licence to enter business fields of the former state monopolists. The licensing process is very strict and therefore criticised as a de facto entry barrier. Moreover, Deutsche Post is exempt from value-added tax (VAT). Japan Post will also receive some preferential tax treatments until 2017 and is exempt from certain traffic rules (as is Deutsche Post), customs procedures and safety regulations (Cohen 2004).

Deutsche Post has been regularly criticised for using profits from the lucrative and regulated letter post business and from the sale of real estate to finance its expansions into new markets. As mentioned above, Japan Post has a de facto monopoly in mail delivery as well, and there is also potential that it will use the profits from this operation for cross-subsidising in the future. At the moment, mail delivery is a loss-making business for Japan Post and fundamental restructuring is needed:

> If Japan Post wants to emulate this strategy [of Deutsche Post], however, it must transform its mail delivery arm and make it quite profitable by using new management techniques and restructuring its operations. It may also need to grab a larger share of the domestic parcel delivery market. (Cohen 2006, p. 18)

Critics believe that Japan Post is already using interest revenues from postal savings, especially from older FILP-related accounts with high and guaranteed rates, to finance its recent expansion activities (Cohen 2006).

Although there exist differences in detail, the overall privatisation process in Japan and Germany shows great similarities, even when it comes to the unlawful use of cross-subsidising to finance the expansion into new international markets. The following section will now give an overview of the international expansion efforts of Japan Post.

Japan Post's move into foreign markets

Turning now to the internationalisation of Japan Post, particularly its regional expansion strategy, the first step towards internationalisation was entry into the international express delivery market. Japan Post handles 9.35 million items of outbound and 5.51 million items of inbound Express Mail Service (EMS) mail (priority international mail; in fiscal year 2004). Yet the market for cross-border express delivery in Japan is – like in most Asian countries – dominated by the global players UPS, FedEx, DHL and TNT with a combined market share of around 70% (Figure 4) (Cohen 2006, Japan Post 2006).

The market for air cargo in Asia exhibits clear growth potential. Air cargo includes freight (scheduled, charter and express) and mail. Scheduled and express freight represents the largest share of the market, with express delivery growing particularly quickly over the past decade, almost twice the growth rate of total cargo traffic (Schreindorfer 2006). The Courier, Express, Parcel (CEP) market in the Asia-Pacific region has an annual size of Euro (€) 56 billion (2003). Of this, the international express business accounted for €3.2 billion. China (including Hong Kong) and Japan represent 63% of the international

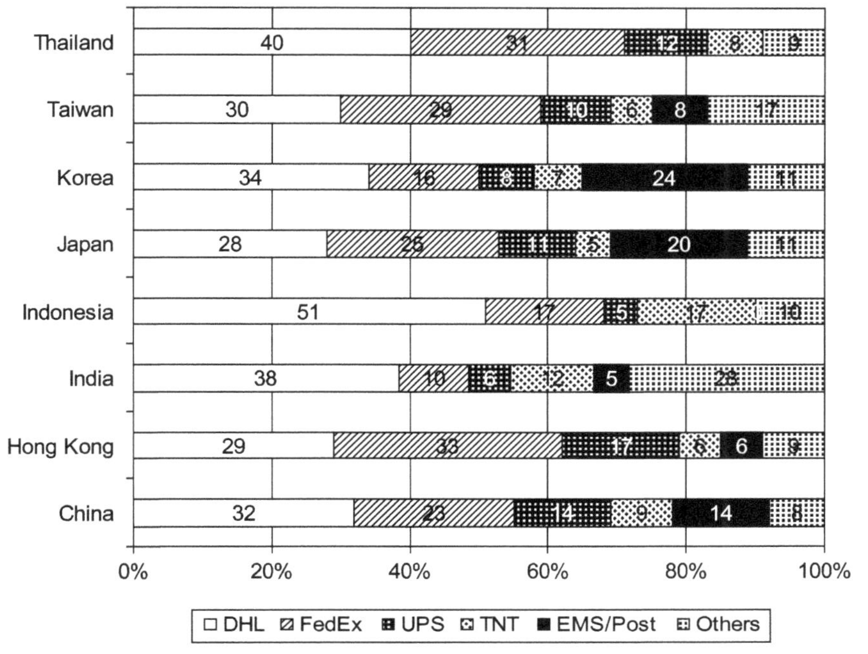

Figure 4. The international postal express market in selected Asian countries.
Source: Price (2006).

express market in Asia. According to a forecast by Airbus (2005), air freight will grow until 2025 at an average annual growth rate of 6%. However, estimates suggest that the air cargo market in China and in the rest of Asia will grow at an average annual rate of 10.1% and 8.5%, respectively. While in 2005, the domestic US market was the largest single cargo market, Airbus predicts that in 2025 the largest markets will be air freight between China and the United States, as well as between China and Europe. Moreover, it is expected that China's domestic express delivery market will continue to grow even faster, with an annual average rate of 12.5% until 2025. Airbus expects that the existing full-service companies DHL, FedEx and UPS will expand their current activities in China substantially (Airbus 2005, DPWN 2005, Schreindorfer 2006).

Therefore, it is perhaps not surprising that Japan Post moved precisely into this growing market. In October 2005, Japan Post began a cooperation with Japan's all-cargo carrier All Nippon Airways (ANA). The cooperation resulted in a joint cargo airline that was established in February 2006 and began operation in August 2006. The new joint venture under the name AJV (ANA & JP Express) offers logistics, freight management and services in relation to express delivery. ANA is, with 51.7%, the majority shareholder of AJV, while Japan Post holds 33.3%. The other minority shareholders are Nippon Express (10%) and Mitsui O.S.K. Lines (MOL; 5%). AJV started its operation with ANA's fleet of three Boeing 767-300F cargo aircrafts flying from Tokyo, Nagoya and Osaka mainly to Shanghai and some other destinations in China (including Hong Kong, Dalian, Tianjin, Qingdao and Xiamen). ANA Cargo was the largest Japanese airfreight carrier before the merger, with a 20% share of the airborne cargo market between Japan and China in 2005 (ANA 2005). In October 2006, AJV added a fourth aircraft to its fleet and expanded its services to Chicago. AJV is expected to be operating a total of 10 freighters by 2009 (ANA 2006a, b).

In the eyes of Japan Post, the new venture has the following tasks (Japan Post 2006):

(1) scheduled international cargo transportation;
(2) non-scheduled international cargo transportation and freighter aircraft operations;
(3) air cargo agency services.

The motivation for Japan Post to form an alliance with ANA was clearly outlined in the *Nikkei Weekly*:

> the cargo delivery market has been rapidly expanding in China and other Asian countries, prompting Japan Post's effort to enter the business as soon as possible. It intends to build its own international distribution channel through the tie-up with ANA. (*Nikkei Weekly* 2005)

ANA, on the other hand, was motivated to expand into air cargo following the stagnation of its passenger operations due to limited landing slots at Narita International Airport (formerly New Tokyo International Airport) and Haneda Airport (formerly Tokyo International Airport). ANA Cargo contributed only to around 10% of group revenues in the early 2000s and therefore holds potential for growth. The partner, Nippon Express, brought its experience as an international provider of air cargo logistics into the joint venture. Nippon Express also operates a global delivery service for urgent documents and cargo known under the brand 'Pelican'. The company can also utilise its network of 1087 offices in Japan and 301 offices overseas. Nippon Express has 10 branch offices in China. The expected role of MOL is not particularly clear at first sight, however. MOL is basically active in marine shipping and runs a large fleet (more than 700 ships) of containerships as well as car, bulk, and liquefied natural gas (LNG) carriers, cruise ships and ferries. However, MOL offers not only port-to-port freight delivery but calls itself a 'logistic service provider'. Companies active in cargo forwarding, warehousing and land transportation also belong to the MOL group. MOL has a tightly woven network of branch offices, especially in Asia. One can imagine that, in addition to MOL's general expertise in logistics, its land transportation and warehousing operations fit especially well into the strategy of AJV (Cohen 2006, Japan Post 2006, MOL 2006, Nippon Express 2006).

In 2005, Japan Post formed a strategic alliance with the Dutch mail and express service provider TNT NV. With the aim of developing an international premium express product for Japanese customers, TNT and Japan Post formed a joint venture in Japan. According to a TNT press release:

> TNT brings in its international express activities from and to Japan, the contribution of Japan Post is in its strong domestic market position and the close business relations to all large enterprises of the country. (TNT 2005)

As a next step, the two partners will develop and strengthen their cooperation in the Asia-Pacific region. TNT has already built up a network of 25 own and 50 franchised service locations in China (as of 2005). In 2006, TNT acquired the Hoau Group, China's biggest private road logistics supplier with a network of 1100 depots and 56 hubs (*Shanghai Daily* 2006).

From the view of Japan Post, TNT provides the (not fully developed) link between Asia and the European markets. TNT's strength lies in its intercontinental air freight network in connection with a land transport network in the European industrial nations. In the six largest European CEP markets, TNT ranks third with a market share of 11% behind DHL (20%) and La Poste (12%). Unlike DHL, TNT has concentrated its activities in express delivery and has sold its bulk traffic as well as contract logistics businesses in 2005 (Granzow and Reichstein 2006).

The internationalisation strategies of Deutsche Post and Japan Post compared

Deutsche Post World Net performed a four-stage strategy to achieve its transformation into a global mail, logistics and express service provider (see Manners-Bell 2003, Cohen 2004):

Change in management structure and investment in mail and express delivery infrastructure

These measures were mainly concentrated in its home market in Germany. Beside some cost-cutting and productivity-improving measures, this also included the integration of East Germany's postal services after unification. The first phase was completed in 1997.

Expansion of its 'geographic scope and capabilities' through an ambitious international acquisition strategy (Manners-Bell 2003)

The acquisition phase started with Danzas. Through Danzas, Deutsche Post acquired other logistic companies like Nedlloyd ETD (Royal Nedlloyd's European Transport and Distribution activities), Sweden's ASG, and later American freight forwarder Air Express International (AEI). Other major acquisitions included DHL and Airborne Inc. Meanwhile Deutsche Post created a European express parcel network (EuroExpress) through acquisitions of, or partnerships with, existing domestic parcel companies. The second phase was basically completed in 2001, although some acquisitions have been made subsequently.

Integration of the newly acquired companies and Deutsche Post's operations into a single global network under the brand name DHL

In order to ease the integration of all companies under one brand, in 2002 DHL started the strategic programme STAR (comprising more than 100 separate projects to achieve uniform branding, harmonise sales structures, standardise the product range and optimise functions such as procurement and information technologies across business units), aimed at creating intrinsic value and raising profitability through the improved use of internal synergies. The programme proved successful. DHL recorded rising group operating and net profits in the period 2003–2005 (Datamonitor 2006).

Expansion and strengthening of the global network especially in China and the Asia-Pacific region

DHL had already entered the Chinese market in 1986 as the first foreign freight service provider and has dominated the forwarding business in China since then with its joint venture, DHL Sinotrans. By 2007, the company had a market share of 40% in China. In 2004, DHL opened its new Central Asia Hub in Hong Kong. Another central hub for North Asia is planned for 2009, either in Shanghai or Incheon (South Korea). DHL plans to grow in the Chinese logistics market by 30–35% each year (CRI 2006, Price 2006).

Japan Post basically followed a similar strategy of expanding into the express delivery business. However, there are at least four important differences. Firstly, Japan Post's activities have been until now on a much smaller scale. The investment in the joint venture with ANA amounts to only 10 billion Yen (€680 million) in contrast to the €10 billion that DHL spent on its acquisitions. For the (planned) joint venture with TNT, no data are available so far. However, Japan Post is still in the initial phase of its international expansion and it is not yet clear if other acquisitions will follow. Given the enormous scale of Japan Post's financial operations, the company clearly has the financial potential for further expansion. Secondly, Japan Post has so far concentrated only on express delivery, while DHL acts as a full-service provider with activities in contract logistics, ocean freight, logistic solutions and so forth. Japan Post may follow the strategy of TNT, which concentrated on express delivery. The reasons were poor performance of the contract logistics operation, as well as the fact that TNT lacked the appropriate size for a full-service provider (Granzow and Reichstein 2006). The same may be true for AJV at the moment but Japan Post clearly has the potential for expansion into other markets. Cohen (2006) argues that Japan Post could easily draw US$2 billion per annum from its revenues in postal savings and mail delivery. This would add up in three to five years to an investment sum of US$10–12 billion, exceeding the amount Deutsche Post has used for its massive investment. Thirdly, Japan Post has not yet established a global network but seems to be concentrating initially on expanding business in the Asia-Pacific region. Japan Post has already entered a second phase, that is the development of ties between Asia-Pacific and Europe through the alliance with TNT on the one hand, and between the Asia-Pacific and the United States through a new AJV connection since October 2006 on the other. These are the routes with the highest growth potential worldwide. However, with these expansions Japan Post is directly challenging the major routes of its main competitors, FedEx and UPS on the Asia-Pacific to USA routes and with DHL on the routes to Europe. It remains to be seen if Japan Post can survive the already fierce and growing competition in these markets. Fourthly, in contrast to Deutsche Post, Japan Post has not expanded its network primarily by means of acquisitions but instead has formed strategic alliances. Nippon Express and MOL could be invited by Japan Post to increase their involvement in AJV. Both companies have extensive forwarding and delivery networks especially in the Asia-Pacific region. However, these alliances have obvious drawbacks. These networks do not operate under one single brand name and all partners pursue their own individual business strategy. Thus, coordination could become extremely difficult. Moreover, the scope to exploit synergies is also limited.

As the expansion strategy of Japan Post has just started relatively recently, it is too early to draw firm conclusions. However, it is obvious that the pace of Deutsche Post's expansion was much faster and the scale of investment much larger than by Japan Post, giving Deutsche Post the necessary size to challenge its major competitors. It also had a first mover advantage in the Chinese market and could expand its network prior to the entry of major competitors.

Figure 5 gives an overview of the expansion strategies of Japan Post and Deutsche Post in comparison with major competitors using the dimensions of 'service range' and 'reach', that is the degree of internationalisation (Dodgson *et al.* 2004). One can observe that each of the operators shown has moved towards greater internationalisation of their business in recent years, but only DPWN and TNT developed into international full-service providers. With TNT's move towards specialisation in 2005, DPWN remains the only full-service provider to operate on a global scale. All other companies have applied an internationalisation strategy only for parts of their business, mostly into logistics or express mail, or both. The majority of firms carried out their internationalisation strategy through acquisitions or the formation of joint ventures. The expansion strategy of Japan Post is therefore 'mainstream' but different from DPWN, which has a rather unique position.

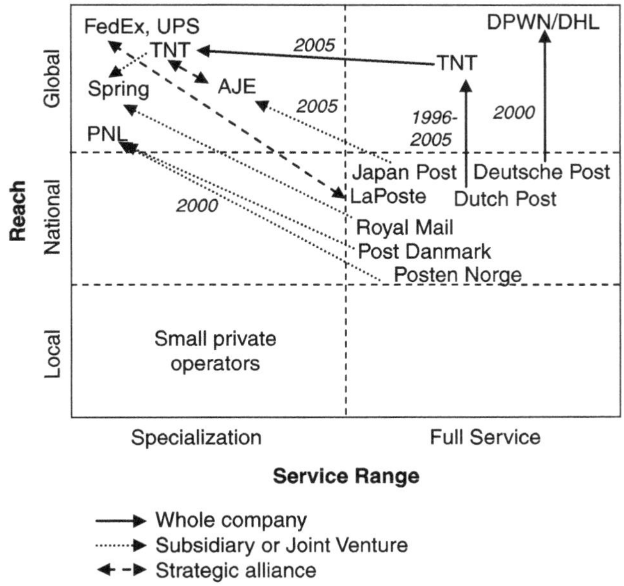

Figure 5. Expansion strategies of major postal operators.
Note: The order of companies in the cell 'National/Full Service' does not imply a ranking in terms of (inter)nationalisation.
Source: Author, based on Dodgson *et al.* (2004).

Generally speaking, Japan Post and Deutsche Post used the deregulation of postal services to diversify their activities into non-universal services, particularly into logistics and express mail, in combination with an internationalisation of their business portfolio. Yet there are some important differences that can be attributed largely to historical and legal specifics, as well as to geography and cultural idiosyncrasies. While Germany has always been integrated into Europe due to its central location and its important role as a transit country, Japan has been much less integrated as a result of its peripheral position as an island country. Thus, both the Japanese economy as a whole, and the postal and logistics service sectors in particular, are much more concentrated on the domestic market (for example, Japan's export to GDP ratio is only 9.7% compared with 31% for Germany). For both countries, the Second World War disrupted communication and trading links with neighbouring countries. However, while Germany became re-integrated – at least with its Western neighbours – relatively quickly, Japan remained for decades surrounded by closed economies (China, North Korea and, to a lesser extent, South Korea). Therefore, Japanese companies established production and supply ties with Southeast Asian countries prior to the opening of the Chinese market. Yet these ties remained relatively loose compared to the economic integration that took place in Western Europe in the post-war period.

From a regulatory perspective both postal operators faced similar changes to their ownership structure, from being part of the civil service to becoming a private company, with the state as a major shareholder initially but with a (planned) reduction of its stake over time. Due to a different regulatory scope Japan Post was not the dominant player in the parcel service segment prior to privatisation. In contrast, DPWN could use its monopolistic position in the parcel and letter mail segments as a backbone for global expansion.

Although Japan Post has never been part of a *keiretsu* network, its pattern of expansion suggests that the company intends to service mainly Japanese customers for their business in or with China. Thus, it seems fair to suggest that Ström's (2004) observation of 'introvert service supply' is also applicable for Japan Post.

As a result of late privatisation, Japan Post became a latecomer in the express mail market, which is basically divided among the major players. However, as this market is expected to grow quickly in future, it is possible that Japan Post can gain an increased share of the market. Furthermore, it is likely that the move into the express market is only the first step and that further acquisitions will follow.

Conclusions

This study contributes to the literature on the internationalisation of Japanese companies by examining the privatisation of Japan Post and its international expansion into new businesses and market segments. This is achieved using a comparative analysis of the German postal administration, Deutsche Bundespost. The studies reveal many similarities between the privatisations of the former postal administrations in Germany and Japan. Both were split into separate enterprises and were granted preferential treatment, even after the end of privatisation process. It is also possible to argue that Japan Post mimicked aspects Deutsche Post's strategy for expanding into new markets.

However, the expansion of Japan Post has been concentrated in the express delivery market and there is no sign that it plans to become a full-service provider like DHL. With its joint venture, AJV, Japan Post has primarily adopted a regional approach to international expansion, with the Asia-Pacific region a key focus. Further expansion into the intercontinental express business is already under way. It is not yet clear how the alliance with TNT will develop, but it has the potential to further drive international business. Basically, the strategy of Japan Post is very much in line with the strategy of a majority of European postal operators, which have all moved towards specialised regional or global services.

The business strategy adopted by Japan Post can be best described as vertical and horizontal integration on a regional scale. The limited reach and the pattern of expansion suggested a customer-following strategy. Japan Post seems to concentrate on Japanese companies. This strategy points to the assumption that Japan Post follows the traditional 'introvert service supply' approach typical of Japanese service suppliers, although further research on this issue is advisable. In contrast, the strategy of Deutsche Post is much more market-oriented and directed towards a broad set of customers.

From a corporate governance perspective, Japan Post's strategy is in line with the behaviour of other private (or privatised) companies in this sector. The use of its (still) monopolistic power to achieve global goals clearly does not help to enhance confidence among other market actors that a level playing field is already established. However, the measures already introduced and planned are likely to improve transparency and accountability of the succeeding entities of the former state monopolist. Moreover, as Japan Post moves into foreign markets, it will probably face fierce and increasing competition from major players like DHL, FedEx and so forth.

The major wave of postal privatisations occurred in the late 1980s and early 1990s. This provided former postal administrations like DHL, La Poste and TNT with an edge over Japan Post. Japan Post now has a clear latecomer disadvantage as most market positions are already taken. Until 2017, Japan Post still has access to the immense assets of its savings and life insurance business and it is most likely that these funds will be used for further global expansions either in express delivery or into new markets. It would not be surprising to see a major takeover by Japan Post in the near future.

Notes

1. The basic theory assumes that all companies can use technology only under identical conditions, pursue no product differentiation and apply the same business strategy. Only then would companies produce at higher costs. Empirical analysis is furthermore hindered by methodological problems, as the real cost function of the industry is almost impossible to determine. Empirical proof for economies of scale in postal services can be found only for delivery of letter post and parcels at the final destination (for a more detailed discussion, see Knorr 1993: 37ff).
2. Japan's Economic Minister Heizo Takenaka met Deutsche Post's CEO Klaus Zumwinkel in 2004, and Japan's Prime Minister Koizumi discussed the privatisation experience of Deutsche Post with Zumwinkel several times (Deutsche Post 2004, *Die Zeit* 2005).
3. Under the Postal Service Law the delivery of first and second class mail was an exclusive right of Japan Post, while parcel delivery was basically not regulated. Before Yamato entered the parcel delivery market in 1976, the business was dominated by Japan Post and Japan National Railway. With a number of innovative services Yamato was able to gain a market share of more than 20% within five years (Mizutani and Uranishi 2003).
4. For example, the MIC demands that a private competitor must set up an 'appropriate' number of mail boxes. It is assumed that a competitor establish at least 100,000 mail boxes in order to meet the requirements of the Ministry, which would make an investment of around 11.1 billion Yen necessary.
5. Until the 1990s, funds of the FILP were primarily assigned to the Japan Development Bank and other state-owned financial institutions under industrial policy criteria. Since then FILP funds have been mainly distributed via special accounts and 'FILP Agencies' (state- or semi state-owned financial institutions with specific promotion tasks) under structural and economic policy initiatives (promotion of small and medium enterprises, housing and road construction, agriculture and so forth).

References

Ahmadjian, C. and Song, J., 2004. Corporate governance in Japan and South Korea: two paths of globalisation. Working Paper No. 221, Center on Japanese Economy and Business Columbia Business School.

Airbus, 2005. *The global market forecast 2006–2025*. Available from: http://www.airbus.com/en/corporate/gmf/ [Accessed 22 December 2006].

All Nippon Airways, 2005. Establishing a firm position in conjunction with the growing market!! *ANA CARGO*, Autumn. Available from: http://www.ana.co.jp/cargo/information/bimonth/crg302005e/pdf/cargo_no30e.pdf [Accessed 27 December 2006].

All Nippon Airways, 2006a. *ANA & JP Express announces the third party allotment of new shares*. Press release. Available from: http://www.ana.co.jp/eng/aboutana/press/2006/060427.html [Accessed 27 December 2006].

All Nippon Airways, 2006b. *Developing a new cargo strategy with freighters as the key component!! ANA CARGO* Spring 2006. Available from: http://www.ana.co.jp/cargo/information/bimonth/crg312006e/pdf/cargo_no31e.pdf [Accessed 27 December 2006].

Amyx, J., Takenaka, H., and Toyoda, A.M., 2005. The politics of postal savings reform in Japan. *Asian perspective*, 9 (1), 23–48.

ANA, *See* All Nippon Airways.

Aoki, M., 1984. Aspects of the Japanese firm. *In*: M. Aoki, ed. *The economic analysis of the Japanese firm*. Dordrecht: North Holland, 3–43.
Aoki, M., 1990. Towards an economic model of the Japanese firm. *Journal of economic literature*, 28 (1), 1–27.
Aoki, M., 2001. *Toward a comparative institutional analysis*. Cambridge, MA: MIT Press.
Bastian, N., 2006. In Japan entsteht neuer Finanzriese. *Handelsblatt.com*, 1 August 2006 [Accessed 22 December 2006].
BMWT, *See* Bundesministerium für Wirtschaft and Technologie (Federal Ministry of Economics and Technology).
Bundesministerium für Wirtschaft and Technologie, 2002. *Das Postwesen im Umbruch - Ziele und Perspektiven der deutschen Postpolitik*. Available from: http://www.bmwi.de/BMWi/Redaktion/PDF/C-D/das-postwesen-im-umbruch-ziele-und-perspektiven-der-deutschen-postpolitik,property=pdf,bereich=bmwi,sprache=de,rwb=true.pdf [Accessed 1 January 2007].
Campbell, J., 1998. A new framework for postal services in the European Union. *Collected papers on international postal reform*, June 2006, 3–26. Available from: http://www.jcampbell.com/articles/CP_intl_reform.pdf [Accessed 2 January 2007].
Cargill, T. and Scott, H., 2006. Postal savings in Japan and mortgage markets in the US. *FRBSF economic letter*, 03, 3 March 2006.
China Radio International, 2006. *DHL expandiert in China*. Available from: http://german.cri.cn/401/2006/04/30/1@47911.htm [Accessed 2 January 2007].
Cohen, R., 2004. *Trade and competition issues raised by the liberalization of state-owned monopolies: the example of Deutsche Post's cross-subsidization of its express delivery operations*. Washington, DC: Economic Strategy Institute.
Cohen, R., 2006. *Policy challenges and the privatization of Japan Post*. Washington, DC: Economic Strategy Institute.
Cornett, M., *et al.*, 2003. The impact of corporate governance on performance differences in privately-owned versus state-owned banks: an international comparison, Mimeo.
CRI, *See* China Radio International.
Deutsche Post, 2004. Japanischer Minister Takenaka trifft Zumwinkel, 1 January 2004.
Deutsche Post World Net, 2005. *Investor's factbook*. Available from: http://investors.dpwn.de/sitecentral_resources/attachments/content_documents/factbook/entire_dp_fact.pdf [Accessed 20 December 2006].
Deutsche Post World Net, 2006. *Group's website*. Available from: http://www.dpwn.de/dpwn?tab=1&skin=hi&check=yes&lang=de_EN&xmlFile=300000221 [Accessed 20 December 2006].
DHL, 2006. *DHL company profile*. Available from: http://www.cn.dhl.com/publish/cn/en/about/history.high.html [Accessed 2 January 2007].
Die Zeit, 2005. Groß und abgeschottet. *Die Zeit* 42, 13 October.
Dodgson, J., *et al.*, 2004. Economics of postal services: final report. A report to the European Commission, DG-MARKT, July, London: NERA.
DPWN, *See* Deutsche Post World Net.
Dyck, A., 2000. Privatization and corporate governance: principles, evidence and future challenges. Working paper, Harvard Business School.
Granzow, A. and Reichstein, R., 2006. TNT macht DHL mächtig Dampf. *Handelsblatt.com*, 28 November.
Haak, R., 2001. Internationalization of Japanese companies: recent strategies towards China – a theoretical approach. Working paper 01-04, Deutsches Institut fuer Japanstudien (DIJ). Available from: http://www.dijtokyo.org/doc/WP_01-04.pdf [Accessed 10 November 2007].
Hall, P.A. and Soskice, D., 2001. An introduction to varieties of capitalism. *In*: P.A. Hall and D. Soskice, eds. *Varieties of capitalism. The institutional foundations of comparative advantage*. Oxford: Oxford University Press, 1–71.
Hunter, J., 2005. Understanding the economic history of postal services: some preliminary observations from the case of Meiji Japan. CIRJE Discussion Papers. Available from: http://www.e.u-tokyo.ac.jp/cirje/research/03research02dp.html [Accessed 4 January 2007].
Japan Center for Economic Research, 2005. *Postal privatization in Japan and the future of banks and life insurers*. Japan financial report, 13.
Japan Post, 2006. *ANA and Japan Post announce new airline*. Available from: http://www.post.japanpost.jp/english/news/join3.htm [Accessed 27 December 2006].

Knorr, A., 1993. *Monopol oder Wettbewerb bei den Postdiensten*. Fuchsstadt: Verlag René F. Wilfer.

La Porta, R., Lopez-de-Silanes, F., and Shleifer, A., 2002. Government ownership of banks. *The Journal of Finance*, 57 (1), 265–301.

Lemoine, W. and Dagnæs, L., 2002. Globalization and networking organisation of European freight, forwarding and logistics provider. *In*: *Second international conference on cooperation and competition*, 19–21 September, Växjo University.

Maclachlan, P., 2004. Post Office politics in modern Japan: the postmasters, iron triangles, and the limits of reform. *Journal of Japanese studies*, 30 (2), 281–313.

Manners-Bell, J., 2003. *Building a global logistics leader: Deutsche Post's acquisition strategy*, Transport Intelligence White Paper, April.

Ministry of Internal Affairs and Communications, 2006. Concerning the promotion of the privatization of Japan Post for a smooth transition to the new company following privatization. *Communications news*, Biweekly Newsletter of the MIC (15 September), 17 (11), 3–4.

Mitsui O.S.K. Line, 2006. MOL Services. Available from: http://www.mol.co.jp/services-e/index.html [Accessed 28 December 2006].

Mizutani, F. and Uranishi, S., 2003. The post office vs. parcel delivery companies: competition effects on costs and productivity. *Journal of regulatory economics*, 23 (3), 299–319.

MOL, *See* Mitsui O.S.K. Line.

Nikkei Weekly, 2005. Japan Post, ANA to join hands in international distribution. *Nikkei Weekly*, 24 October.

Nippon Express, 2006. Available from: http://www3.nittsu.co.jp/EDOC/SERVICE/service_e.html [Accessed 28 Dec 2006].

Porges, A. and Leong, J.M., 2005. *The privatization of Japan Post: Ensuring both a viable post and a level playing field*. Washington, DC: Sidley Austin Brown & Wood LLP. Available from: www.sidley.com/db30/cgibin/pubs/PRIVATIZATION_OF_JAPAN_POST.pdf [Accessed 22 September 2006].

Price, S., 2006. Presentation on the DHL express capital markets day, 5 December, New York. Available from: http://investors.dpwn.de/sitecentral_resources/attachments/content_documents/veranstaltungen/2006/de/CMD_12052006/7_Asia_Pacific_Scott_Price_CMD.pdf [Accessed 4 January 2007].

Sappington, D. and Sidak, G., 2003. *Competition law for state-owned enterprises*. Available from: http://www.criterioneconomics.com/docs/competition_law_stateowned.pdf [Accessed 3 January 2007].

Scher, M., 2004. *Policy challenges and the reform of postal savings in Japan*. Center on Japanese Economy and Business, Working Paper 211. New York: Columbia University.

Schreindorfer, D., 2006. Air cargo industry. Henry find research, February. Available from https://www.biz.uiowa.edu/henry/Files/2006_Reports/Air_Cargo.pdf [Accessed 26 December 2006].

Shanghai Daily, 2006. TNT buys stake in domestic road firm. *Shanghai Daily*, 30 September. Available from: http://www.chinadaily.com.cn/bizchina/2006-09/30/content_700538.htm [Accessed 04 January 2007].

Sharkey, W., 1982. *The theory of natural monopoly*. Cambridge: Cambridge University Press.

Sommer, C., 2005. Sie war eine Behörde ohne Zukunft. Heute ist sie ein weltweit agierender Milliarden-Konzern. Trotzdem hat die Deutsche Post AG noch einiges vor sich. *Brand eins*, 6 (5), 22–33.

Ström, P., 2004. Japanese professional business service firms in the UK: competitiveness and client relationships. *In*: *16th Conference RESER*, 23–24 September, Castres.

TNT, 2005. *Japan Post and TNT join forces*. Press release, 31 October. Available from: http://group.tnt.com/pressreleases/pressfinancial/tnt/Japan_Post_and_TNT_join_forces.asp [Accessed 4 January 2007].

Walke, A., 2004. Postprivatisierung in Japan: eine kritische würdigung. *In*: *Japan aktuell*. Hamburg: Institut für Asienkunde, 501–509.

Watanabe, S., 2006. Legal analysis of controversy on privatization of Japan's postal services system: what is the purpose and effect to privatize public corporations? Available from: http://www.law.harvard.edu/programs/pifs/LLMpapers/LLMPaper_swatanabe_.pdf [Accessed 15 October 2006].

Wiwattanakantang, Y., 2006. Big business owners and politics: investigating the economic incentives of holding top office. CEI Working Paper Series, Center for Economic Institutions, Institute of Economic Research, Hitotsubashi University.

Yamazawa, I., 2003. East Asian regionalism and Japanese business strategy. IUJ Research Institute Working Paper 04-1 Asia-Pacific Series. Available from: http://www.iuj.ac.jp/research/wpap04-1.pdf [Accessed 10 November 2007].

Pre-clusterization in emerging markets: the Toyota group's entry process in China

F. Hatani

Manchester Business School, University of Manchester, Manchester, M15 6PB, UK

Introduction

This study introduces a new pattern of foreign entry by Japanese multinational enterprises (MNEs), which can be labelled 'pre-clusterization'. Pre-clusterization is defined as an advanced form of network-based foreign entry, by which supplier firms in a business group enter an emerging market and begin to cluster in the location that the core firm targets *before* the full entry of the core firm. Although it has been assumed that Japanese *keiretsu* suppliers follow the foreign direct investment (FDI) of their core firms, there have been evolutionary changes in their internationalization pattern against the background of global competition, notably in the context of fast-growing developing countries – that is, emerging markets, which is manifested as an alternate approach to market entry timing.

FDI activities in the idiosyncratic environment of emerging markets have attracted a large volume of research. One of the main streams in this area focuses on the entry timing of MNEs in order to examine their performance (Buckley and Casson 1981, Lieberman and Montgomery 1988, 1998, Kerin *et al.* 1992, Mascarenhas 1992, Luo and Peng 1998). Others focus on an interorganizational network, in which a group of firms are connected with each other to fulfil specific roles within their group, and to facilitate achievement of their common goals (Gomes-Casseres 1994, Provan *et al.* 2007). Such networks can be seen in various industries, such as Apple Computer's network of software developers, Benetton's international store chain and Toyota Motor's production system (Lorenzoni and Baden-Fuller 1995). The evolutionary view of MNEs suggests that internationally active business groups create a competitive advantage in unfamiliar environments by applying the tacit knowledge they have developed (Kogut and Zander 1993, 1995). MNEs can obtain information on foreign markets through business linkages with familiar group members (Delios and Henisz 2000). Guillén (2003) also suggests that early entrants of a business group can convey the best entry mode to following entrants.

However, the study on how a network of MNEs adapts its entry strategy for emerging markets is still underdeveloped. There is a need to update previous analyses because of changes in the international market, as well as the development of activities of MNEs. This inductive study incorporates network analysis into the internationalization model to explore the recent pattern of the foreign entry of a multinational business group and the increasing pace of its capacity building in a new market. This study analyzes the process of pre-clusterization using the case of the entry process of the Toyota Group (Toyota Motor and its affiliates and subsidiaries) into China. By doing so, the study attempts to inform the entry strategies of MNEs for emerging markets. Although some previous studies emphasize early mover advantages in the emerging Chinese market (Luo 1995, Luo and Peng 1998), the findings of this study demonstrate the importance of network-level strategic actions and the speed of capacity building, rather than entry timing per se.

This study is in seven sections. The next section reviews the literature on the internationalization of MNEs. The third section describes the research methods used in this study. The fourth section investigates the pre-clusterization of the Toyota Group in China. The fifth section summarizes the findings with a comparison between the entry processes of the Toyota Group in China and their previous entries into more developed markets such as the United States. The sixth section analyzes why and how pre-clusterization happens and offers a conceptual framework for it, along with three propositions that are derived from the discussion. The final section provides conclusions and suggests avenues for future research.

Literature review

Five streams of literature help to explain the phenomenon of pre-clusterization by Japanese firms.

Internationalization process model

FDI decisions represent critical strategic moves by MNEs, which are jointly determined by the use and development of their resources and capabilities (Caves and Mehra 1986). One of the major frameworks of foreign entry is the internationalization process model (or stages theory) proposed by Johanson and Vahlne (1977). The traditional concept of the model suggests that firms develop engagement in foreign markets by gradually increasing their commitment of resources and knowledge transfer from international trade to the stages of sales subsidiaries, manufacturing in joint ventures and wholly owned operation (Johanson and Wiedersheim-Paul 1975, Johanson and Vahlne 1977, 1990).

Although the model has been supported by a number of empirical studies, a firm would not necessarily take the stages step-by-step but could enter directly into new markets by establishing large-scale local production (Hedlund 1986, Nordström 1991). Forsgren (1989) also argues that the internationalization process model is valid only when a firm is still at the early stage of internationalization, lacking sufficient knowledge and experience in foreign entry. Also, if a firm is in a network, it can learn from and share local information with other member firms (Imai 1987, Chang 1995, Delios and Henisz 2000), rather than gradually learn by doing on its own. Moreover, MNEs today are likely to have more experience and higher capabilities for building up their production capacities in foreign markets than was the case a few decades ago through rapidly globalizing business activities and their learning within and outwith networks.

In this regard, Johanson and Vahlne (1990) acknowledge that the concept of the internationalization process model needs to be developed in view of an ever-changing world. Addressing key problems of the traditional model of the internationalization process, Calof and Beamish (1995, p. 116; emphasis added) define internationalization as 'the process of *adapting* firms' operations (strategy, structure, resource, etc.) to international environments'. In addition, Delios and Henisz (2003) suggest that the internationalization process model can be developed by incorporating a more comprehensive conceptualization of national institutional environments. In particular, the institutional contexts of emerging markets are markedly different from those of the advanced countries. The study of the entry strategies of MNEs in an emerging market context will provide both new practical options for entry strategy and concomitant academic implications.

Entry strategies for emerging markets

Underdeveloped market institutions, as well as political and economic uncertainty that characterize many emerging markets, offer new challenges to MNEs (Hoskisson *et al.* 2000). According to North (1990), institutions can be defined as 'rules of the game in a society', which include formal institutions (laws, regulations, policies) and informal institutions (social conventions and cultural norms). Due to the idiosyncrasies of multifaceted institutions in each host country (Henisz 2003), the traditional 'global strategy', which is formulated in the developed country context, may not work adequately in emerging markets (Wright *et al.* 2005). It is therefore important to recognize how different institutional factors impact on the strategies of different firms (Wright *et al.* 2005).

In emerging markets, government institutions play a particularly important role in MNEs' FDI decisions (Brewer 1992, Henisz and Delios 2001, Chung and Beamish 2005), because host governments can alter their policies quickly, and when FDI policies in host countries change, MNEs may also need to change their entry strategies (Loree and Guisinger 1995). However, while the changeable nature of regulatory institutional environments in emerging markets impact MNEs' strategies, MNEs can respond strategically to the complex influences of policy variables (Henisz and Delios 2001, Chung and Beamish 2005).

Henisz (2003) argues that the ability to manage institutional idiosyncrasies is one of MNEs key abilities. On the one hand, MNEs tend to tailor their entry strategies for host countries with foresight to ensure the best outcome (Delios and Henisz 2000). On the other hand, although a restrictive government may influence both the MNE's ownership structures and entry timing, the degree to which restrictive policies deter entry can often depend on characteristics of the MNE or the proposed venture (Gomes-Casseres 1990). Oliver (1991) suggests, furthermore, that institutional processes can often facilitate, rather than constrain, the strategic behaviour of firms in a given environment.

Entry timing and growth speed in emerging markets

In emerging markets, in particular transitional economies, timing of entry is critical for MNEs (Luo and Peng 1998). It could be argued that firms that have entered a given market early benefit from: (1) technological leadership; (2) pre-emption of scarce assets; and (3) establishment of entry barriers for latecomers (Kerin *et al.* 1992). Luo and Peng (1998) suggest that in emerging markets, early movers can achieve higher performance in aspects such as higher profitability, stability and market expansion in the long term, and emphasize the benefits of early entry, in reference to the Chinese automotive industry. However, their study neither considers the effect of a unified capability of network firms nor sufficiently examines the mixed result of the performance of MNEs in the local market.

In regard to MNEs' entry timing and performance in the Chinese market, Yan (1998) provides a more comprehensive picture: Kraft entered China in the 1980s, but its plants have been suffering poor performance; Pepsi entered China at almost the same time as Coca-Cola, but its market position significantly lags behind Coca-Cola's; Peugeot was one of the early entrants into China, entering into a joint venture with the Guangzhou municipal authorities but which, after losing tens of millions of dollars each year since 1995, sold its stake in the joint venture in 1997 (before returning in 2001).

Another example of poor performance of the early entrants into China is Volkswagen (VW), a pioneer in the Chinese automotive industry. Although VW held more than 50% of the market share in China around 2000, its share plunged from 32% in 2003 to 26% in 2004 (Kühl and Reinking 2005), and decreased further to 19% in 2005 (News Net Asia 2006). Although VW is still the leading foreign manufacturer in the Chinese market (in terms of vehicle numbers produced), the German carmaker has rapidly been losing its early mover advantage in China since competition became more intense as a result of the entry of other foreign carmakers and the rise of domestic producers. Although slow entry and a gradual shift of operation modes based on the traditional internationalization model may not be the most effective way to compete in the rapidly changing business environment typical of emerging markets, early entry does not necessarily yield lasting advantages.

Even Lieberman and Montgomery (1998), the representative contributors to the first-mover advantage literature, point out the disadvantages of early entry, such as missing the best opportunities that may arise later or by acquiring inappropriate resources, both of which could become significant drawbacks as the market evolves. In the idiosyncratic environment of transitional economies in particular, early entrants may incur substantial costs (Yan 1998). In the early stages of transition, for example, markets are often still highly regulated, and marketing activities and delivery costs may be more expensive due to underdeveloped supporting infrastructures. Thus, there is no guarantee that the potential advantages of early entry will serve well during the long-term in a changing market environment (Lieberman and Montgomery 1998). Success in emerging markets hinges upon whether or not firms can make a series of successful short-term moves rather than simply being early movers (Yan 1998). Isobe *et al.* (2000) also point out that successful early movers have not only entered the market early but also aggressively develop the necessary infrastructure by themselves.

Network-based entry

From the network perspective, foreign entry is defined as 'the whole process by which firms enter foreign markets over long time periods and not just the characteristics of the entry decision and modes of entry' (Axelsson and Johanson 1992, p. 219). Business networks will to a large extent influence the internationalization behaviour of member firms in the whole process. The central concern of the network approach is the action possibilities of firms and their strategies in different markets (Johanson and Mattsson 1987). MNEs in a network can formulate dynamic entry processes that are more effective based on shared experience and by adapting their capabilities (Chang 1995, Delios and

Henisz 2000). The foreign investments of large MNEs therefore tend to trigger a series of FDI in potential markets by other firms in the network.

In addition, foreign investors can speed up their entry pace based on their accumulated knowledge about the markets, which is called 'experiential knowledge' (Barkema *et al.* 1996). According to Chandler (1977, 1980), intensive capital utilization and faster throughput backed by coordination, which he called 'economies of speed', are the most important factors for modern corporations. Developing the concept in industrial organization analysis, Sturgeon (2002) also argues that the advantages of economies of speed, together with economies of scale, in production networks surpass those of any single firm.

Clustering to compete

For production networks, a key issue for keeping up with and surviving the competition is how efficiently member firms can build up their supply clusters in a new environment. A cluster is defined as a geographic concentration of interconnected firms and institutions in a particular field (Porter 1998). A network, on the other hand, may or may not locate itself in a particular location as a network is more about interactions between firms rather than geographical proximity.

Being part of a cluster has several benefits, such as more productive sourcing inputs and efficient transportation, assets in information sharing, and complementarities with others in a cluster (Porter 1998, Kenney and Florida 2004). Due to the institutional and economic advantages of clusters, suppliers in the same industry or related industries tend to position their operations in a certain location. The study by Kenney and Florida (1993), for example, shows that FDI by Japanese auto-parts suppliers in North America are concentrated around places where the assembly plants of their core firms are located.

In the process of the cluster configuration of a particular business network during a specific period, buyer-supplier relationships also play a role. As Ellis (2000) argues, foreign market entry, in this context, is a function of ongoing inter-firm interactions between the core firm and its network firms. Thus, cluster building in a new market involves strategic actions taken by both the core firm and the supplier firms in its network. Due to the unstable and underdeveloped business environments of emerging economies, the synergy of the strategies of existing member firms in a given network is crucial to achieving speedy cluster building and to make their network-based entry successful.

The following sections report the ad hoc entry strategy – which can be termed 'pre-clusterization' – of a large business network in an emerging market. Based on a case study of the entry into China of the Toyota Group, firstly, the process of pre-clusterization is articulated, followed by an analysis of how and why pre-clusterization can happen.

Methodology

In this research, the case study is used to investigate the dynamics within a single setting (Eisenhardt 1989). Although most previous studies of Japanese FDI have been predominantly based on quantitative analysis (Chang 1995, Belderbos and Sleuwaegen 1996, Tan and Vertinsky 1996, Zhou *et al.* 2002), exploratory case research is more suitable for articulating processes made by a specific inter-firm network during a short time span. According to Weick (1996), qualitative research is useful to analyze implicit assumptions and new relationships. Glaser and Strauss (1967) also suggest that empirical reality permits the development of a testable theory.

The Toyota Group was selected as a case because it is a distinctive exemplar of a well-integrated supply network (Womack *et al.* 1990, Dyer 2000, Dyer and Nobeoka 2000). Moreover, Toyota's latecomer status in China and the efforts of its suppliers to speed up the process of capacity building in one of the world's fastest-growing markets provides an ideal case for examining the development of the entry strategy of a multinational network.

Semi-structured interviews with firms in the Toyota Group were conducted in both Japan and China between January and April 2003, shortly after Toyota launched its full operation in Tianjin, China. The sample firms, besides Toyota itself, were identified as supplier firms which met all three of the following criteria: (1) being an affiliate or subsidiary of Toyota; (2) being a member of Toyota's suppliers association, *Kyoho-kai* (since membership of *Kyoho-kai* requires one billion yen or above of direct and indirect business with Toyota per annum, not all Toyota affiliates and subsidiaries are necessarily registered in the association); (3) having an operations base in China. There were approximately 50 supplier firms that met these criteria at the time of a pilot study in 2002. For interviews, the author narrowed down the scope of sample firms, focusing on Toyota's 'group companies', which historically have the closest organizational ties with Toyota, in order to obtain indepth information concerning inter-firm relationships in the network. The author visited the headquarters of Toyota, together with six Toyota group companies in Japan, and their 15 operation units (holding companies or production plants) in China.

The number of interviewees totalled 42 (20 in Japan and 22 in China). Each interview lasted at least 90 minutes, but most lasted approximately two hours. The interviews focused on: (1) the background and incentives for their FDI in China; (2) key activities in their entry processes; and (3) their interactions with other group members in China. Information of recent developments of the Toyota Group in China was supplemented by follow-up contact with some of the previously interviewed sample firms as well as by a review of newsletters they provided and their official press releases. Integration of this four-dimensional approach, involving the core firm, suppliers, their decision-making in the home country, and their activities in the host country, is an effective way to analyze the network-based entry process.

Data analysis

Toyota group in China: background

Compared with Western carmakers, the attitude of Japanese carmakers towards the Chinese market has been more cautious. Although Japanese carmakers were the early movers into Southeast Asia (METI 2001), they were slow to take action in the Chinese market, mainly because of the uncertainty and complexity of the business environment in China. In particular, Toyota was concentrating decisively on boosting its market share in the North American market during the 1980s, judging that it was too early to produce passenger cars in China.

Toyota's late entry into China was also associated with an external factor; in 1994, acknowledging China's development and market potential, Toyota officially announced its intention to enter the country. Initially, Toyota wished to establish its production base in China's most advanced city, Shanghai. However, the company lost the bid for a joint venture (JV) with the local leading carmaker, Shanghai Automotive Industry Corporation (SAIC), to General Motors (GM) in 1995.

After failing to secure the joint business with SAIC, Toyota was obliged to form a technical tie-up for joint engine production with Tianjin Automotive Xiali Co Ltd, a small local carmaker in severe financial distress. At that time, Toyota was not permitted to produce passenger cars in China, because the Chinese government's new Auto Industry Policy, implemented in 1994, had declared a moratorium on the launching of new major automotive assembly ventures during the ninth five-year plan for 1996–2000 (Arnold 2003).[1] Consequently, Toyota had to endure absolute latecomer status, particularly vis-à-vis VW, which had entered China in 1984.

In May 2000, Toyota finally obtained the government permission required to produce passenger cars based on production in a 50-50 joint venture with Tianjin Auto, and began its production of passenger cars in late 2002. By that time, most major carmakers had already entered China based on tie-ups with local carmakers (Table 1).

With this background, Toyota's group suppliers confronted an unfamiliar situation in the 1990s; despite China's large market potential, Toyota did not have an assembly plant there and it was not clear when the core firm's local operation would start.[2] This idiosyncratic condition (in comparison to other international entries of the Toyota network) required that the member firms in the Toyota Group devise an alternative entry strategy for China.

Pre-clusterization near 'virtual assembly plants'

Despite the uncertainty, however, production units transplanted by Toyota suppliers have mushroomed in China since the mid-1990s. Clustering prior to the full entry of the core firm was a new challenge for Toyota suppliers. Unlike previous FDI in Southeast Asia and later in the United States, Toyota did not give direct instruction or hands-on support to them for their FDI in China, partly because Toyota itself did not know when the company would obtain approval for passenger-car production from the Chinese authorities.

Toyota suppliers' initial steps to enter China were supported by favourable incentives offered by Special Economic Zones (SEZs) in China, which provided foreign suppliers with some choices for locations. After Toyota's equity participation in an auto-parts factory of Tianjin Auto in 1996, more Toyota suppliers started deploying themselves around there, expecting that Toyota would construct its assembly plant in the vicinity in the near future. In other words, they began to pre-cluster near Toyota's 'virtual assembly plant', which was an anticipated transplant assembly plant that did not exist at the time of the suppliers' FDI decisions.

Table 1. Major automakers' passenger cars joint ventures (JVs) in China (1984–2002).

Year*	Company	Local partner
1984	VW	Shanghai Automotive Industry Corporation (SAIC)
1985	Peugeot	Guangzhou Automobile
1988	VW	First Automobile Works (FAW)
1992	Citroën	Dongfeng Motor
1993	Suzuki	Chongqing Changan Automobile
1997	GM	SAIC
1998	Honda	Guangzhou Automobile
2000	Toyota	Tianjin Auto**
2002	Toyota	FAW

Notes: *The year of establishment of the first JV for passenger cars (excluding JVs for buses and trucks); **Toyota's partner for its first passenger-cars assembly JV changed as a result of FAW's acquisition of the Tianjin Auto in 2002.
Source: various news sources, press releases and companies' websites.

When Toyota came to an agreement on its assembly plant in 2000, 18 local units of Toyota suppliers were already in the Tianjin area.[3] In the Shanghai area, moreover, there were also 18 local units operated by group suppliers as of the end of 2001, when Toyota set up a replacement parts supply centre in the city. In Shanghai, VW had an established supply cluster, called the 'Shanghai VW Auto Parts Industry Zone', which encompassed its JV with SAIC. As of early 2002, VW had 25 suppliers in the zone (10 first-tier and 15 second-tier suppliers),[4] which means that the Toyota Group had caught up with the supply cluster of the first mover in terms of the total number of group suppliers in China before Toyota's full entry.

In late 2002, there were a total of 56 operation units of Toyota's group suppliers in China, 34 in Tianjin and 22 in Shanghai. Since Toyota's passenger-car production in China was finally launched in October 2002, group suppliers have accelerated their FDI in the country. Although the minimum local content requirement in China is 40%, pre-clustered group suppliers enabled Toyota to achieve a local content ratio of well above 60% from the outset. Towards the end of 2002, the conventional follow-up FDI of suppliers led to the number of their operation units surging from 34 to 50 in the Tianjin area and from 22 to 47 in the Shanghai area.

Meanwhile, the pre-clusterization of Toyota suppliers had also been happening in China's southern city, Guangzhou. In February 2004, Toyota established a joint venture for engine production with Guangzhou Automobile Group and announced the establishment of its second joint assembly plant in Guangzhou in September. As of mid-2004, 15 local operation units of Toyota's key suppliers were present in the Guangzhou area. As Figure 1 illustrates, the Toyota Group has configured three production clusters in China to cover three key regions of the country.

Toyota suppliers' pre-clustering capability

It is worth noting that some key suppliers in the Toyota Group acted proactively, entering China even before Toyota's technical tie-up with Tianjin Auto.

For example, Denso Corporation, a Toyota group company and one of the world's leading suppliers of automotive technology, systems and components, began its FDI plan for China in the late 1980s. Denso established its first joint venture for the production of air conditioners and compressors in a coastal city, Yantai, in 1994. When Toyota took an equity share in an auto-parts plant of Tianjin Auto in 1996, Denso quickly redirected its subsequent FDI to the Tianjin area. Another Toyota group company, the automobile parts manufacturer Aisin Seiki Co. Ltd, also started an FDI project in China prior to Toyota's official announcement of FDI in China. Aisin Seiki set up a project team for Chinese business in 1993 and established five JVs in China before Toyota's full entry.

Until Toyota's prospective assembly plant in Tianjin became real, however, the suppliers that initiated pre-clustering had to endure poor performance based on small economies of scale with limited volumes of orders from other foreign carmakers that had entered China earlier than Toyota. Nevertheless, they regarded their initial FDI in China at this stage as 'scouting' FDI; the main task of which was to study the local business environment and to obtain market information.

One characteristic of the Toyota Group is that Toyota's first-tier suppliers organize their own supplier groups under their umbrellas, which are actually subunits of Toyota's supply network. The entry of Toyota's key suppliers motivated the second-tier suppliers in their networks. In other words, the synergy between the core firm's centripetal force and competitive group suppliers realized pre-clusterization while speeding up the whole

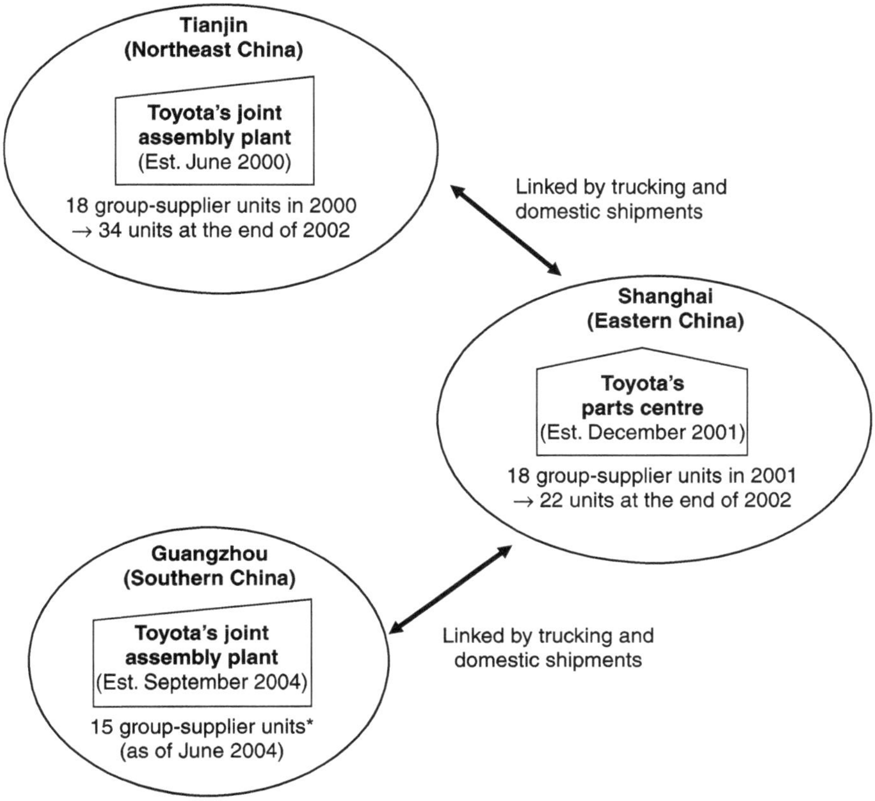

Figure 1. Toyota's supply clusters in China.
Note: Northeast China includes Beijing, Tianjin, and three provinces, Hebei, Henan and Shandong, whereas East China includes the Shanghai city area, Zhejiang province and Jiangsu province. The numbers of operation units exclude Toyota's own affiliates for auto-parts production, while including group suppliers' technical tie-ups with local firms. *The number of local units of group suppliers in Guangzhou was counted based on information from press releases, newsletters and media sources of sample firms.
Source: Based on an internal document of Toyota Motor Corporation.

process of the network-based entry. The idiosyncratic regulatory environment in China seems to have provided a rare opportunity for this well-integrated supply network to develop a new capability for foreign entry.

Toyota's management of pre-clusterization

Besides key suppliers' proactive actions, one of the settings for the pre-clusterization of the Toyota Group has likely been the steady commitment of the core firm to the Chinese context. Although Toyota's full entry into the Chinese market was late, the company had a long preparation period for it; for instance, Toyota had established technical schools, training centres and authorized service stations in China since 1980.

Another incentive for supplier firms in the Toyota Group was Toyota's informal supplier management system. To organize suppliers in a context without tangible production linkages, Toyota established a locally based liaison group in China. An original form of the liaison group was created in 1995 under the name 'Tianjin *Kyoho* Liaison Group' by seven of Toyota's key first-tier suppliers. The liaison group was open to Japanese firms in any sector operating in the Tianjin area to facilitate a wider range of information exchange and networking opportunities. The number of members steadily increased as the FDI of Japanese firms grew in the area. As of April 2000, just before Toyota obtained permission for passenger-car production from the Chinese government, 24 business units of Japanese firms were registered on the members list (Tanaka 2001).

When passenger-car production was approved, however, Toyota dissolved the liaison group and reorganized it into a new group, the 'Tianjin Auto Parts Liaison Group' (*Toyota Tensin buhin renrakukai*) in 2001, limiting its membership to auto-parts suppliers in the Toyota Group. Rules governing membership of the new liaison group were stricter than for the previous one. Members were required to be joint ventures established by group suppliers in which Toyota and Toyota Industries – from which Toyota originated – had to hold a total equity share of 30% or above. In the same year, Toyota also set up a liaison office in Shanghai in order to organize local meetings in the Shanghai area to coordinate the increasing number of Japanese firms there. Through this liaison office and regular meetings, group suppliers have managed to maintain close communication and information sharing with each other, although there is no Toyota assembly plant in Shanghai.

Although informal meetings are nothing new in the Toyota Group, Toyota's arrangement for information sharing among member firms locally was important for improving their local operations and giving them confidence in doing business in a context with no tangible business orders from the core firm. It was also crucial for Toyota itself to accentuate its presence among group suppliers in order to encourage them to endure until Toyota started full production of passenger cars in China.

The growth momentum of a latecomer: the race goes on

An analysis of the Chinese market once led to speculation that it would be very difficult for latecomers to sell more than 100,000 units of vehicles a year there, as the early movers had established their dominant positions (*The Economist* 1996, cited in Luo and Peng 1998). However, it was too early to make a judgmental observation on the rapidly changing market. The game was far from over. In the first half of 2005, within less than three years of launching the assembly plant in China, Toyota's annual sales reached just over 100,000 vehicles in China (Just-auto.com 2005). Toyota had achieved double-digit growth, while VW, the first mover into the Chinese car market, registered a 70% plunge in year-on-year deliveries to dealers in early 2005 (EIU viewswire 2005).[5]

Discussion

Behavioural change in network firms

The case study described above indicates a notable behavioural change among Japanese *keiretsu* firms. *Keiretsu* networks are defined as 'institutionalized relationships among firms based on localized networks of dense transactions, a stable framework of exchange, and patterns of periodic collective action' (Gerlach 1992, p. 3). Focusing on Japanese *keiretsu* firms as a distinctive case, the sequential FDI of business networks has been well studied. Empirical studies have shown that Japanese suppliers entered foreign markets where their core firm 'had set up its assembly operation' (Banerji and Sambharya 1996, Belderbos and Sleuwaegen 1996). However, as evidenced by this case study, Toyota's first-tier suppliers have proactively entered China, rather than adopting the 'follow-the-leader' strategy common to their entry into Southeast Asia in the 1960s and 1970s, and North America in the 1980s.

Until recently, the follow-the-leader attitude of Japanese suppliers was indeed persistent. Even after experiencing significant success based on network-based foreign entry into Southeast Asia, many suppliers in the Toyota Group had initially still been reluctant to construct transplants in the competitive North American market. Toyota therefore needed to support group suppliers in various ways – for instance, by providing financial support and introducing potential local partners to group suppliers for their JVs – in order to encourage them to enter the United States to supply Toyota.

Not even Toyota's prime supplier, Denso, which had been active in internationalization, was an exception. It adopted a follower FDI strategy when the company first started to internationalize in the 1960s and in its subsequent FDI, in the United States in the 1970s, for example. For instance, although Denso entered North America by establishing a sales company, Denso Sales California, in 1972, much earlier than Toyota's first JV with GM (which was New United Motor Manufacturing Inc. – NUMMI – formed in 1983), Denso Sales California was actually established with Toyota's financial support. Denso's first transplant factory in Michigan was set up in 1984 in direct response to Toyota's official announcement of the plan to establish a wholly owned Toyota assembly plant in the Midwest.

While directly helping the FDI of key suppliers in the United States, Toyota also coordinated small- and medium-sized equipment manufacturers and plant facility contractors in its association to help them to establish a JV together to provide maintenance services to the Toyota Group in the United States. Other Japanese carmakers also made similar hands-on arrangements when they first entered North America in the 1980s. Honda, for example, provided financial assistance to four of its Japanese suppliers to form a transplant (Kenney and Florida 1993); Mitsubishi Motors requested that its suppliers enter the US and as a response, 18 Mitsubishi suppliers jointly set up a venture company in Japan and, subsequently established a transplant in Illinois a year later (Chusho Kigyo Sogo Jigyodan 2000). During the 1980s, the FDI activity of Toyota group suppliers more or less followed, or at best 'accompanied', that of the core firm, entering a new market after the establishment of a local assembly plant by the core firm.

However, group suppliers gradually accelerated their internationalization processes to keep up with Toyota's expansion in international markets, such that their FDI became concurrent with the subsequent FDI of the core firm and later was further accelerated to facilitate pre-clusterization. In particular, Toyota's first-tier group suppliers had developed the capabilities required to conduct FDI, together with gaining a greater competitiveness than they had in preceding decades, which enabled pre-clusterization of the Toyota Group. Figure 2 shows a comparison of their previous entry process, for instance, in the United States, and the recent case in China.

Conceptual framework

As the case study shows, suppliers in a well-integrated network can enter a foreign market even *before* the establishment of the core firm's assembly unit, forming a supply cluster near the potential location. By pre-clustering, network firms could ensure that the core firm's supply chain would be ready when it began local production. In the case that the core firm is a latecomer in an emerging market, pre-clusterization of network firms is particularly effective for enabling the core firm to overcome latecomer disadvantages and catch up quickly with competitors who entered the market earlier.

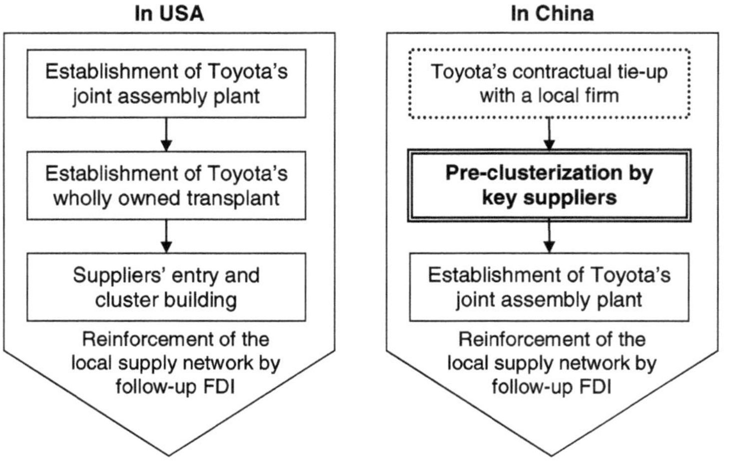

Figure 2. Comparison of the entry process of the Toyota Group.

Since emerging markets are markedly different in regime, degree of progress and stage of development (Hoskisson *et al.* 2000), it is crucial for MNEs to effectively formulate their strategies in a more dynamic way, rather than at the individual firm level, by utilizing the whole set of competencies of the network to meet the requirements of idiosyncratic settings. Moreover, as MNEs develop new knowledge through past experience, they can replicate the process of evolutionary acquisition and recombination of knowledge (Kogut and Zander 1993). The repetition of certain activities can be routinized and firms can then carry out those activities more swiftly than before and in a more effective way. This network evolution can be seen as a driving force underlying pre-clusterization. Table 2 illustrates a framework of pre-clusterization by network firms.

There appear to be three major factors in the occurrence of pre-clusterization other than the general benefits of production clusters. First, the core firm should have significant influence on member firms in the network, which often requires the core firm to have a strong international market position and excellence in supply chain management in order to motivate key suppliers, especially at Stages 1 and 2 in the process of pre-clusterization.

At the early stage of pre-clusterization, a network needs some interactive functions to connect member firms. In the case of the Toyota Group, informal meetings organized by Toyota facilitated interactions among group firms while substantiating network relationships. In a large network in particular, coordination through joint planning or power exercised, or both, by the focal entity over others is important in the activities of member firms (Pfeffer and Salancik 1978, Johanson and Mattsson 1987), because member firms can vary in size, expertise and capabilities. Without the core firm's centripetal force and coordination, FDI could be fragmented rather than clustered.

Wrong (1968) argues that through frequent successful acts of control that have been carried out in the past, the focal entity has the capacity to control others, and the capacity to control can modify the behaviour of others even without exercising direct fiat. As the case of the Toyota Group in China suggests, the core firm does not necessarily achieve pre-clusterization by force. The important point here is to encourage and coordinate network members in effective ways. Considering these factors, the following suggestion can be made:

Table 2. Framework of pre-clusterization.

	Stage 1	Stage 2	Stage 3	Stage 4	Stage 5
Incentives for pre-clusterization of suppliers in an emerging market	– The core firm's interest in entry – Potentiality of supply markets – Suppliers' own competitiveness	– The core firm's FDI plan – Any form of the core firm's commitment to the new market	– Decision concerning the core firm's location	– Establishment of the core firm's assembly plant	– Production in the core firm's assembly plant begins
Entry process of the network					
Key suppliers (mainly first-tier)	···→	Pre-clusterization	→	→	Follow-up FDI →
Second and lower-tier suppliers				···→	Follow-up FDI →

Proposition 1: If the entry of the core firm into a targeted market is delayed, but the market power or strategies of the core firm (or both) have a strong influence on the network firms, pre-clusterization occurs.

Pre-clusterization is also associated with the organizational capability of member firms. As early FDI by Toyota's key suppliers demonstrates, the process of pre-clusterization can be accelerated and enhanced by the ability of individual suppliers to advance their business projects in a given emerging market while planning the long-term growth trajectory of the network as a whole. Thus, network members, or at least a critical mass of them, must be capable of designing and implementing their own FDI plans in line with the strategy of the core firm, and have sufficient competitiveness and competencies themselves in order to put their plans into practice, rather than passively waiting for hands-on guidance from the core firm. Although, from the perspective of cost effectiveness, suppliers' entries into an uncertain and competitive market without the core firm might be seen as irrational, such a strategy could be rational if adopted by a critical mass of firms in the network.

Furthermore, the closer the supplier is to the core firm of the network, the more influence and information the supplier is likely to receive from the core firm. Accordingly, key suppliers – mainly first-tier suppliers – are likely to take action at an early stage of a network-based entry, such that proactive FDI by those key members encourages pre-clusterization of a network (Stage 1). In addition, capable network firms pay close attention to the interests and needs of the core firm and react quickly to any form of commitment by the core firm in a targeted market, such as the core firm's contractual tie-up with a local firm, establishment of a parts facility, or even its lobbying activities towards those purposes (Stage 2). At Stage 3, key suppliers are likely to need to identify not only the most effective location for their FDI,[6] but also what and how they will supply in detail.

Proposition 2: If the entry of the core firm into a targeted market is delayed, but key supplier firms in the network can lead the collective action of the network, pre-clusterization occurs.

Finally, the relational linkages among network members are essential for promoting pre-clusterization and for sequentially enhancing the clusters' capacities. Although initial collective actions in an inter-firm network may begin informally (Aldrich and Fiol 1994), as the number of actors taking the same action increases, the particular course of action is institutionalized and becomes 'obligatory action' (March 1981). Thus, alongside the increase of network members that have entered prior to the full entry of the core firm, other members in the network are likely to follow the collective action fairly quickly if they know – based on shared experience – how their network-specific clusters should be built. Accordingly, a well-integrated network with shared knowledge can speed up the whole process of cluster building in the foreign market and enable the cluster to be ready just in time for the start of the full operation of the core firm.

Proposition 3: If the entry of the core firm into a targeted market is delayed, but its business network is well integrated vertically and horizontally, pre-clusterization occurs.

At this stage, network firms need a clearer time frame for pre-clusterization to justify their collective move. For Toyota suppliers, an implicit target time to enter China was around 2000, when the Chinese government's moratorium on the approval of new large car assembly projects would end. As the number of member firms increases from Stage 4 towards Stage 5 in response to the core firm's entry, the coordination of suppliers by the core firm, as well as self-coordination by the suppliers themselves, becomes critical in a different way from the earlier stages. This is the period when the network needs to examine how pre-clustered supply capacity can be integrated with follow-up FDI.[7]

Implications

As Caves and Mehra (1986) posited in their study of MNEs in the US manufacturing industry in the 1970s, a large inflow of FDI to a fast-growing market is a catch-up game. Lieberman and Montgomery (1998) point out that first-mover advantages are moderated by differences in the resources and capabilities of firms. Also, White and Linden (2002) suggest that market success depends on the total organizational capability with which firms respond to new competitive environments. In particular, if production in an industry involves a number of different types of firms, the net effect of the advantages or disadvantages of an inter-firm network become significant. Thus, a successful strategy for a high-velocity market hinges on the integrated competitiveness of a network as a whole.

Through past foreign entries, many Japanese auto-parts suppliers have increased their competitiveness and are able to take action that is more proactive than the conventional network-based entry of Japanese *keiretsu* firms. The case indicates that as a business network internationalizes, it must evolve to cope with global competition and to meet a range of needs in new markets. Given the high level of unified capability of network members, the early entry of the core firm per se may not be the necessary determinant of high (network) performance in emerging markets.

To achieve high performance in emerging markets in the long term, it is essential for the core firm of the network to coordinate its suppliers and their resources in order to maximize the network's competitiveness, even though the context of emerging markets may not allow the core firm to orchestrate suppliers in conventional ways. Meanwhile, suppliers must increase their own international competitive advantages. In the challenging context of emerging markets, in which a number of global players may rush in more or less concurrently, network suppliers have complex tasks to confront, not only in competing with their competitors but also in balancing relationships with various customer firms while ensuring the reinforcement of their ties with their prime core firms. In the context of this particular study, this synergistic action between core firms and their suppliers is vital to revive and reinforce Japan's competitiveness in the international arena. Achieving this synergy in a wider geographical area should ultimately further strengthen their performances in the global market.

Conclusions

This country- and industry-specific case study sought to contribute to the study of the network-based entry of multinational business groups in the context of emerging markets. The business strategies that MNEs implement for emerging markets need closer examination and a broader view of their inter-firm relationships. If the capabilities and resources of member firms in a network are effectively coordinated, their collective actions can generate a new strategy to overcome disadvantages associated with emerging market contexts.

The pre-clusterization by the Toyota Group in the Chinese automotive market shows that a well-integrated inter-firm network does not always take the form of conventional follow-up FDI by suppliers. Supply capacity can be built up prior to the full entry of the core firm and the network can speed up the growth momentum in a new market despite the relative latecomer status of the core firm. In hierarchical industries, such as the automotive industry, the competence of the network as a whole and the speed of its capacity building, rather than early entry per se, are key factors for advancing market share in emerging markets.

Several restrictions limit definitive conclusions, however. This study of an idiosyncratic phenomenon bears the common limitation of qualitative case research, that is the difficulty of raising the level of generality of the theory (Eisenhardt 1989). On the one hand, the Toyota Group's entry process into China represents an ad hoc strategy related to the unique network capability of the Toyota Group. On the other hand, the pre-clusterization of the Toyota Group was also a consequence of FDI policy change in China in the 1990s in particular. Thus, the issues of whether other large business groups, or supply networks in other industries or in other country contexts, will show evidence of pre-clusterization prior to the entry of the core firms, and under what conditions this might occur, remain to be tested. In addition, the motivations for pre-clustering may not necessarily be to serve the core firm exclusively. As touched on in the Implications section, various other factors, such as competition among supplier firms and the diversification of their customer bases, may also be involved. It is reported, for example, that Toyota suppliers have been even more proactive in Central Europe, but to increase their own market shares rather than simply to serve their core firm (Hatani 2006). Future research should investigate the determinants for FDI by supplier firms and their growth strategies in emerging markets in more depth.

Nonetheless, pre-clusterization clearly illustrates an important and previously unreported aspect to the evolution of multinational networks' entry processes. It also reconfirms the value of network-level competitiveness to cope with uncertainty in emerging markets. Furthermore, pre-clusterization is not a one-shot phenomenon, but an important process in the entry of multinational business networks, which may have a significant impact on supply systems and local competition in emerging economies. Considering the complexity of inter-firm relationships and growing FDI in emerging economies, there appears to be room to further refine the model of foreign market entry to provide deeper insight into the international business strategies of multinational network firms in markets characterized by uncertainty.

Notes

1. GM's joint venture with SAIC was based on a decision made in 1995. Honda's JV, established in 1998, was an exception because it was not a new JV but a takeover of Peugeot-Guangzho's existing assembly plant.
2. Although Toyota has had an assembly joint venture in Sichuan since 2000, it was initially an assembly plant for buses, not for passenger cars.
3. Based on an internal document. The number excludes Toyota's own parts plants.
4. Based on an internal document. Although VW has some suppliers outside the zone, the Shanghai VW Auto Parts Industry Zone is the central ring of VW's cluster, in which most major suppliers of VW are located.
5. In particular, VW had inherited inefficient production lines from its JV partner and this may have contributed to its poor performance. The author is grateful to a reviewer for highlighting this additional facet to the problems that first-movers can encounter in emerging markets.
6. Several suppliers mentioned that when it is difficult to recruit skilled labour, locating 'too close' to the transplant of the core firm may not be the best location because of the tendency of good workers to prefer to work at the plants of assemblers.

7. There will be, as pointed out by one reviewer, a limit to how long pre-clustered network firms will be willing or able to sustain a reduced return on market entry, while waiting for the core firm to enter.

References

Aldrich, H.E. and Fiol, C.M., 1994. Fools rush in? the institutional context of industry creation. *Academy of management review*, 19 (4), 645–670.

Axelsson, B. and Johanson, J., 1992. Foreign market entry – the textbook vs. the network view. *In*: B. Axelsson and J. Easton, eds. *Industrial networks: a new view of reality*. London: Routledge, 218–234.

Banerji, K. and Sambharya, R.B., 1996. Vertical keiretsu and international market entry: the case of the Japanese automobile ancillary industry. *Journal of international business studies*, 29 (1), 89–113.

Barkema, H.G., Bell, J.H., and Pennings, J.M., 1996. Foreign entry, cultural barriers, and learning. *Strategic management journal*, 17 (2), 151–166.

Belderbos, R. and Sleuwaegen, L., 1996. Japanese firms and the decision to invest abroad: business groups and regional core networks. *Review of economics and statistics*, 78 (2), 214–220.

Brewer, T.L., 1992. An issue-area approach to the analysis of MNE-government relations. *Journal of international business studies*, 23 (2), 295–309.

Buckley, P.J. and Casson, M., 1981. The optimal timing of a foreign direct investment. *The economic journal*, 91, 75–87.

Calof, J.L. and Beamish, P.W., 1995. Adapting to foreign markets: explaining internationalization. *International business review*, 4 (2), 115–131.

Caves, R.E. and Mehra, S.K., 1986. Entry of foreign multinationals into US manufacturing industries. *In*: M.E. Porter, ed. *Competition in global industries*. Boston: Harvard Business School Press, 449–481.

Chandler, A., 1977. *The visible hand: the managerial revolution in American business*. Cambridge: Belknap/Harvard University Press.

Chandler, A., 1980. The growth of the transnational industrial firm in the United States and the United Kingdom: a comparative analysis. *Economic history review*, 33 (3), 396–410.

Chang, S.J., 1995. International expansion of Japanese firms: capability building through sequential entry. *Academy of management journal*, 38 (2), 383–407.

Chung, C.C. and Beamish, P.W., 2005. The impact of institutional reforms on characteristics and survival of foreign subsidiaries in emerging economies. *Journal of management studies*, 42 (1), 35–62.

Chusho Kigyo Sogo, Jigyodan, ed., 2000. *Kaigai Tenkai Chusyo Kigyo Jittai Chosa: Jirei-hen* [*Survey of foreign expansion of small-and-medium sized enterprises: cases*]. Tokyo: Chusho Kigyo Sogo Jigyodan [Japan Small and Medium Enterprise Corporation (JASMEC)].

Delios, A. and Henisz, W., 2000. Japanese firms' investment strategies in emerging economies. *Academy of management journal*, 43 (3), 305–323.

Delios, A. and Henisz, W.J., 2003. Policy uncertainty and the sequence of entry by Japanese firms, 1980–1998. *Journal of international business studies*, 34 (3), 227–241.

Dyer, J.H., 2000. *Collaborative advantage: winning through their extended enterprise supplier networks*. Oxford: Oxford University Press.

Dyer, J.H. and Nobeoka, K., 2000. Creating and managing a high-performance knowledge-sharing network: the Toyota case. *Strategic management journal*, 21, 345–367.

Eisenhardt, K.M., 1989. Building theories from case study research. *Academy of management review*, 14 (4), 532–550.

EIU viewswire, 2005. *China automotive: Passat, passed, passé* [online]. Available from: http://www.viewswire.com [Accessed 19 June 2005].

Ellis, P., 2000. Social ties and foreign market entry. *Journal of international business studies*, 31 (3), 443–469.

Forsgren, M., 1989. Foreign acquisitions: internalization or network interdependency? *Advances in international marketing*, 3, 141–159.

Gerlach, M., 1992. *Alliance capitalism: the social organization of Japanese business*. Berkeley: University of California Press.

Glaser, B. and Strauss, A., 1967. *The discovery of grounded theory: strategies of qualitative research*. London: Weidenfeld and Nicholson.

Gomes-Casseres, B., 1990. Firm ownership preferences and host government restrictions: an integrated approach. *Journal of international business studies*, 21 (1), 1–22.

Gomes-Casseres, B., 1994. Group versus group: how alliance networks compete. *Harvard business review*, July/August, 62–74.

Guillén, M., 2003. Experience, imitation, and the sequence of foreign entry: wholly owned and joint-venture manufacturing by South Korean firms and business groups in China, 1987–1995. *Journal of international business studies*, 34 (2), 185–198.

Hatani, F., 2006. Emerging markets as a self-inducing institution: flexible strategy mix for Central Europe. Presented at *The Academy of International Business (AIB) annual conference*, June, Beijing, China.

Hedlund, G., 1986. The hypermodern MNC – a heterarchy? *Human resource management*, 25 (1), 9–35.

Henisz, W.J., 2003. The power of the Buckley and Casson thesis: the ability to manage institutional idiosyncrasies. *Journal of international business studies*, 34 (2), 173–184.

Henisz, W.J. and Delios, A., 2001. Uncertainty, imitation, and plant location: Japanese multinational corporations, 1990–1996. *Administrative science quarterly*, 46 (3), 443–475.

Hoskisson, R.E., *et al.*, 2000. Strategy in emerging economies. *Academy of management journal*, 43 (3), 249–267.

Imai, K., 1987. The corporate network in Japan. *Japanese economic studies*, 16, 1–37.

Isobe, T., Makino, S., and Montgomery, D.B., 2000. Resource commitment, entry timing, and market performance of foreign direct investments in emerging economies: the case of Japanese international joint ventures in China. *Academy of management journal*, 43 (3), 468–484.

Johanson, J. and Mattsson, L.G., 1987. Interorganizational relations in industrial systems: a network approach compared with the transaction-cost approach. *International studies of management and organization*, 17 (1), 34–48.

Johanson, J. and Vahlne, J.E., 1977. The internationalization process of the firm – a model of knowledge development and increasing foreign market commitments. *Journal of international business studies*, 8 (1), 23–32.

Johanson, J. and Vahlne, J.E., 1990. The mechanism of internationalization. *International marketing review*, 7 (4), 11–24.

Johanson, J. and Wiedersheim-Paul, F., 1975. The internationalization of the firm: four Swedish cases. *Journal of management studies*, 12 (3), 305–322.

Just-auto.com, 2005. *China: Toyota raises sales target* [online]. Available from: http://www.just-auto.com/news [Accessed 28 September 2005].

Kenney, M. and Florida, R., 1993. *Beyond mass production: the Japanese system and its transfer to the US*. Oxford: Oxford University Press.

Kenney, M. and Florida, R., eds., 2004. *Locating global advantage: industry dynamics in the international economy*. California: Stanford University Press.

Kerin, R.A., Varadarajan, P.R., and Peterson, R.A., 1992. First-mover advantages: a synthesis, conceptual framework, and research propositions. *Journal of marketing*, 56 (4), 33–52.

Kogut, B. and Zander, U., 1993. Knowledge of the firm and the evolutionary theory of the multinational corporation. *Journal of international business studies*, 24 (4), 625–645.

Kogut, B. and Zander, U., 1995. Knowledge, market failure, and the multinational enterprise: a reply. *Journal of international business studies*, 26 (2), 417–426.

Lieberman, M.B. and Montgomery, D.B., 1988. First-mover advantages. *Strategic management journal*, 9 (Summer special issue), 41–58.

Lieberman, M.B. and Montgomery, D.B., 1998. First-mover (dis)advantages: retrospective and link with the resource-based view. *Strategic management journal*, 19 (2), 1111–1125.

Loree, D.W. and Guisinger, S.E., 1995. Policy and non-policy determinants of US equity foreign direct investment. *Journal of international business studies*, 26 (2), 281–299.

Lorenzoni, G. and Baden-Fuller, C., 1995. Creating a strategic center to manage a web of partners. *California management review*, 37 (3), 146–163.

Luo, Y., 1995. Business strategy, market structure and performance of international joint ventures: the case of joint ventures in China. *Management international review*, 35 (3), 241–264.

Luo, Y. and Peng, M.W., 1998. First mover advantages in investing in transitional economies. *Thunderbird international business review*, 40 (2), 141–163.

March, J.G., 1981. Decisions in organizations and theories of choice. *In*: A.H. Van de Ven and W.F. Joyce, eds. *Perspectives on organization design and behavior*. New York: Wiley, 205–244.

Mascarenhas, B., 1992. Order of entry and performance in international markets. *Strategic management journal*, 13 (7), 499–510.

METI. *See* Ministry of Economy, Trade and Industry.

Ministry of Economy, Trade and Industry, 2001. White paper on international trade 2001 [online]. Available from: http://www.meti.go.jp/english/report [Accessed 4 November 2002].

News Net Asia, 2006. China: passenger car sales in 2005 [online]. Available from: http://nna.asia.ne.jp [Accessed 28 February 2006].

Nordström, K., 1991. *The internationalization process of the firm – searching for new patterns and explanations*. Stockholm: Institute of International Business.

North, D.C., 1990. *Institutions, institutional change and economic performance*. Cambridge: Cambridge University Press.

Oliver, C., 1991. Strategic responses to institutional processes. *Academy of management review*, 16 (1), 145–179.

Pfeffer, J. and Salancik, G., 1978. *The external control of organizations*. New York: Harper.

Porter, M.E., 1998. Clusters and the new economics of competition. *Harvard business review*, 76 (6), 77–90.

Provan, K.G., Fish, A., and Sydow, J., 2007. Interorganizational networks at the network level: a review of the empirical literature on whole networks. *Journal of management*, 33 (3), 479–516.

Sturgeon, T.J., 2002. Modular production networks: a new American model of industrial organization. *Industrial and corporate change*, 11 (3), 451–496.

Tan, B. and Vertinsky, I., 1996. Foreign direct investment by Japanese electronics firms in the United States and Canada: modelling the timing of entry. *Journal of international business studies*, 27 (4), 655–681.

Tanaka, A., 2001. Tenshin kisha shudan no japanaizeishon: Nihon-teki kigyo gurupu keisei eno michi [Japanization of the Tianjin Auto Group: the road to the creation of a Japanese-type business group]. *In*: H. Shiomi, ed. *Ikoh-ki no Chugoku Jidosha Sangyo* [*The Chinese automotive industry in transition*]. Tokyo: Nihon Keizai Hyoron-sha, 15–47.

Weick, K.E., 1996. Drop your tools: allegory for organizational studies. *Administrative Science Quarterly*, 41 (2), 301–313.

White, S. and Linden, G., 2002. Organizational and industrial response to market liberalization: the interaction of pace, incentive and capacity to change. *Organization studies*, 23 (6), 917–943.

Wright, M., *et al.*, 2005. Strategy research in emerging economies: challenging the conventional wisdom. *Journal of management studies*, 42 (1), 1–33.

Wrong, D.H., 1968. Some problems in defining social power. *American journal of sociology*, 73 (6), 673–681.

Yan, R., 1998. Short-term results: the litmus test for success in China. *Harvard business review*, 76 (5), 61–71.

Zhou, C., Delios, A., and Yang, J., 2002. Locational determinants of Japanese foreign direct investment in China. *Asia Pacific journal of management*, 19 (1), 63–86.

Product adoption and innovation diffusion: the case of Japanese marketing to China

S.A. Horn

Department of East Asian Studies, School of Modern Languages and Cultures, University of Leeds, Leeds LS2 9JT, UK

Introduction

Japanese foreign direct investment (FDI) expanded substantially during the 1990s. A significant proportion of capital was directed towards China, which quickly emerged as the pre-eminent number one destination of Japanese trade and investment in Asia (JETRO 2007). In recent years, there has been a notable shift away from Japanese-owned, labour-intensive assembly production in China. Japanese multinational enterprises (MNEs) are increasingly active in localising their research and development (R&D), as well as their capital-intensive and knowledge-intensive production in China (NKS 2006a, p. 4). While the first wave of Japanese FDI in the modern era (1991–1996) was manufacturing-/assembly-driven (reflecting the prominence of China in the international division of labour), a new wave of investment is well underway. Since China's accession to the World Trade Organization (WTO) in December 2001, investment in production for sale within China exceeds production for export (third-country, reversed imports), signalling a qualitative and quantitative change in investment strategies of Japanese firms. This is consistent with the view that Japanese affiliates in China have positioned themselves in order to not only use the country as a global workshop and export platform, but also increasingly as a target market.

Literature review, theoretical perspectives and research framework

Following the well-established effects of market liberalisation,[1] the Chinese marketing environment has indeed undergone dramatic changes. This shift is ultimately symbolized by the increasing centrality of consumption in individual lives and with it the emergence of a consumer society in China. Changes in demand are underpinned by a surge in the spending power of Chinese consumers: estimates predict that by 2015 more than 80% of Chinese urban households will cross the US$3500 annual income threshold, rising to 90% by 2025 (Farrell *et al.* 2006), and therefore can be categorized as affluent/aspirational. While regional contrasts in general and the urban-rural divide in particular remain, Japanese manufacturers and retailers are gradually building up the infrastructure in China, with a view to capitalizing on the advent of a large Chinese consumer market. The influx of Western-style shopping environments ('retailtainment') and flagship stores, the dramatic rise in advertising spending (China has surpassed Germany and the UK and is set to replace Japan as the world's second largest advertising market after the US, according to NKS 2006b, p. 2) and the omnipresence of luxury brands (China has established itself as a major market for luxury brands, surpassing Japan as main market, Anon. 2005a) all symbolise the advent of China's market-led economy.

Since 2002, Japan's FDI in production for sale within China exceeds export-oriented investments (JETRO 2006). The shift from a production-orientation to a market-orientation is a key dimension of the reconfiguration of China's position in the global strategies of Japanese corporations (Kô 2000, p. 242). With a saturated domestic market on the one hand, and the envisaged mass consumer market on their doorstep on the other, Japanese corporations are increasingly monitoring this future market. A recent survey among Japanese consumer goods manufacturers revealed that firms are cautiously planning to extend their operations to China despite the instable environment, counterfeiting[2] and anti-Japanese sentiments (NKS 2005a, p. 5, NKS 2006c, p. 13). In theory, a number of reasons should contribute to the future competitiveness and strong performance of Japanese firms vis-à-vis local and foreign competition in China: (1) traditional export-orientation; (2) advanced technology; (3) global distribution system; (4) established manufacturing bases in China itself; (5) experience with the local environment; (6) well-defined global brands; and (7) extensive global marketing competence. However, things are not so easy. Brand rankings are important indicators for both retailing forecasts (top-of-mind and loyalty, for example) and recruitment (employer attractiveness). In Chinese brand rankings, Japanese corporations are less prominent than other international brands. According to the Nomura Research Institute there are only two Japanese corporations listed in the top 50 valued brands in China: Sony is ranked 26th and Matsushita 46th (Konomoto 2006, Nakajima 2006, p. 72). While advanced technology and quality of Japanese products are generally valued by Chinese consumers, the overall evaluation is poor. One explanation is that some Japanese firms do not live up to their international marketing reputation. Japanese brands have consistently received much media coverage, reinforcing negative publicity. Further to this, a persistent anti-Japanese sentiment is prevalent. Public opinion has flared up on several occasions, such as in the case of Japan's bid to become a permanent member of the UN Security Council or when former Prime Minister Koizumi visited the Yasukuni shrine in 2005. These issues shape the attitude of Chinese consumers towards Japanese corporations and brands (Ishii 2005, p. 35, Jin 2006, p. 67, NKS 2006b, p. 2, Kumon 2006). Examples of direct consequences included mass demonstrations, consumer boycotts against Japanese goods and the banning of Japanese goods by local retailers.

Doing business in China can be a thorny path for foreign firms in general, but as the examples illustrate, for some Japanese corporations it seems thornier than for others. This is not to say that local business does not follow pragmatic rules, and obstacles are certainly not unique to Japanese corporations. Many Japanese corporations have in fact been very successful in learning how to adapt to the new rules of engagement in this emerging consumer market, as the following two examples demonstrate.

(1) The premium brand Aupres was the key to success in the Chinese market for the Japanese cosmetic manufacturer Shiseido. While giving the brand an exclusive European connotation through the choice of the brand name, Shiseido was careful to use Chinese models and stress the fact that Aupres was developed specifically for Chinese women in its marketing. At the same time, the company used the well-known Shiseido corporate brand as an indicator of quality and exclusivity. Piggy-backing on the Aupres success, Shiseido introduced a range of medium-priced brands for the Chinese market. Retail channels are carefully chosen to reflect the brand appeal of each product line. While the Aupres brand and other high-end Shiseido lines are sold through specialty stores, flagship stores and upscale department stores, other product lines are available through department stores, supermarkets and convenience stores (Anon. 2005a, NKS 2005b, p. 9, Prasso 2005). Currently the company is in the process of expanding its retail network and aims to be among the top three foreign manufacturers in the Chinese cosmetics market.

(2) Mazda, the automobile manufacturer, has also successfully targeted Chinese luxury markets. Mass marketization and price wars with low-cost Chinese brands were avoided by concentrating on premium segments. On the basis of extensive consumer research the brand was carefully developed, after-sales services introduced (Shanghai Support Centre) and products tailored to the taste of customers. Retail sales per dealership in China are now among the highest in the whole Mazda network (NKS 2005c, p. 23). Currently the company is intensifying its engagement by localizing manufacturing (together with affiliated Hiroshima supply chain partners) to secure the highest quality for the Chinese market.

As the above examples indicate, corporate strategies must match consumer profiles and reflect how and why new (product) ideas spread through cultures. The identification and targeting of early adopters (with the potential of trickle-down effects) is key to successful market entry and marketing in China, because they are the ones who select products and technologies first, based on their openness to new ideas. In turn, early adopters act as agents and multiplicators for the majority and consumer laggards, resulting in a bell-curve shaped spread of innovation diffusion (Katz 1957, Rogers 2003, Katz and Lazarsfeld 2005).

Embedded within the question of opinion leadership, this study seeks to establish the fundamental forces now shaping the marketing reality for Japanese operations in China. The most essential aspects of contemporary China are the advent of consumerism and the influx of modern lifestyles via global brands (the particularly successful diffusion of Japanese premium luxury brands is a case in point). As a manifestation of Chinese consumer behaviour it is obvious that the attitude towards (non-Chinese) innovations, as symbolized by these global brands, is of particular relevance for firms operating in China, including Japanese corporations. Following acculturation theory (Berry 1980), reactions may range from open resistance to wholehearted integration into local life. However, the reality of China's vast regional and socioeconomic differences begs the question whether product diffusion theory firmly established in a Western context can be applied to this emerging consumer market. This places this study in the context of Appadurai's (1990) concept of global idea diffusion and extends the seminal work of Steenkamp *et al.* (1999) on the antecedents of international consumer innovativeness. With reference to the idiosyncrasies of the Chinese market, the review deals with the dynamics (and barriers) by which new products diffuse through the population. With their rapid product development strategies and speed-to-market approaches, Japanese firms are particularly dependent on consumer acceptance and product adoption. This makes them an ideal showcase with regard to understanding the effects of cosmopolitanism and nascent ethnocentrism in China on corporate behaviour. By means of these two acculturation paths the study sheds light on how Japanese firms enforce their Chinese market presence amidst the consumer poles of openness to, and rejection of, the influx of foreign brands.

Findings

Key findings are discussed from two perspectives: the proclivity of Chinese consumers to (i) accept and (ii) reject Japanese brands.

Consumscapes: adoption and product diffusion

China's economy continues to grow into double-digit figures. The increase in income and spending power signals the long-awaited advent of the ultimate mass market. Shifts in social status (and with it consumer lifestyles) have not gone unnoticed by Japanese retailers and consumer goods manufacturers, many of which are entering quickly to claim a stake in this highly lucrative market. The onset of a middle class with real spending power will change the global marketing map considerably (*The Economist* 2006, O'Leary 2007). With its decisive role in product diffusion, Japanese manufacturers and retailers are now recognizing the importance of the dimension of innovativeness (openness and rejection to change as extreme poles). The attitude towards adoption/innovation directly impacts on the diffusion of leading-edge technology products in China. Due to their technology-intensive portfolio of products, the identification of socioeconomically innovative clusters (and potential barriers) is crucial for the successful marketing planning of Japanese firms in China, as they seek control over diffusion patterns. To state the obvious: because of its diversity and size, China must be treated as a continental entity (with ramifications on integration and differentiation approaches). The Chinese consumer market is as heterogeneous as any other market in the world. It is highly diverse both in terms of socioeconomics and geography. Both emerge as key variables in the diffusion of innovation in their role as fundamental local lifestyle shapers in China.

Socioeconomic demography in China

In 2007, the total population of China stood at 1.321 billion. Of course, lifestyles vary across the different age and gender brackets but there is a common thread of growing willingness to consume, which is detectable in the main demographic groups. It is important to note, however, that location is a key dimension of socioeconomic disparity. The trend of a rural-urban income divide (with an income difference of 40%) is predicted to intensify exponentially in the next decade. High-income (more than US$10,000) and medium-income (US$2500–4000) households are primarily located in metropolitan areas (Anon. 2005b). This coincides with the recent influx of Japanese convenience store formats, reflecting increases in disposable income paired with changes in urban lifestyles. Following deregulation, top Japanese franchise formats, such as convenience stores (7-Eleven, Lawson), fast food chains (Mos Food, Yoshinoya) and services (such as hair stylist Asakura) have heavily extended their presence in major conurbation areas

(NKS 2004, p. 4, NKS 2007b, p. 4) and are currently planning to shift their focus to second- and third-tier regions (NKS 2006i, p. 6). Even within metropolitan areas such as Beijing, stark income differences exist. Accordingly, the Japanese retail group Seven & I has developed its convenience store chain 7-Eleven in key areas of affluence (following a dominance strategy to take control of the market) as can be seen in Figure 1.

China's socio-demographic diversity translates into a fragmented and fluctuating consumer market with highly contrasting segments. The analysis and definition of target segments are the basics of marketing in any market, but Japanese firms show a particular strength in defining target segments and brand positioning. Their marketing apparatus is geared towards rapid product development, short product lifecycles and staccato product introduction. This speed-to-market approach is also key to their success in China. They pay meticulous attention to consumer innovativeness and rely on their ability to keep track of the fast-paced changes of Chinese consumers' lifestyles. Word-of-mouth communication plays a major role in their strategy and with it the identification of early adopter segments that have the ability to act as a carrier for product diffusion. While the goalposts of income threshold are being constantly moved in China, Japanese firms target wealthier segments that can afford their products in the hope of trickle-down effects. Generally, Japanese corporations divide the Chinese market into three consumer clusters: nouveaux riches, middle class and blue collar. Educated, in full employment and affluent (more than US$7000 income), it is the first cluster and the upper echelon of the second cluster in particular that they target (Kwak 2004, p. 224), leaving the mass market to domestic firms for the present.

Due to the limited predictability of socio-demographic variables, Japanese market research companies that have followed Japanese business partners to China (NKS 2005d, p. 9, NKS 2006d, p. 4, NKS 2007a, p. 2) enrich this with qualitative information around lifestyle, motivation and values (among others). Despite the level of socio-demographic

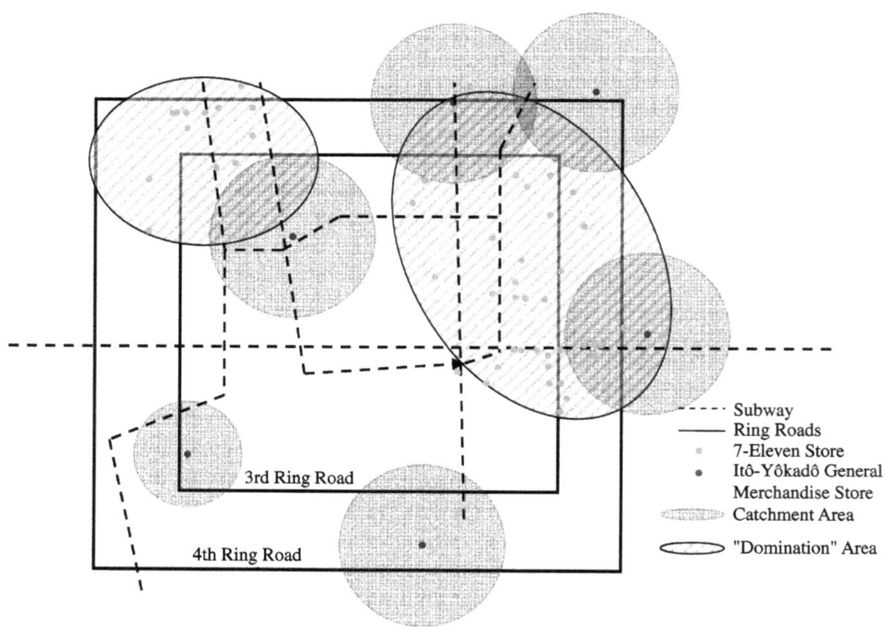

Figure 1. 7-Eleven and Itô-Yôkadô retail outlets in Beijing city centre: a stylised map.
Source: Compiled from data available on the 7-Eleven homepage, China.

fragmentation, two major trends can be isolated in order to shed light on current consumer lifestyles that influence and determine innovativeness. These will for the time being be restricted to affluent urban areas, although trickle-down effects can be anticipated in other regions of (metropolitan) China.

Me-ism and individuality. Young Chinese consumers have quickly shed communist thoughts of putting society and community before the self and individuality. With the advance of market-oriented work and life patterns, they are increasingly focused on self-satisfaction and on expressing their individuality. A longitudinal study conducted by the research organisation Gallup found that self-satisfaction has advanced to become the primary motivator for private consumption in first-tier Chinese cities, while the number of respondents agreeing to statements such as 'work hard and get rich' and 'never think of self; give in service of society' has dropped quite sharply between 1994 and 2004 (McEwen *et al.* 2006). A recent study among women aged between 20–49 years in urban China mapped out five segments and found the largest concentration of people (33%) in a cluster called 'life-seeker', which depicts an individualistic and independent lifestyle (Anon. 2005b). This finding is further confirmed by a cluster analysis of changing lifestyles among Hong Kong women, who in this context can be seen as a role model for other Chinese women. The largest cluster in this study, dubbed 'individualist', scored particularly high on socioeconomic independence and the pursuit of freedom from traditional Chinese values among respondents (Sin *et al.* 2001).

The trend towards a more individualistic society in China concerned increasingly with conveying individualism through consumption is a clear indication of the move towards consumerism that characterizes other, far more advanced, consumer societies like Japan or the US. From the perspective of innovation research, this trend is helping to establish the breeding ground for opinion leaders.

Aspirations and preparation. Chinese consumers tend to save a disproportionally large part of their total income compared to other consumer societies (a trend that has accelerated due to changes in the welfare system). While this is partly in response to the necessity to build up resources for old age and illness, it also reflects a specific consumer lifestyle, which is generally more concerned with the future than the present. A comparative study by Hakuhôdô (2003) found that in the Chinese cities surveyed, over 81% of respondents would choose to prepare for the future instead of enjoying the here and now, whereas in Tokyo, 52% were inclined to put pleasure in the present first. However, the belief in savings for the future is set to change. With the rapid increase of disposable income, it is the younger generation that increasingly exhibits a tendency of openness to hedonistic lifestyles (Horn 2005) and a readiness to spend money. Although, disposable income alone does not contribute to product diffusion, the increasing willingness to spend money is a vital stepping stone towards the manifestation of a consumer society. Embedded within these dynamics, sub-segments with the potential to kick-start new trends are emerging.

(i) Children and young adults. Increases in disposable income in combination with effects of the one child policy has stimulated a spending boom for this age bracket. Related markets such as clothing, toys, fast food and so forth have consequently witnessed both increases in sales and fierce brand competition (NRS 2004a, p. 5). For example, by making use of local planning and design departments, the Japanese consumer electronic company Sony tailored its Walkman P series to Chinese consumers and launched it successfully to this target group (NKS 2006e, p. 13). The Japanese fashion brand Honey's has also successfully targeted this young Chinese segment by developing sales outlets as part of a store-in-store strategy (NKS 2006f, p. 4). Local appeal is the key strategy of Kirin Beverages, which is also targeting young Chinese consumers. With TV commercials and promotional sales events, localized packaging and product adaptation, Kirin is currently focusing on the segment of urban adolescents (NSS 2006a, p. 24). Mirroring the enthusiasm for Japanese lifestyles in other Asian markets, this group is very open to Japanese brands.

(ii) Young professionals. With the start into working life (depending on educational background), disposable income rises and with it the willingness to spend money. This age bracket is the breeding ground for new consumer trends (for example, males with regard to digital equipment, see NRS 2004a, p. 5). The general openness also extends to global brands in general and Western luxury brands, in particular. Japanese firms such as Matsushita or Kanebo have identified this segment as the main driver of innovation (and therefore of brand diffusion) and have started to actively engage with this group (through market research, communication, tailoring products and so forth). The Japanese fashion brand Sanyo for example has identified female office clerks as their main target group in China. Next to its own brand 'Fragile', Sanyo has licensed the Hong Kong based upscale designer brand Johanna Ho to reflect local consumer interests. Using a store-in-store concept, Japanese department stores have been chosen as the main retail channel (NKS 2006g, p. 20). With a view to loyalty, retention and brand diffusion relationship marketing are at the core of Sanyo's China strategy. Some young professionals are key to a large number of consumer trends, appealing to this segment is crucial for Japanese corporations – even more so considering future possibilities (elevator brands) when this segment reaches a more mature age and thus the ability to access higher income levels. This segment already has considerable spending power, and the combination of relatively high first incomes on the one hand and few responsibilities, on the other, makes them extremely attractive to marketers. Moreover, in contrast to the overall inclination of Chinese consumers to save a large part of their income and worry about the future, this age group has started to mirror American consumer lifestyles by taking out loans in order to finance their desires (Qiong 2005). Combining both individuality and the willingness to consume, successful targeting of this group is central to the success of Japanese firms in China.

(iii) Middle-aged adults. With age rises income. Being the biggest consumer cluster in Chinese society middle-aged adults have attracted considerable attention lately. The economic situation of this demographic segment has been largely affected by recent improvements in the standard of living. Their disposable income has risen sharply. Three sub-groups stand out in particular: (1) Entrepreneurs: private enterprise owners and managers of state owned enterprises (SOEs) are the backbone of the rapid growth of the Chinese economy. Originating in many cases from rural provinces with little to no income, members of this socioeconomic cluster have climbed the social ladder through diligence and rigor leading to a high social status perception. Currently concentrated in the commercial centres of Shanghai and Guangzhou, the size of this group is set to increase in line with growing economic prosperity. Due to their role model function, members of this group are highly desirable targets from a product innovation perspective. They have the necessary means and motivation to become early adopters. Many of them may be considered as nouveaux riches who like to openly consume, with the potential of triggering information flows. Additionally, this consumer cluster is arguably used to independent thinking and thus does not shy away from consumption experiences off the beaten track. (2) Experts: highly educated and (increasingly) well travelled, this segment uses specialist know-how to work at various government-funded institutions (professors, technicians, lawyers, etc.). As their skill profile is in high demand, their already well-established social status and image has further increased in recent years. Members of this group are carriers of foreign ideas and lifestyles, disseminating their overseas experience (which they have acquired during their education and profession) to the Chinese society as a whole. While only a relatively small socioeconomic segment, this cluster is key to innovation diffusion. It holds modern values and with their fundamentally positive attitude towards Western lifestyles and products, it has the potential to impact other segments. (3) Salarymen: ordinary office workers are a blueprint of the emerging middle class. Members of this group hold mid- and low-level positions in government organizations, private businesses or foreign firms. This segment comprises both lower and higher socioeconomic strata and thus shows a certain inconsistency. While for some members it serves as an aspirational spring-board towards social 'white collar' status (in particular, rural migrants), for others it has become a symbol of increased competition and social downward mobility (in particular, early retirees in the context of restructuring of state-owned enterprises). With economic transition in full swing, this cluster is set to grow exponentially. Two scenarios are possible: either it develops into an undifferentiated super-cluster of the emerging Chinese middle class or – more likely – it fragments into a number of nuanced sub-segments with distinct values and lifestyles. While not innovators themselves, members of this group with their aspirational mindset may form the critical mass of mainstream and laggards in product diffusion in China.

While not being as innovative as their younger counterparts, middle-aged Chinese consumers tend to be interested in upscale goods and services, tailored to their needs and lifestyle circumstances. Numerous Japanese brands have actively targeted this segment, including Yamanashi-based Hakubaku (the Japanese cereal manufacturer) who recently introduced a luxury dry noodle brand designed for Chinese consumers only (in the coastal regions). Produced under license near Beijing, the packaging and name, *shang pin long xian* (high sense, dragon flavour), reflects the local lifestyle demand (NKSCK 2006, p. 24). Japanese companies are also targeting middle-class households as in the case of Kanebô Cosmetics. Next to the export of its upmarket brands 'Impress' and 'Lunasol', Kanebô specifically developed the skincare brands 'Aqua' and 'Ex' for Chinese consumers, tailoring brand and packaging appeal to local tastes (NSS 2006b, p. 25, NKS 2007c, p. 30). It is important to note that many key workers and decision takers (managers, engineers, doctors and so forth), and therefore opinion leaders, can be found in this age bracket. While a general openness to foreign influences (and brands) can be assumed, this group will equally enjoy local products and services. Nissan is actively engaging with these target segments and has fine-tuned its brand and corporate identity to local needs (for example, in respect of the design of dealerships and so forth). The Japanese car manufacturer takes great care in sales staff selection and training. Nissan perceives sales personnel as the company's face to customers and goes to great lengths to influence word-of-mouth communication in China; for example, a contest for the best Nissan sales representative is aired on Guangzhou TV (NKS 2006h, p. 5).

Geographic segmentation

If age has become a decisive factor in Chinese lifestyle consumption (as it is in other societies), the aforementioned location factors play an even bigger role in determining consumer behaviour. Recent lifestyle studies by Japanese advertising think tank Hakuhôdô attest vast regional value and lifestyle differences across China. From a product innovation perspective, respondents from the regions of Beijing, Guangzhou, Shanghai and Wuhan showed the highest openness to new products (Anon. 2003).

Population density and the degree of urbanization vary largely in China and this has a strong impact on consumer lifestyles (Chinawork 2002). With their orientation towards coastal regions, conurbation areas are characterized by prosperous cities and regions that attract the bulk of investment (and connected with this have also been the target of mass migration of workers from rural areas). Most inner regions of the country have a low population density and are largely dependent on agriculture (with the notable exception of the province Sichuan, one of China's major industrial bases). Therefore, geography shapes economic ability and general lifestyle characteristics of social clusters (with regards to, for example, disposable income, values, environment). As such, geography has become a fundamental variable for the segmentation and investment strategies of Japanese corporations. Seiko uses geographic segmentation in its go-to-market approach. Key to the marketing strategy is the introduction of the watch manufacturer's super luxury brands 'Credor' and 'Grand Seiko'. Targeted at the affluent nouveaux riches (middle-age bracket), these brands are only available in specialist stores in Shanghai (NSS 2006c, p. 21).

The extent of the difference between super-rich young urbanites and traditional rural lifestyles runs like a thread through discussions on consumerism in China and has to be at the heart of an analysis of modern Chinese consumption. Western and Japanese manufacturers have developed their retail networks accordingly. The first wave of investment was directed towards the coastal and metropolitan areas (also as part of investment regulations).

Yet, the effects of these economic gravity centres are increasingly diffusing from metropolitan areas to second-tier and rural regions. Two major triggers of these developments have become apparent in this context: rural migration and commuting (better-paid work in the megalopolis leads to exposure to city consumerism, leading to carriers of modern lifestyles), and role modelling of first-tier lifestyles that are transcending into neighbouring areas (Wang 2005). Supported by government initiatives to encourage local development (for example, the promotion of North-East territories), Chinese retailers have been able to extend already existing networks beyond the major conurbation areas. While the top 20 retailers in China are typically found in the North-East and Yangtze River regions (Onda and Higashi 2004, p. 42), many Japanese firms choose to concentrate their operations in specific regions. For example, the Japanese beverage manufacturer Suntory launched its Oolong Tea brand in 1997 only to the Shanghai region. Geographical disadvantages (after all, this region is the birth place of Oolong Tea) were compensated by successful brand differentiation. Suntory Tea was positioned as a non-traditional lifestyle product (on-the-go drink being the unique selling proposition), also distinct from competitors through a premium price strategy. After the initial unadapted version failed, local market research resulted in fine-tuning to local tastes (less sugar, advertising, pet bottle) to appeal specifically to young Shanghai consumers (Matsui 2006). Over the last decade the brand was carefully developed (with brand extensions, extension of customer base) while maintaining the strategy of regional targeting. Only in 2007 did the firm start to redefine its areas of operations and plans to extend its activities to the metropolitan area of Beijing (thereby continuing with its selective Chinese market strategy).

A further example is Aeon, one of the first Japanese-associated retailers in China to establish a wholly foreign-owned subsidiary in 2004. The Aeon group plans to expand its China business via affiliated store formats and retail brands such as Jusco Supermarkets and Aiku. From their bases in metropolitan areas the new network (50–100 stores are planned), complemented by infrastructure investments, will target specific inland regions (NRS 2004b, p. 5). Despite this extension, Aeon follows a regional concentration pattern, as Figure 2 shows, with a strong presence in the Guangdong region. This 'dominance strategy', an inherent copy of the Japanese retail business model, is contrasted by Western firm activities. Like Chinese competitors, retailers such as Carrefour follow a geographical dispersion approach and are in the process of diffusing their networks further (Figure 3).

As inland regions catch up with the development of economic powerhouses on the coast they become increasingly attractive. Accordingly many Japanese manufacturers have set sight on a regional expansion from Eastern to Western China (that is, coastal regions to inland). This can be demonstrated in the case of Japanese beer breweries. Aiming at synergy effects, closeness to customers and speed, a number of Japanese brewery firms developed manufacturing bases and logistic infrastructure across China's coastal regions in the mid-1990s. They are currently extending their base to the North-East (Heilongjiang, Jilin and Liaoning), South China Sea (Guangdong, Pearl River Delta) and East China Sea (Yangtze Delta) (NKS 2005e, p. 2). Numerous Japanese retail channel developments such as in the brewery industry are under way using the latest technology. The fashion retailer Onwards Kashiyama is implementing a point-of-sale database system (in more than 100 of its shops) for product tracking and customer analysis (NRS 2006, p. 15). Shiseido has so far concentrated its operations in Beijing and Shanghai, but is now in the process of developing nationwide retail outlets with more than 5000 stores planned by 2008 (Izumi 2005, Kanayama 2007). As these examples illustrate, Japanese firms are at the forefront of retail infrastructure developments in China. Selective coastal investments are followed by an inland roll-out of retail formats.

These geographical diffusion patterns reflect the central-periphery paradigm of 'consumscapes'.[3] With the influx of sophisticated local brands and Western retail formats, more demanding and cosmopolitan consumer clusters are emerging in China with halo-effects of first-tier urban settings. Japanese retailers assist in trickling down the

Figure 2. Aeon (Jusco-Supermarket) outlets in China (2007).
Source: Compiled from data available on the China Aeon homepage.

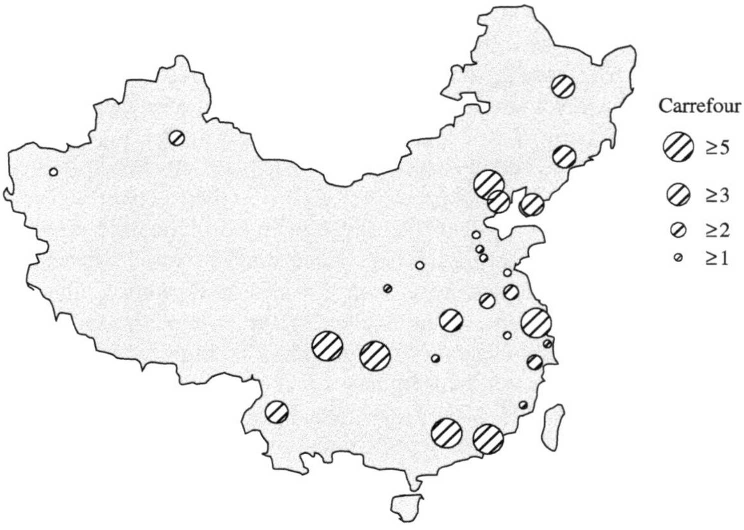

Figure 3. Carrefour's hypermarket outlets in China (2007).
Source: Compiled from data available on the China Carrefour homepage.

modern values and lifestyles by expanding their operations to second- and third-tier cities in order to establish a nationwide retail network with an eye to potential future earnings. Despite anticipated lifestyle diffusion, stark disparities between regions remain. The analysis of the Chinese consumer market must start with the existing differences between the main urban regions such as Beijing, Guangzhou and Shanghai and more rural settings, which are still lagging far behind.

Nostalgia and consumer ethnocentrism

Consumer innovativeness is a key challenge for all foreign firms operating in China. Japanese firms have successfully tailored their strategies to consumer clusters with a high potential for innovation diffusion, carefully taking into account underlying socioeconomic and geographic facets. However, discussions around new product adoption and diffusion should not only include individuals and clusters, but also show interest in novelty. At the other end of the spectrum, ethnocentrism is equally shaping Chinese consumptive behaviour. Economic transitions evoke insecurity and may trigger barriers to new product diffusion. Instead of beliefs in progress and modernity, changes are generally perceived as threat scenarios. Consumer ethnocentrism is neither unique to Chinese consumers nor limited to transitional economies. It is rather a more general reaction towards perceived change (either as a result of felt restrictions or positive attitudes towards the past) as numerous 'buy national campaigns' highlight (for example, the denunciation of Toshiba products in the US in the 1980s in front of the White House). However, it is a fundamental force that is shaping the Chinese consumer's evaluation of Japanese brands (Park 2004, p. 86), both in terms of image and anti-Japanese sentiments. A recent survey by China Research highlights the problems Japanese firms are facing in terms of negative country of origin (COO) evaluations. While products themselves carry positive connotations (such as regarding high-quality, advanced technology), Japanese firms lag behind other foreign competitors with respect to overall appeal and social image (Jin 2006, p. 68), however, socio-demographic variations exist. The image of Japanese firms suffers particularly among young Chinese (Searchina 2007, p. 30). Japanese firms are aware of the potential repercussions on their long-term success in this important future market (in fact, organizations like JETRO and Keidanren have started to address the problems for Japanese companies in China by running special seminars on crisis management).

At the individual level, nostalgic attitudes and predispositions often involve negative feelings towards change. As the influx of new products is a vehicle for change, they are challenging the status quo. Reactions are strong if the current lifestyle is under threat (for example, as a consequence of retirement, loss of influence). In combination with diffusion of foreign ideas and lifestyles (as is often the case in transitional economies), as part of global pathways, associations with 'foreignness' lead to ethnocentric behaviour including consumption. Chinese consumers have recently shown an impressive trend towards embracing modern products and lifestyles. In some cases, however, this is combined with an ethnocentric tendency to prefer local produce.

While foreign brands symbolize central aspects of modernity, prestige and cosmopolitanism (Ger and Belk 1996, Alden *et al.* 1999), Chinese brands have closed the gap, as evidence presented in Table 1 indicates. This is signalling a fading symbolic value of foreign brands in China (Zhou and Hui 2003), with Japanese corporate brands lagging far behind. This is not to say that the success story of Japanese brands in China will come to an abrupt end (fast-food chains and luxury items in particular are highly popular). However, with the rise of local brands such as Lenovo and Haier a noticeable shift has occurred; modernity and prestige do not necessarily come with the (open) consumption of foreign brands or services, but can be evoked via local brands. Chinese firms employ modern brand-building techniques and have started to challenge the negative image of 'Made in China' products that are typically associated with low-quality, inexpensive mass produce. These home-grown global brands will appeal to clusters of Chinese consumers

Table 1. Employer image ranking among Chinese graduates.

Rank	Corporate name and nationality	Ownership structure in China
1	Haier (China)	Listed company
2	IBM (USA)	Foreign capital 100%
3	Procter & Gamble (USA)	Joint venture
4	Lenovo (China)	Listed company
5	Huawei (China)	Private enterprise
6	China Mobile (China)	Listed company
7	Microsoft (USA)	Foreign capital 100%
8	LG Electronics (Korea)	Foreign capital 100%
9	Siemens (Germany)	Foreign capital 100%
10	GE (USA)	Foreign capital 100%
11	Samsung (Korea)	Foreign capital 100%
12	China Telecom (China)	Listed company
13	Intel (USA)	Foreign capital 100%
14	TCL (China)	Listed company
15	Nokia (Finland)	Foreign capital 100%
16	Motorola (USA)	Foreign capital 100%
17	Hewlett Packard (USA)	Foreign capital 100%
18	Mars (USA)	Foreign capital 100%
19	Sinopec (China)	Listed company
20	Unicom (China)	Listed company

Source: Adapted from Nakamura (2006).

that have a generally favourable attitude to change, but prefer local and national products as part of an underlying trend towards 'back to your roots' and nostalgia. If they are to continue to succeed in China, Japanese firms must not underestimate facets of this ethnocentric consumerism evidenced among more or less powerful opinion leaders. By addressing these ethnocentric tendencies, some Japanese are already successful in incorporating a localized appeal. Shiseido has based its success in China on its stand-alone brand 'Aupres'. This product was developed with its joint venture partner solely for the Chinese market (deviating from the otherwise global approach of this cosmetic manufacturer). Local expertise is part of the core product identity (also taking centre stage in advertising campaigns), and serves as the main differentiator from other (Western) upmarket brands. Similarly, beverage manufacturer Suntory ascribes its success not only to its localization approach and smart targeting, but also on a local culture positioning. In its advertising communication, the firm relies primarily on local themes that draw on Chinese theatre, music and cuisine.

In contrast to the aforementioned segments characterized by an overarching openness to change, some clusters have the potential of kick-starting trends in the opposite direction that goes beyond the somewhat negative associations of Japanese firms. While the younger age groups show a general openness to change, a recent study by Horn (2005) suggests a more diverse picture.[4] In this study, young Chinese consistently scored high on the Schwartz (1992, 1994) conservation scale consisting of the values of conformity, tradition and security. Steenkamp *et al.* (1999) show that high scores in conservation will have a negative impact on innovativeness. Interestingly, the Chinese sample also scored relatively high on the stimulation aspect of the openness to change scale. With opposing values leading to psychological conflicts, it is apparent that young Chinese follow a dual strategy vis-à-vis the influx of modern values and lifestyle, with the preservation of the status quo at the centre of consumer behaviour but associated with a general willingness to welcome Western values (transcended by these global brands), as long as they do not interfere with the status quo of local lifestyles. This dual attitude resurfaces with regards to the willingness to welcome innovations from abroad, as indicated in the Horn (2005) survey. Less than one-third of the respondents revealed a willingness to engage with foreign ideas. In contrast, the majority had mixed feelings towards innovativeness, ranging from hesitance to outspoken resistance. This coincides also with findings on the cultural openness scale consisting of seven items (Sharma and Shimp 1995) used by Horn (2005) that demonstrates comparatively low scores for the Chinese sub-sample. Contrary to the assumption that adolescents are a hotbed for new ideas, this survey shows a relatively low interest in engaging and interacting with foreign cultures. Although these two studies are only a snapshot of current societal changes, the findings suggest that, even in this assumed 'progressive' socio-demographic cluster, barriers to foreign lifestyles and values exist.

The underlying tendency towards duality in openness and conservation are complemented by further clusters that are not likely to act as multiplicators of foreign innovations. People in the older age clusters, in particular, belong to the losers of China's economic catch-up. Many of them have lost their job in the wake of the recent transformation of state-owned enterprises. Moreover, being born into the time of the Cultural Revolution this segment has traditionally a very low education background and, therefore, little potential for re-training. Due to these specific factors, very few members of this segment have the necessary spending power to participate in the newly developing lifestyles. Even though seniors and pensioners remain generally unaffected by current shifts in lifestyles, Japanese firms are nevertheless beginning to address these segments. Yakult, for example, has been highly successful with its sales strategy in Guangzhou.

It primarily relies on door-to-door sales and word-of-mouth communication (replicating the Japanese marketing concept of the 'Yakult Lady', whose visits act as an important relationship point). Extending its good reputation, the health drink manufacturer is currently developing a delivery service (NSS 2004, p. 1). However, pensions are generally low and in many cases merely cover the daily necessities. In the foreseeable future, this age bracket is likely to become less attractive for Japanese brands.

It is apparent that gradual changes to the dimensions of openness to change and conservation play a major role in Chinese economic transition. Many Japanese corporations active in China are aware of these underlying tendencies, particularly with a view to the sensibilities vis-à-vis the influx of foreign values and ideas symbolized by brands (as part and parcel of the emerging consumer society). The phenotypological positive attitude towards foreign brands is confounded by inherent conservatism. This resulting consumer ethnocentrism (reflected in increased preference of local brands) confirms surveys that attest to young Chinese high patriotism scores (NSKG 2005). Low individualism and consumer ethnocentrism are correlated (de Mooij 2006, p. 120). China's low score on this Hofstede (1980, 1997) dimension may therefore help to explain nascent ethnocentric consumer behaviour, for example, vis-à-vis Japanese brands as in the case of anti-Japanese sentiments.

Discussion

The targeting of early adopters is a key ingredient of Japanese marketing approaches, both in Japan and abroad. The inherent rapidity of product development and staccato market introduction makes Japanese firms dependent on quick market access and a positive consumer attitude towards product innovations. In the melange of the socio-demographically and geographically diverse Chinese consumer society, the topic of innovation diffusion becomes paramount for the market considerations of Japanese marketing practitioners. The wave-like pattern is usually projected through opinion leaders and early adopters buying the product first, followed by mainstreamers and laggards. Due to China's location and economic transition factors, distinct geographic and socio-demographic trickle-down effects complement this pattern. Drawing from the Japanese MNE experiences in China, a number of factors contribute to the importance of successful product introductions for future growth and profitability of Japanese firms in China. At the same time these are responsible for unique local patterns of innovation diffusion evident in the country.

Despite the novelty and influx of Western and Japanese products and lifestyles, Chinese consumers are by no means easy to please with out-of-date technology. They are well informed about global product developments (the number of internet users has risen dramatically, as has the number of Chinese tourists abroad; Yamatani 2006) and demand for the newest technology is on a par with Western consumers. The expectations vis-à-vis retail formats are equally high and have led Japanese firms to introduce high-end formats in China.

Currently, Japanese product innovation is spreading from metropolitan to urban areas and from there into neighbouring regions. While similar patterns can be detected in industrialized countries (opinion leaders are 'naturally' located in metropolitan areas and are therefore targeted by trend scouts and research companies), the disparity of wealth and innovation is more accentuated in China. The economic transition in geographic stages is unique to China and should be part of the marketing equation. Many Japanese manufacturers and retailers are aware of this dynamic behaviour and focus on the importance of halo and cascade effects in their marketing strategy. Anticipating inherent word-of-mouth communication mechanisms to channel information flows during and after market introduction are often in place for brand-building purposes. However, no distinct pattern can be detected as geographical diffusion is linked to the business model. While some Japanese retailers follow a dominance strategy, other firms are currently rolling out their activities across China.

In industrialized societies, the correlation between product innovation and revenues is well established (Farley 1997). In the case of China, product-lifecycles are increasingly short, with immediate knock-on effects on research and development (R&D). This also spirals into marketing as manufacturers rely more and more on successful product launches. Western corporations are beginning to follow this approach of rapid market introduction and development and have shortened the product life cycles dramatically. Characterized by staccato-style product innovation and market introduction patterns, the marketing of Japanese firms is already fine-tuned to obtaining short-term revenues (Horn 2006, Horn and Horn 2007). Furthermore, Japanese firms are adapting marketing to local product diffusion patterns making use of the unique geographical diversity of the Chinese market.

The development of socio-demographic layers fundamentally influences product diffusion in China. A crucial element of this process is communication, both within and between socioeconomic segments. Additionally, product diffusion is strongly linked to the socioeconomic context (the higher the socioeconomic position of a cluster, the earlier the adoption of innovations). Those higher in the social structure are more likely to be early adopters of new technology (as they are able to afford to pay for information), while those lower in the social structure are more likely to be followers. There is currently only eclectic information on Chinese consumers available in this respect. While at an aggregated level, disposable income has risen sharply, the spread across clusters is currently unclear. With the ongoing economic transition, the socioeconomic stratification will be in flux for the foreseeable future. In this non-transparent state Japanese firms are playing to their strengths and are targeting luxury and upmarket segments (and in doing so are also addressing aspirational consumption). By leveraging geographic segmentation, retail channels are carefully selected to implement positioning and develop brands. As there appears to be only limited communication between the different consumer segments in China, strategies are in place that aim to support word-of-mouth communication (for example via viral marketing and TV competitions).

Access to market information is vital for success in foreign markets. While Japanese research companies have conducted ad hoc studies in China from the beginning of the 1990s, investments into the local research infrastructure have increased rapidly since China's access to the WTO. Most of the major Japanese market research firms and advertising agencies have now a strong presence in key regional areas for test marketing. Not only have Japanese specialist firms intensified their engagement in China (using advanced sampling techniques, online surveys and so forth), but also Japanese manufacturers and retailers themselves have mechanisms in place to continuously monitor consumer trends (point-of-sale system, antenna shops and so forth) (Horn 2006). The fundamentals of information-gathering mechanisms for understanding the emerging consumer market are therefore firmly in place.

Implications for business and management practices

Japanese retailers are at the forefront of the development of the Chinese consumer market. They are currently developing distribution channels beyond the consumer hotbeds in coastal China, and act as physical carriers of retail innovations and gateways to other parts of China for Western lifestyle brands. Piggy-backing on these distribution channels Japanese products will increasingly find their way to Chinese consumers, thereby further enforcing innovation diffusion and product adoption.

Closely related to product diffusion in China and of particular relevance to foreign brands is the question of openness to change. Key carriers and barriers have been identified in this respect. While 'made in ...' philosophies might lose their impact on consumer perceptions, products remain important carriers of national identities (McCracken 1991, 1993). In many respects, country images have replaced the country-of-origin appeals. Often patriotism translates into ethnocentric consumer behaviour with a direct impact on foreign firms. Due to the negative country image (NRI 2006, p. 25), many Japanese corporations find themselves in a precarious situation with respect to China. A distinct pattern of negative images on the one hand and – with a highly sensitized public – a ruthless exposure of Japanese marketing mistakes on the other (Japanese corporations repeatedly are in the Chinese media for PR incidents), mean that Japanese companies have to tread very carefully in this market. While exceptions often prove the rule in most cases, Japanese brands are successfully overcoming hurdles and are appealing to Chinese consumers. On a product choice level, Japanese brands are commonly category leaders, indicating a strong Japanese market presence, on the one hand, and stiff competition for US or European MNEs on the other. As Japanese firms in China face a multitude of barriers on a corporate level, including low employer attractiveness, weak social image and low overall appeal, they seemingly have found the right formula of corporate and product brand segregation. In deviating from their brand architecture in the home market (Horn 2001), Japanese consumer good manufacturers are often able to successfully identify and target clusters with the potential of opinion leadership relying on socioeconomic and geographic segmentation techniques. Instead of relying on their corporate brand, Japanese firms are establishing single, global culture positioned brands (following Western-style crystal strategy) for maximum efficiency. Moreover, with a view to their strategic relevance as innovation carriers in China, Japanese corporations focus on luxury and upmarket products, due to their superior quality. Even everyday products, such as instant ramen, can become luxury goods. In this way they also negate local competition (low-cost alternatives, me-too products). From a well-defined brand identity base, Japanese firms are able to address changes in the consumer cluster composition (such as rise of disposable income, migration). As psychological dimensions (intangible assets) will increasingly determine Chinese consumer behaviour, Japanese firms are likely to continue to exploit the positive image on a product level (reliance, trust, superior quality) and extend it in the medium- to long-term to middle-class/non-luxury segments. It is likely that the launch of top-of-the-range brands will be followed by products targeted at the upper-middle class. This trickle-down strategy includes geographical expansion to second- and third-tier regions of China as part of a market diffusion strategy and customer base extension. In this system the future role of Japanese corporate branding in China is, as yet, unclear.

Conclusions

The majority of Japanese products are strongly positioned (and communicated) as global culture brands, taking into account anti-Japanese sentiments on a corporate brand level. If necessary then foreign culture positioning, with clues to the country of origin, is used (for example to convey superior craftsmanship, technology and so forth, particularly in the B2B sector). Underlying consumer ethnocentrism and cosmopolitanism, both influential and strong purchase decision factors in China are, in this way, anticipated and made part of the Japanese product diffusion strategy. It remains to be seen, however, how the attitude towards foreign brands (including Japanese) as carriers of foreign lifestyles will change in light of improvements to the marketing repertoire of Chinese firms. Some Chinese companies are already very successful in implementing modern branding techniques and have closed the gap to global consumer brand champions. Their popularity (in China and increasingly abroad) reflects not only immanent ethnocentric consumer behaviour but, also indicates that Chinese consumers may potentially evolve towards a preference of localized brand profiles. This conflicts with the notion that consumers in transitional economies typically have a positive attitude towards global brands (reflected in current global culture positioning of Japanese brands). Japanese firms will need to find an answer to the nascent ethnocentrism paired with changes in attitudes towards brands with a global or foreign culture positioning. As the Chinese market advances to become a central pillar of the new global system, Japanese MNEs will continue to carefully monitor China's unique product diffusion patterns. In adapting and extending their local brand presence to evolving shifts in local innovativeness, corporate Japan will further strengthen their market positions in China.

Notes

1. Rising incomes and larger spending power have led to changes to spending patterns in favour of lifestyle products as the following data indicate (increases between 1997 and 2004): medicine and healthcare (156.0%), housing (138.5%), education and entertainment (129.0%), transport and communication (125.9%), and household durable goods (101.4%) (Access Asia 2005). This coincides with a substantial rise in disposable income per capita in China between 1997 and 2003 (Deloitte 2005). This highlights that, although living standards and wages are continuously rising, consumer aspirations and desires are rising even faster. This desire for modern lifestyles is increasingly attended to by (foreign) retailers, who have rushed into China since its accession to the WTO (for further details see Horn and Horn 2007).
2. Many Japanese brands are subject to counterfeiting. Honda, for example, faces a Chinese company named 'Hongda' that imitates the famous CR-V brand (NKS 2006a, p. 4). The motorcycles of the same company are also subject to design infringements. One of its models was copied more than 20 times by local competitors.
3. In his seminal work on the global diffusion of ideas, Appadurai (1990) identifies five central carriers: ethnoscapes (movement of people), technoscapes (movement of technology), finanscapes (movement of money), ideoscapes (movement of ideas) and mediascapes (movement of media images). With the rise of consumerism, Horn (2005) shows that the global movement of brands and consumption needs to be added.
4. Valuable insights into Chinese consumer behaviour in terms of product adoption and innovativeness can be drawn from an empirical research project recently conducted in East Asia (for full details see Horn 2005). Shedding light on Asian consumer acculturation strategies on the dimensions 'desire to participate in global culture' and 'desire to uphold local identity' (with the inherent strategies assimilation, integration, marginalisation and separation) more than 500 volunteers were interviewed in Japan, People's Republic of China and South Korea. With a view to the understanding of the impact on younger clusters as potential change agents the interviewees were all aged below 25.

References

Access Asia, 2005. *Retailing in China 2004: a market analysis*. Bristol, Shanghai: Access Asia Limited.

Alden, D., Steenkamp, J.B., and Batra, R., 1999. Brand positioning in Asia, North America, and Europe: the role of global consumer culture. *Journal of marketing*, 63 (1), 75–87.

Anon., 2003. Chinese Seikatsusha [Chinese consumers] [online]. *Hakuhôdô global habit 2003*. Available from: http://www.hakuhodo.co.jp/english/news/e/ [Accessed 14 Jan 2007].

Anon., 2005a. China to be top consumer of luxury brands [online]. Available from: http://www.china-embassy.org/eng/gyzg/t225956.htm [Accessed 17 Jan 2007].

Anon., 2005b. Chinese women score lowest brand loyalty. *Media Asia* [online]. 23 September. Available from: http://www.brandrepublic.com/News/518215// [Accessed 17 Jan 2007].

Appadurai, A., 1990. Disjuncture and difference in the global cultural economy. *In*: M. Featherstone, ed. *Global culture: nationalism, globalization and modernity*. London: Sage, 295–310.

Berry, J.W., 1980. Social and cultural change. *In*: H.C. Triandis and R.W. Brislin, eds. *Handbook of cross-cultural psychology: social psychology*, Vol. 5. Boston: Allyn and Bacon, 211–279.

Chinawork, 2002. *Chûgoku Tôshi Mâketingu Senryaku Mappu* [*Strategy map for Chinese marketing investments*]. Tokyo: Chinawork.

de Mooij, M., 2006. *Consumer behaviour and culture*. Thousand Oaks: Sage Publications.

Deloitte, 2005. China's consumer market: opportunities and risks [online]. Available from: http://www.deloitte.com/dtt/cda/doc/content/DTT_DR_China_Consumer_Jul05.pdf [Accessed 17 Jan 2007].

Farley, J., 1997. Looking ahead at the marketplace: it's global and it's changing. *In*: D. Lehmann and K. Jocz, eds. *Reflections on the futures of marketing*. Cambridge, MA: Marketing Science Institute, 15–35.

Farrell, D., Gersch, U., and Stephenson, E., 2006. The value of China's emerging middle class [online]. *The McKinsey quarterly*. Available from: http://www.mckinseyquarterly.com/home.aspx [Accessed 3 Jan 2007].

Ger, G. and Belk, R., 1996. I'd like to buy the world a Coke: consumptionscapes of the less affluent world. *Journal of consumer policy*, 19 (3), 271–304.

Hakuhôdô, 2003. Chûgoku Shuyô 8 Toshi 20 dai 30 dai no Seikatsusha no Kachikan to Shôhi Chôsa [online]. Available from: http://www.hakuhodo.co.jp [Accessed 8 Jan 2007].

Hofstede, G., 1980. *Culture's consequences: international differences in work-related values*. Beverly Hills: Sage Publications.

Hofstede, G., 1997. *Lokales Denken, Globales Handeln* [*Local thinking, global acting*]. Munich: C.H. Beck.

Horn, S., 2001. Konsumgütermarketing in Japan [Consumer good marketing in Japan]. *In*: GfK, ed. *Jahrbuch der Absatz- und Verbrauchsforschung*. Berlin: Duncker & Humboldt, 391–405.

Horn, S., 2005. *Interkulturelle Kompetenz im Zugang zu Japanischen Konsumenten* [*Intercultural competence in accessing Japanese markets*]. Wiesbaden: Deutscher Universitäts-Verlag.

Horn, S., 2006. Marktforschung in Japan [Market research in Japan]. In: *Proceedings of the 18th German Japanese studies conference*, September, Bonn, 39.

Horn, S. and Horn, K., 2007. Retailing and consumption in China. *In*: M. Jovanovic, *et al.*, eds. *System transformation in comparative perspective*. Berlin: LIT-Verlag, 333–364.

Ishii, H., 2005. *Chûgoku Shijô de Motomerareru 'Senryakuteki Kôhô'* [*Expections from strategic PR in China*] [online]. Nomura Research Institute, 34–47. Available from: http://www.nri.co.jp/opinion/chitekishisan/2005/pdf/cs20051104.pdf [Accessed 9 Jan 2007].

Izumi, A., 2005. Chûgoku 5000 Ten ni Kakeru [Placing a bet with 5,000 stores in China]. *Nikkei Business*, 14 February, 62–64.

Japan External Trade Organisation, 2006. *JETRO White Paper on international trade and foreign direct investment*. Tokyo: Jetro.

Japan External Trade Organisation, 2007. Japanese trade and investment statistics [online]. Available from: http://www.jetro.go.jp/en/stats/statistics/bpfdi_01_e.xls [Accessed 14 Jan 2007].

JETRO, *See* Japan External Trade Organisation.

Jin, J., 2006. Chûgoku ni okeru Kigyô PR Senryaku no Arikata. *Economic review*, 10 (4), 66–91.

Kanayama, R., 2007. Chûgoku Zenshi 5000 Ten no Senmonten wo Mesashu Shiseidô [Shiseidô aims to open 5.000 speciality stores]. *Ekonomisuto*, 10 April, Tokyo: Mainichi Shinbunsha, 94–95.

Katz, E., 1957. The two-step flow of communication. *The public opinion quarterly*, 21 (1), 61–78.

Katz, E. and Lazarsfeld, P.F., 2005. *Personal influence: the part played by people in the flow of mass communications*. Edison, NJ: Transaction Publishers.
Kô, R., 2000. *Nihongata Mâketingu* [*Japan-style marketing*]. Tokyo: Chikura Shôbô.
Konomoto, S., 2006. *Chûgoku Shôhisha no Burando Ishiki* [*Brand consciousness of Chinese consumers*]. Shanghai: Searchina Sôgô Kenkyûjo.
Kumon, T., 2006. Nikkei Kigyô no [Chûgoku Kaisha he no Koken] wo Apîru [Contributions to Japanese corporate appeal] [online]. *Searchchina.ne.jp*, Chûgoku Jôhôkyoku, July. Available from: http://news.searchina.ne.jp/disp.cgi?y=2006&d=0706&f=column_0706_004.shtml [Accessed 21 January 2007].
Kwak, Y., 2004. *Muttsu no Senryaku kara Manabu Chûgoku Shinsutsu Kigyô no tame no Bijinesu Moderu* [*Selecting from three strategies: business models of China market investors*]. Tokyo: Yuigaku Shôbô.
Matsui, T., 2006. Burandingu in Chaina [Branding in China]. Y. Yamashita, ed. Tokyo: Tôyô Keizai Shinpôsha, 75–108.
McCracken, G., 1991. Culture and consumer behaviour: an anthropological perspective. *Journal of the market research society*, 32 (1), 3–11.
McCracken, G., 1993. The value of a brand: an anthropological perspective. *In*: D. Aaker and A. Bowl, eds. *Brand equity and advertising: advertising's role in building strong brands*. Hillsdale, NJ: Lawrence Erlbaum Associates, 125–139.
McEwen, W., *et al.*, 2006. Inside the mind of the Chinese consumer [online]. *Harvard business review*, March. Available from: http://search.ebscohost.com/login.aspx?direct=true&db=bth&AN=19707486&lang=fr&site=bsi-live [Accessed 8 January 2007].
Nakajima, H., 2006. *Chûgoku ni okeru Kigyô Burando Kôhô no Jûyôsei* [online]. Tokyo: Nomura Research Institute, 72–73. Available from: http://www.nri.co.jp/opinion/chitekishisan/2006/pdf/cs20060806.pdf [Accessed 28 January 2007].
Nakamura, K., 2006. *Saichû Nikkei Toppu Kigyô no Hyôka* [*Evaluation of top Japanese firms in China*] [online]. The 21st century China research institute. Available from: http://www.21ccs.jp/china_watching/KeyNumber_NAKAMURA/Key_number_24.html [Accessed 14 January 2007].
Nihon Keizai Shinbun, 2004. Famima, Rôson, FC Kasoku. *Nihon Keizai Shinbun*. Nihon Keizai Shinbunsha, 10 December, p. 4.
Nihon Keizai Shinbun, 2005a. Shutten 'Shôkyokuteki' 9 Wari. *Nihon Keizai Shinbun*. Nihon Keizai Shinbunsha, 29 June, p. 5.
Nihon Keizai Shinbun, 2005b. Shiseido, Kesshôhin 5000 Ten. *Nihon Keizai Shinbun*. Nihon Keizai Shinbunsha, 1 September, p. 9.
Nihon Keizai Shinbun, 2005c. Kôkyûkan Tamochi Chûgoku Shijô Kaitaku. *Nihon Keizai Shinbun Chihô Keizaimen*. Nihon Keizai Shinbunsha, 11 November, p. 23.
Nihon Keizai Shinbun, 2005d. Dokuji Monitâ 20man Nin Tsunoru. *Nihon Keizai Shinbun*. Nihon Keizai Shinbunsha, 2 June, p. 9.
Nihon Keizai Shinbun, 2005e. Santorî Shangai Jiban Katame. *Nihon Keizai Shinbun*. Nihon Keizai Shinbunsha, 20 January, p. 2.
Nihon Keizai Shinbun, 2006a. Chûgoku de R&D Kyôka. *Nihon Keizai Shinbun*. Nihon Keizai Shinbunsha, 23 March, p. 4.
Nihon Keizai Shinbun, 2006b. Chûgoku, Sekai Nii no Kôkoku Shijô ni. *Nihon Keizai Shinbun*. Nihon Keizai Shinbunsha, 3 July, p. 2.
Nihon Keizai Shinbun, 2006c. Chûgoku Shijô wo Dô Miru ka? *Nihon Keizai Shinbun*. Nihon Keizai Shinbunsha, 17 July, p. 13.
Nihon Keizai Shinbun, 2006d. Nihon Kigyô Muke Monitâ Shôkai. *Nihon Keizai Shinbun*. Nihon Keizai Shinbunsha, 2 October, p. 4.
Nihon Keizai Shinbun, 2006e. Chûgoku Muke Wôkuman. *Nihon Keizai Shinbun*. Nihon Keizai Shinbunsha, 5 April, p. 13.
Nihon Keizai Shinbun, 2006f. Chûgoku de Choku Eiten Tenkai. *Nihon Keizai Shinbun*. Nihon Keizai Shinbunsha, 18 January, p. 4.
Nihon Keizai Shinbun, 2006g. 25-35sai OL wo Kaitaku. *Nihon Keizai Shinbun*. Nihon Keizai Shinbunsha, 31 August, p. 20.
Nihon Keizai Shinbun, 2006h. Kôdôryoku, Supîdo ni Odoroki. *Nihon Keizai Shinbun*. Nihon Keizai Shinbunsha, 6 January, p. 5.
Nihon Keizai Shinbun, 2006i. Ôte Konbini Chûgoku Shutten Gensoku. *Nihon Keizai Shinbun*. Nihon Keizai Shinbunsha, 18 August, p. 6.

Nihon Keizai Shinbun, 2007a. Chûgoku de no Kôhô Katsudô Shien. *Nihon Keizai Shinbun*. Nihon Keizai Shinbunsha, 14 February, p. 2.

Nihon Keizai Shinbun, 2007b. Gaishoku, Chûgoku de Shutten Kasoku. *Nihon Keizai Shinbun*. Nihon Keizai Shinbunsha, 18 January, p. 4.

Nihon Keizai Shinbun, 2007c. Chûgoku Senyô Burando ni UV Shôhin. *Nihon Keizai Shinbun*. Nihon Keizai Shinbunsha, 31 January, p. 30.

Nihon Keizai Shinbun Chihô Keizaimen, 2006. Chûgoku de Kôkyû Kanmen Hanbai. *Nihon Keizai Shinbun Chihô Keizaimen*. Nihon Keizai Shinbunsha, 27 April, p. 24.

Nikkei Ryûtsû Shinbun, 2004a. Bunseki Chainîzu. *Nikkei Ryûtsû Shinbun*. Nihon Keizai, Shinbunsha, 29 June, p. 5.

Nikkei Ryûtsû Shinbun, 2004b. Ion, Chûgoku ni Tôkatsu Kaisha. *Nihon Ryûtsû Shinbun*. Nihon Keizai Shinbunsha, 14 September, p. 5.

Nikkei Ryûtsû Shinbun, 2006. Chûgoku Zenten ni POS Haibi. *Nikkei Ryûtsû Shinbun*. Nihon Keizai Shinbunsha, 24 April, p. 15.

Nikkei Sangyô Shinbun, 2004. Yakuruto 'Nisshiki' de Kôryaku. *Nikkei Sangyô Shinbun*. Nihon Keizai Shinbunsha, 18 May, p. 1.

Nikkei Sangyô Shinbun, 2006a. Chûgoku de 'Seicha' 2.2bai Nerau. *Nikkei Sangyô Shinbun*. Nihon Keizai Shinbunsha, 3 March, p. 24.

Nikkei Sangyô Shinbun, 2006b. Chûgoku de mo Hanbai. *Nikkei Sangyô Shinbun*. Nihon Keizai Shinbunsha, 24 April, p. 15.

Nikkei Sangyô Shinbun, 2006c. Chûgoku de Udedokei Kakuhan. *Nikkei Sangyô Shinbun*. Nihon Keizai Shinbunsha, 28 August, p. 21.

Nikkei Shinbun Kôkoku Guide, 2005. Chûgoku Bijinesu ni okeru Otoshiana to Chansu [online]. *Nikkei Shinbun Kôkoku Guide*. Nihon Keizai Shinbunsha, September 05. Available from: http://www.nikkei-ad.com/cb/corporate_brand/topic0508_2.html [Accessed 17 Jan 2007].

NKS, *See* Nihon Keizai Shinbun.

NKSCK, *See* Nihon Keizai Shinbun Chihô Keizaimen.

Nomura Research Institute, 2006. *Chûgoku Shijô de no Kigyô Burando Senryaku*. Tokyo: Nomura Research Institute.

NRI, *See* Nomura Research Institute.

NRS, *See* Nikkei Ryûtsû Shinbun.

NSKG, *See* Nikkei Shinbun Kôkoku Guide.

NSS, *See* Nikkei Sangyô Shinbun.

O'Leary, N., 2007. The new superpower: China's emerging middle class [online]. *Adweek*, January 1. Available from: http://www.adweek.com/aw/magazine/article_display.jsp?vnu_content_id=100352622 [Accessed 19 Jan 2007].

Onda, T. and Higashi, M., 2004. *Chûgoku ni okeru Ryûtsûgyô Kisei Kanwa no Inpakuto* [*Impact of the deregulation of Chinese distribution*]. Tokyo: Nomura Research Institute, 40–53.

Park, S., 2004. *Burando ni okeru Kantrî obu Orijin no Eigyô* [*Brand management of country of origin*]. Thesis (PhD), Faculty of Commerce, Waseda University. Tokyo: Yoshida Hideo Memorial Foundation.

Prasso, S., 2005. Battle for the face of China [online]. *Fortune*, 12 December. Available from: http://money.cnn.com/magazines/fortune/fortune_archive/2005/12/12/8363110/index.htm [Accessed 22 Jan 2007].

Qiong, W., 2005. China's workplace tweens. *The China business review*, November–December, 30–33.

Rogers, E., 2003. *Diffusion of innovations*. London: Free Press.

Schwartz, S., 1992. Universals in the content and structures of values: theoretical advances and empirical tests in 20 countries. *In*: M. Zanna, ed. *Advances in experimental social psychology*, 25. Orlando: Academic Press, 1–65.

Schwartz, S., 1994. Beyond individualism/collectivism: new cultural dimensions of values. *In*: U. Kim *et al.*, eds. *Individualism and collectivism: theory, method, and applications*. Thousand Oaks: Sage Publications, 85–119.

Searchina, 2007. *Chûgoku Shôhisha no Seikatsu Jittai 2007–2008 [Chinese consumer living condition 2007–2008]*. Shanghai: Searchina Research Institute.

Sharma, S. and Shimp, T., 1995. Consumer ethnocentrism: a test of antecedents and moderators. *Journal of the academy of marketing science*, 23, 21–36.

Sin, L. *et al.*, 2001. Chinese women at the crossroads: an empirical study on their role orientations and consumption values in Chinese society. *Journal of consumer marketing*, 18 (4), 348–367.

Steenkamp, J.B., Hofstede, F., and Wedel, M., 1999. A cross-national investigation into the individual and national cultural antecedents of consumer innovativeness. *Journal of marketing*, 63 (2), 55–68.

The Economist, 2006. Ready for warfare in the aisles [online]. *The Economist*, 3 August. Available from: http://www.economist.com [Accessed 17 Jan 2007].

Wang, J., 2005. Bourgeois bohemians in China? Neo-tribes and the urban imaginary. *The China quarterly*, 183 (September), 532–548.

Yamatani, Y., 2006. *Chûgoku Intânetto Hatten Genjô Tôkei Hôkô* [*Statistical information on the internet expansion in China*] [online]. Available from: http://internet.watch.impress.co.jp/static/others/travel/050223/index.htm [Accessed 9 Jan 2007].

Zhou, L. and Hui, M., 2003. Symbolic value of foreign products in the People's Republic of China. *Journal of international marketing*, 11 (2), 36–58.

Why Japanese multinationals failed in the Chinese mobile phone market: a comparative study of new product development in Japan and China

T. Marukawa

Institute of Social Science, University of Tokyo, Tokyo, Japan

Introduction

Japanese multinational enterprises (MNEs) have been characterized as having a centralized organization, in which most strategic assets, resources and decisions are concentrated at their headquarters in Japan, while overseas operations are treated merely as pipelines to deliver products and services to global markets (Bartlett and Ghoshal 1998, Whitley *et al.* 2003). Typically, the innovation process is managed in the same manner, by which new product and process development activities are almost always undertaken at the headquarters and are subsequently transferred to the overseas operations. Japanese MNEs might occasionally modify their innovations to meet the specific needs of overseas markets, but generally with much reluctance. Although many Japanese MNEs have deployed their research and development (R&D) facilities abroad since the 1980s – for example to tap research resources or to appease political pressure in the host market (Cairncross 1994) – the basic structure of the innovation process remains largely unchanged.

By adopting such a centralized and innovative process, MNEs bear a risk of being insensitive to the local needs of overseas markets (Bartlett and Ghoshal 1998). The risk of maladjustment is even larger when not only consumer demand but also the distribution system differs in the overseas market from the MNE's home country, because the distribution system that stands between consumers and the manufacturers can often influence consumer demand. With respect to Japanese MNEs in particular, the centralized innovation process often makes it difficult for them to adapt to a foreign market where consumer demand and the distribution system are radically different from those in Japan. These differences can, at the same time, create room for local firms, which usually have poorer resources than MNEs, to expand their presence. Local firms, with better knowledge of the preferences and distribution system of the host nation, may be able to win market share against MNEs by creating innovative capabilities that are more adaptive and responsive to local conditions.

Given this backdrop, the purpose of this study is to assess the difficulties that Japanese MNEs can experience in developing new markets when the innovation process is centralized. This is done using a case study of Japanese mobile telephony companies and their expansion into the Chinese market. The study describes in detail differences in the product innovation and distribution systems of the Japanese and Chinese mobile telephony sectors, and shows how difficult it can be for Japanese electronics manufacturers to adapt to the Chinese market, and how local Chinese firms, despite a paucity of resources when they first appeared, have been able to out-compete Japanese MNEs in the Chinese market.

In the next section, data are presented to demonstrate that Japanese telephony manufacturers have underperformed in China relative to their foreign and local counterparts, and a number of possible explanations are discussed. This is followed by a statement of a research proposition derived from the theory of the innovation processes of MNEs which this study will evaluate. The fourth section describes the methodological approach to data collection, and this is followed by a brief account of the development of the Chinese mobile phone industry. In the fifth section, a comparison is made of the mobile phone distribution systems in Japan and China, while the sixth section presents a comparison of production development activities of Japanese and Chinese mobile phone manufacture based upon primary data collected in interview. The seventh section analyzes how Japanese phone makers have attempted to sell their products in China and gives reasons for the failure of their marketing strategies. This is followed by conclusions and suggestions for further research.

Literature review: theoretical explanations for Japanese MNE performance in China

Little scholarly attention has been paid to explaining the failure of Japanese mobile telephone manufacturers in foreign markets. However, the issue is widely discussed in the trade press and business circles in Japan. In the case of China, this poor performance is evident in data on the market shares of major mobile phone brands (Table 1). In discussions in Japan, three kinds of explanation for the failure have been put forward, which can be summarized as follows.

First, some scholars, including Funk (1998, 2002), argue that differences in the technological standards of mobile phones between Japan and foreign markets has made it difficult for Japanese manufacturers to succeed in foreign markets. During the second generation (2G) of mobile phone services' development, which started in 1993 and still continues today, Japan adopted an indigenous standard, PDC (Personal Digital Cellular), whereas most other countries adopted the Europe-based standard, GSM (Global System for Mobile).[1] To market mobile handsets abroad, Japanese MNEs are required not only to design handsets anew to accommodate GSM technology, but also to pay license fees and royalties, which can amount to 6–10% of the total price of a handset, to the owners of GSM patents. Conversely, European and American manufacturers face the same technical barrier when they try to sell PDC-compatible handsets in Japan. Although the 'technology standards' explanation seems convincing, two recent developments undermine it. Firstly, the Korean mobile phone makers, Samsung and LG, face much the same entry barrier

Table 1. Market shares of major mobile phone brands in China (%).

	1997	1998	1999	2000	2001	2002	2003	2004*	2005	2006
Nokia	2.5	11.7	32.3	25.1	22.3	18.2	11.2	17.0	23.8	30.2
Motorola	68.0	64.0	39.4	35.4	29.3	28.5	9.3	14.3	13.3	22.0
Samsung			–					8.3	9.6	9.6
Bird				3.2	6.4	9.9	13.2	7.8	6.1	5.2
Amoi								4.6	4.2	2.9
Ericsson (SonyEricsson)	5.0	11.4	6.4	9.2	6.5	2.1	1.3	3.9	4.1	5.7
Lenovo									4.1	6.2
TCL				1.0	3.0	8.7	11.2	6.8	3.7	1.1
Konka							5.5	3.9	2.8	1.6
Haier									2.8	1.0
NEC	1.7	1.6							2.1	–
Matsushita	6.6	2.9							1.0	–
Siemens		2.6	6.0	8.1	9.7	4.7	2.4			–
Philips		5.6						2.8		1.2

Notes: Data for 1997 and 1998 are based on production volumes; others are based on sales surveys. *For 2004, the data are for the period January to October.
Source: 1997–1998: China Electronics Industry Yearbook; 1999: China Electronics News; 1999–2003: China Electronics and Information Industry Yearbook 2003; 2004: CCID; 2005: Norson Telecom Consulting (2006); 2006: SINO-MR.

abroad as do the Japanese, because their home market has not adopted GSM either. However, this fact did not prevent them from gaining large market shares internationally, with Samsung having 10.6% and LG having 3.7% shares of the world's GSM market, placing them third and fifth, respectively, among the world's leading handset manufacturers in 2006 (Fuji Kimera Research Institute 2007). Secondly, Chinese mobile phone manufacturers in the Chinese market face higher entry barriers to the GSM market than do the Japanese and Korean manufacturers, because, lacking any sort of proprietary technology, they cannot resort to cross-licensing agreements (when two or more manufacturers with related patents mutually exchange the right to use patented technology and so economize on licensing fees) to gain market access. Nevertheless, at least some Chinese manufacturers have been able to out-compete the Japanese in the Chinese market (Table 2). Cheung (2005) attributes the rise of Chinese handset manufacturers to the standardization of product technology and cooperation between the Chinese firms and locally investing MNEs. Although these factors might explain why Chinese manufacturers were able to narrow the technological gap with MNEs, they do not explain why they were able to out-compete most foreign handset manufacturers, including the Japanese, in the Chinese market.

The second explanation for the poor performance, some might argue, is that the technological capabilities of Japanese manufacturers are simply weaker than their rivals, such as the world's top three mobile phone manufacturers, Nokia, Motorola and Samsung. However, as far as product technology is concerned, this is unlikely to be the case, because Japanese manufacturers have been leaders in mobile phone innovation for many years: for example, they were the first in the world to install colour liquid crystal displays (LCD), cameras, internet browsers, electronic money services and television receivers on a mobile phone handset. Furthermore, the high proportion of the latest third-generation (3G) mobile phone subscribers in Japan, occupying one-third of all 3G subscribers in the world,[2] indicates that the Japanese market has a strong demand for high value-added services and sophisticated handsets, and these are provided by Japanese manufacturers, for the most part.

Third, some commentators suspect that Japanese mobile phone manufacturers have ignored or place little importance on overseas markets. It is true that the major Japanese manufacturers, such as Sharp, Matsushita and NEC, generate more than 80% of their mobile phone sales in Japan (Fuji Kimera Research Institute 2007). However, this is more a consequence of their failure in overseas markets rather than of a strategy to concentrate resources on the domestic market. In the case of China, for example, the fact that Matsushita established a mobile phone production site there as early as 1995 – the same year that Nokia established a production site in China – shows that the Japanese company was as eager as its Finnish rival to gain a dominant position in the Chinese market, at least in the early stages of China's mobile market development. The above three explanations are not convincing, and alternate explanations are therefore required.

Research proposition

Given the characterization in the literature that many Japanese MNEs in the manufacturing sector are highly centralized and use their overseas operations merely to deliver products and services developed in Japan to global markets (see Bartlett and Ghoshal 1998, Whitley *et al.* 2003), this study evaluates the following proposition: the centralized innovation process of Japanese MNEs has made it difficult for them to adapt to the Chinese market, where the demand conditions for mobile handsets are radically different from those in the Japanese market.

Table 2. Volume of subscribers, production and trade of mobile phone handsets in China (million units).

	No. of subscribers	Annual increase of subscribers	Imports[1]	Exports	Production	Worldwide production[2]	Share of China in world production (%)
1989	0.01						
1990	0.02	0.01					
1991	0.05	0.03					
1992	0.2	0.1	0.3	2.6			
1993	0.6	0.5	0.7	3.2			
1994	1.6	0.9	0.4	0.1			
1995	3.6	2.1	0.4	0.5	1.3		
1996	6.9	3.2	–	–	2.0		
1997	13.2	6.4	1.4	1.9	8.9	101.0	8.8
1998	23.9	10.6	1.6	2.2	11.8	163.0	7.2
1999	43.3	19.4	3.0	5.7	20.2	275.0	7.3
2000	84.5	41.2	6.0	22.8	52.5	405.0	13.0
2001	145.2	60.7	7.5	39.7	80.3	380.0	21.1
2002	206.0	60.8	17.2	63.3	121.5	405.0	30.0
2003	269.0	63.0	22.1	95.2	182.3	471.1	38.7
2004	334.8	65.8	12.7	146.1	233.5	643.0	36.3
2005	393.4	58.6	12.7	227.9	303.5	795.0	38.2
2006	461.1	67.7	28.9	385.4	480.1	978.0	49.1

Note: 1. Imports include completely knocked-down components; 2. From Nokia's annual reports.
Source: China Statistical Yearbook, China Electronics Industry Yearbook, Ministry of Commerce (various years).

Methodology

The study is based on the author's interviews at 47 companies conducted in China and Japan during the period 2004–2007. The names of the companies and their divisions interviewed are as follows: (1) the handset management divisions of mobile phone service carriers (namely NTT DoCoMo and China Unicom); (2) the product planning or product development divisions of Japanese mobile phone makers (Casio Hitachi Mobile Communications, Sharp, Toshiba Corporation Mobile Communications Company, Panasonic Mobile Communications and Hitachi); (3) the Chief Executive Officers (CEOs) of the subsidiaries of Japanese mobile phone makers in China (Matsushita Electric China Mobile Communications Company, Tianjin Sanyo and NEC Telecommunications China); (4) the product planning and product development divisions of Chinese mobile phone makers (Amoi, Konka, ZTE, Eastcom, Bird, Panda, Lenovo Mobile and Capitel); (5) the planning divisions of other mobile phone makers in China (UTStarcom and Sony Ericsson Mobile Communications); (6) the planning and marketing divisions of Chinese mobile phone design houses (Techfaith, Yulong, Ginwave, Shanghai Huaqin, Cellon, Longcheer, Sim and Shenzhen Elite); (7) the CEOs of the retailers and wholesalers of mobile handsets in China (Guangzhou Datianxing, Guangxun Dianxun, Shenzhen Telling, Guangzhou Yihaotong, Shenzhen Xinan Anshun and Beijing Putian Taili); (8) the marketing divisions of integrated circuit (IC) chip vendors and parts suppliers (Spreadtrum, Texus Instruments, Renesus Technology, Oki, Datang Mobile, NXP, Shenzhen Shangli, Seiko Epson Corporation and Dongguan Nocin); and (9) four consulting companies and media companies specialized in electronics (GfK Group, iSuppli, Beidou Shouji Wang and Shoujiquan).

Each interview lasted for two hours on average. Semi-structured interviews using a standard questionnaire were conducted at the mobile phone makers, design houses, retailers and wholesalers. The purpose was to understand issues surrounding the evolution of China's mobile phone industry, product development processes in Japan and China, the distribution systems used and overall firm strategy. Interviews with other types of company were unstructured but the questions posed were mainly related to product development and the distribution of mobile phones in China. Due to the rise and fall of business models and firms having been rapid and dramatic in the Chinese mobile phone industry – for example, a few companies interviewed no longer exist at the time of writing – interview questions were modified each year accordingly.

Data analysis

The development of the Chinese mobile phone industry

Mobile telecommunications services were first offered in China in 1987. During the first five or six years, mobile phones were considered a luxury good, which only foreign businessmen could afford to buy, and growth in the subscriber base was very slow (Table 2). Only foreign manufacturers provided handsets in China during this period, among which Motorola had a dominant share, occupying 60% of the market in 1993. The dominant position of Motorola was a result of China's adoption of the Total Access Communication System (TACS), a technology developed by Motorola, as the technical standard for its mobile telecommunications network. The number of subscribers began to grow when the monopoly of mobile phone service operation held by China Mobile came to an end in 1994 and when the second telecommunication carrier, China Unicom, started offering mobile phone services. The latter adopted 2G GSM technology, which had many advantages over TACS. China Mobile also began using GSM in the following year. The adoption of 2G digital technology, which can accommodate several times more phone calls in a limited frequency spectrum than first-generation analogue technology, made the popularization of mobile phones possible. In 2001, the number of mobile phone service subscribers in China reached 145 million, and China became the world's largest mobile phone market in terms of subscriber base.

The policy to promote the domestic mobile phone industry

The adoption of GSM in China helped the European mobile phone makers, such as Nokia, Ericsson, Philips, and Siemens, to expand their market presence. Before 1998, China's mobile handset market was occupied by foreign brands, including the European manufacturers, the US firm Motorola, and the Japanese MNEs, Matsushita and NEC. Hoping to foster an indigenous mobile phone industry, the Ministry of Information Industry of China promulgated an industrial policy, named the 'Opinion on the Promotion of Mobile Phone Industry Development' in 1999. The 'Opinion', which was not communicated widely, obliged foreign handset manufacturers to export more than 60% of their output and to increase the local content of mobile handset production to 60%. It also allowed for subsidies to be given to domestic manufacturers for their R&D activities. The 'Opinion' restricted entry to mobile handset production to those companies that were granted production licenses (Kimura 2006).

The 'Opinion' was a tremendous success from the viewpoint of policy-makers. Domestic handset manufacturers, which were non-existent in 1998, emerged immediately after the promulgation of the 'Opinion', occupying 3% of the market in 1999. Their total share increased to 10% in 2000, to 23% in 2001, to 39% in 2002, and reached 55% in 2003 (Editorial Committee 2000, 2001, 2002, Institute of Industrial Economics 2003). In 2003, a domestic manufacturer, Bird, became the top seller of mobile handsets in China (see Table 1). The discriminatory regulations of the 'Opinion', which obligated only MNEs to export and to raise local content, helped domestic manufacturers to expand market share at the expense of the MNEs. However, the 'Opinion' received few criticisms from the MNEs. The reason for their silence seems to lie in the fact that the obligations of the 'Opinion' coincided with the strategy of major MNEs, who had decided to use China as an export base from which to supply mobile handsets to the industrialized countries. As shown in Table 2, the export of mobile phones grew rapidly after 1999. By 2006, China accounted for nearly one-half of global mobile handset production.

The export requirement of the 'Opinion', however, presented Japanese MNEs with a dilemma. Having only small market shares outside of Japan, the only market to which they could realistically export handsets from China in large volumes was Japan. Yet such a move would have sacrificed employment at their Japanese factories for the expansion of exports from China. Hence, exports were limited, which in turn limited expansion of their sales within China. The local content requirement of the 'Opinion', on the other hand, was not a difficult task to meet for any foreign handset manufacturer, because the Chinese authorities did not impose a strict definition of what constituted local components. In fact, whatever components were bought from a local trading company, irrespective of their place of manufacture, were regarded as 'local components' by the Chinese authorities.

The emergence of Chinese mobile phone makers

Even after taking account of the support of the 'Opinion', the rapid expansion of the Chinese manufacturers remains impressive. A mobile phone handset is undoubtedly a technology-intensive product, dealing with high-frequency radio waves in a small enclosure, while having the functionality similar in many respects to that of a personal computer. It is easy to hypothecate that it must be difficult to acquire the technology and become a competitive mobile phone manufacturer in just a few years.

The reason for the quick expansion of Chinese manufacturers was their use of international outsourcing. During the first few years of their emergence, Chinese makers, such as Bird, TCL and Konka, relied on Korean and Taiwanese mobile phone manufacturers for the design and production of mobile phone handsets. The 'Opinion', which was intended to nurture the domestic mobile phone industry, had the effect of encouraging Chinese manufacturers to import handsets branded with the Chinese manufacturers' names but made by Korean and Taiwanese manufacturers. This was a consequence of a loophole of the 'Opinion': it did not place any local content requirements on domestic manufacturers.

The fact that outsourcing to foreign phone makers became rampant after the emergence of Chinese manufacturers in 1999 is reflected in data on mobile phone imports (Table 2), which increased alongside the expansion of Chinese phone makers' sales. The drop in imports in 2004 coincided with decline in the market share of domestic phone manufacturers, to 38%. It is possible to estimate that 70% of handsets sold by domestic phone manufacturers in 2002 and 50% in 2003, were actually imported, including those in the form of completely knocked-down components.

The history of Bird, or *Bodao*, the largest domestic mobile phone maker, reveals how Chinese manufacturers made use of outsourcing. Bird was established in 1992 as a manufacturer of pagers. After becoming the second largest pager maker in China, the management decided to diversify into the production of mobile phones. Not having the capability to develop and produce mobile phones, Bird sought the support of Sagem, a French electronics company, to provide production technology and completely knocked-down components of mobile handsets. For Sagem, supplying Bird with technology and components was the only way to enter the Chinese market, because it had not been awarded a production license in China.

With Sagem's support, Bird entered the domestic mobile phone market, but the company soon discovered that Sagem's European-style handsets did not fit the tastes of Chinese consumers. Therefore, Bird asked the Korean phone makers, Pantech and Telson, to provide handset design. The production line built using the technological support of Sagem was later transformed into a joint venture with Sagem, with the latter taking charge of production. Bird's advancement to a market-leading position can be attributed to the support it received from the French and Korean firms, which did not have the rights to manufacture and market mobile handsets under their own brand names in China. Along with expansion of production, however, Bird advanced its inhouse development capability. Bird's handsets are now designed partly by its own Chinese development centres in Ningbo and Hangzhou which employ more than 500 staff in total, and partly by Korean and Chinese design houses.

Japanese MNEs began producing mobile handsets in China before the Chinese makers came into existence. As mentioned before, Matsushita started its mobile phone joint venture in 1995, followed by NEC in 1997, and later by Sony, Toshiba, Sanyo, Mitsubishi and Kyosera. Before 1997, Matsushita enjoyed first newcomer advantage in China and held second position in terms of market share. However, since 1998, none of the Japanese manufacturers, except for Sony Ericsson (a joint venture between Sony Corporation and the Swedish telecommunications company Ericsson), which inherited much of its market share in China from Ericsson, has occupied more than 3% of the Chinese market (Table 1). The reason for this, which is discussed in detail below, is that the Japanese manufacturers failed to adjust their product innovation strategy to adapt to the demands and distribution systems of China, which were radically different from those of Japan.

A comparison of product development in Japan and China

This section compares the product development activities of Japanese and Chinese mobile phone manufacturers. Product development activities are the responses of firms to the demand presented to them from consumers, or from the intermediaries that stand between the manufacturers and end-users. Therefore, differences in product development strategy will, to a great extent, reflect differences in demand between Japan and China.

Number of models

The most striking difference between the Japanese and Chinese mobile phone markets is the number of handset models sold. In Japan, there were 83 models on the market as of June 2006, sold by three mobile phone operators (NTT DoCoMo, Vodafone and au, which is marketed by KDDI Corporation and Okinawa Cellular), and a personal handyphone system (PHS) operator (Willcom). Each of the mobile phone makers had fewer than 13 models in their portfolio (Table 3). Mobile phones in Japan form part of the service operators' product line-up: all mobile phones have the corporate logos of the service operators on their case, while the manufacturer's logo appears less conspicuously, or in some instances, not at all.

In China, the leading manufacturers usually sell more than 60 models at a time. Nokia, for example, had 63 models, Motorola had 67, Samsung had 89 and Bird had 67 models as of June 2006. Even NEC, which sold only eight models in their home market, had as many as 59 models in China, gaining only 2.1% of the market. According to *Beidou shouji wang*, an internet handset shop that boasts the extent of its coverage, there were 70 brands in China and 1460 different models of mobile phone as of June 2006. Mobile phones in China always have the manufacturer's logo clearly marked but seldom show the service operator's logo. The difference in the number of models per manufacturer between Japan and China is a reflection of differences in the organization of product line-up. Broadly speaking, in Japan, each operator prepares a product line-up that covers various consumer demands and tastes, whereas, in China, each handset manufacturer prepares its own product line-up. The diversity of income levels and tastes also explains why there are so many types of mobile phones in China.

As there are so many models in China, the average sales volume per model is much smaller than that in Japan. In Japan, phone makers usually set sales targets per model to between 500,000 and one million units. Yet in China, the target is 100,000–200,000 units and, often, actual sales only amount to around 50,000 units on average.

In Japan, the replacement of models strictly follows the service operator's plan. NTT DoCoMo, for example, issues two series of handsets, the '700' series and '900' series, every six months. Three generations of models appear simultaneously in the company's catalogue, which means that one model will be sold for a year and several months. In China, the replacement of models is not planned. Handset manufacturers release new models every month, and sales of each model continue as long as it sells well. The duration of sales usually ranges from five months to two years, but there is no rule. Replacement is left to natural selection in the market.

The process and cost of product development

In Japan, service operators are heavily involved in the development of handsets. It is the operator who plans the line-up of products and determines the concept of each model. In some cases, the operators even provide the exterior design of handsets, but usually the

Table 3. Supply relationships between mobile handset makers and service operators in Japan (no. of models).

	Handset manufacturer															
Service operators	Mitsubishi	Fujitsu	LG Electronics	NEC	Nokia	Matsushita	Sanyo	Sharp	Sony Ericsson	Motorola	Toshiba	Samsung	Kyosera	Hitachi	Casio	Pantech	Nihon Musen
NTT DoCoMo	6	5	1	6	1	7	2	4	3	1							
Vodaphone[1]				2	1			7			6	1					
Au							6		3		3		6	2	1	1	
Willcom							1	2					3				2

Note: 1. Vodafone has now changed its brand to 'Softbank'. 2. The data are based on information collected in June 2006.
Source: Author, based on operators' marketing materials.

entire design is undertaken by the manufacturers. Therefore, the role of manufacturers in Japan can be likened to that of Taiwanese 'original design manufacturers' (ODM) that design and manufacture personal computers for international brands based on the requirements of the latter.

Typically, manufacturers in Japan start planning for a new model around 14 to 18 months prior to the date of release (Figure 1). Planning is based on suggestions received from the service operator about what functions they wish to have installed in future models. For example, operators will tell the manufacturers that they want to have a handset that can receive digital television broadcasting and can be used as electronic money and has a large display. Manufacturers examine the feasibility to realize such requirements with the components and technology that are available to them. Around one year prior to release, service operators formally announce the concept and specification of the handset they want to purchase and invite manufacturers to submit their plans. At that time, manufacturers have already spent several months making a plan, so they quickly submit their plans and compete for the order. The operator compares the plans and decides to whom the order should be placed. After the contract between the operator and manufacturer has been signed, the manufacturer starts circuit design, exterior design, and software development for the handset. Since a detailed and feasible plan has been made during the planning period, the first prototype will be developed quickly, typically within a month or so. However, since new handsets in Japan typically employ many new components, the first prototype is usually problematic. Thereafter, a cycle of trial production, detection of defects, and mending of defects will be repeated several times. During the research interviews, one Japanese manufacturer revealed that it had once had 13 iterations in trial production in order to develop a single model. Normally, the design will be finalized three months prior to product release.

Product development in China is quite different. In particular, it is conducted independently by the manufacturer without the involvement of the service operator. As shown in Figure 1, the time devoted to the development of a single model in China is less than half of that in Japan. The most different aspect is the time assigned to planning.

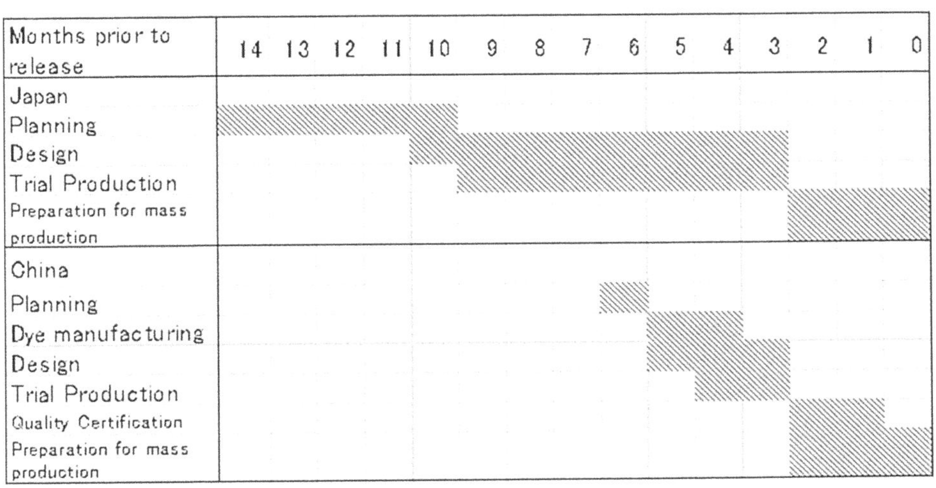

Figure 1. Typical schedule of handset development.
Source: Interviews with Japanese and Chinese handset makers and design houses.

In Japan, planning is as important as the design, because without a good plan manufacturers cannot win orders from the operator. In China, most handsets are sold by manufacturers to consumers without the involvement of operators, so planning involves the manufacturer determining for itself the concept of the new model. Even when Chinese operators purchase handsets from manufacturers and resell them to consumers, operators usually do not decide to buy handsets that are still at the planning stage; they generally select from the handsets that are ready for mass production.

The subsequent design period is also shorter than in Japan, because Chinese manufacturers only use mature components. In some cases they simply make use of the printed circuit board designed for a former model and change the exterior. Designing the case and making the dye for it are often the most important parts of the development process, and usually take approximately two months. Circuit design is conducted simultaneously, which normally takes between one and two months. Only two or three cycles of trial production are needed to finalize a new handset. After the design is fixed and the total amount of units produced reaches 2000, the model must pass through two quality certifications: (1) the 'full-type approval' (FTA) and (2) 'China-type approval' (CTA) conducted by an independent certification organization, which usually take two months in total.[3] If the certification procedures are excluded, it takes only four months to develop a new model in China. In Japan, too, new handsets must pass through quality certification, which usually takes place around six months prior to release but, unlike China, the certification process does not slow the whole development process.[4]

Why is the design process so time-consuming in the case of Japan? The first reason, as mentioned before, is the adoption of several dozens of newly developed components for a new handset for the Japanese market. When adopting a new component, the Japanese manufacturer must certify its quality and durability, and sometimes the component needs to be redesigned several times to achieve the required quality. One Japanese phone maker revealed that it once took more than a year to finalize a new hinge, for example. Secondly, in Japan, the development of software is very time-consuming. To illustrate, 70% of the total man-hours that Japanese manufacturers spend on the development of a handset is occupied by software development. Software cannot be made simply by assembling components. Recently, Japanese manufacturers have been trying to create a common software platform that can be reused by several makers. But even this has not helped them shorten lead times significantly.

The total man-hours needed to develop a new model in China is only around one-quarter of that in Japan. The development cost per model is around 100 million Japanese Yen (converted from Chinese Yuan by official exchange rate) in China, compared with 5 billion Yen in Japan. This is an important reason why Chinese handset makers can achieve a break-even point much lower than that set by Japanese manufacturers.

The procurement of components

A mobile handset consists of various components, including the case, LCD panel, camera module, printed circuit board and integrated circuits (ICs), each produced by specialized manufacturers. There is little difference in the scope of component manufacturers that comprise the Japanese and Chinese mobile phone industries. However, the manner of procuring components from suppliers does differ significantly.

In the case of Japan, the phone manufacturer frequently requests suppliers to customize components. With regards to cameras, for example, Japanese phone makers may require the supplier to shorten their length. To shorten the camera the supplier needs to redevelop the lens and sensors, which requires considerable time and cost. Yet Japanese makers are willing to bear the cost of this because a shorter camera will enable them to make a thinner handset than their rivals, which is a key selling point in Japan. Another component that Japanese manufacturers often require is customization of the display panel. As the LCD is the 'face' of the mobile phone, Japanese makers frequently want to make this aspect different from others in order to differentiate their product offering.

Chinese phone makers, on the other hand, only buy components that are already available in the suppliers' catalogue. At present, they almost never require the customization of components such as cameras and LCDs because customization is often expensive, and Chinese manufacturers are highly cost-sensitive. The customization of an LCD, for example, can require as much as 100 million Japanese Yen – the total amount a Chinese maker typically assigns to the development of one model of handset.

The manner of procuring ICs is also different. In Japan, the service operator and phone makers are deeply involved in the development of new IC chips for mobile handsets. Japanese phone makers are often the first in the world to use the most up-to-date chips. As ICs are highly complex, they may contain many bugs at the moment of their release. This often proves problematic to early adopting handset manufacturers and can require that the IC supplier is called in to fix them. Hence, using a brand new chip is more time-consuming in terms of product development than using a more mature chip, but the manufacturer that is willing to accept this shortcoming may be in a position to develop more advanced handsets than rival firms.

Chinese phone makers, on the other hand, rely on 'platforms' provided by the IC suppliers. A 'platform' is a set of ICs and software that support the basic function of a mobile handset, consisting of a radio frequency IC, which modulates and remodulates the radio waves, a 'baseband' IC that processes the digitalized signals, and operation system software. Along with the platform, IC suppliers provide a 'reference design' for the handset, which includes the list of recommended components that should be assembled along with the platform. Chinese phone makers and design houses depend heavily on reference designs, which Japanese manufacturers never do. Japanese manufacturers generally believe that they can design a circuit that is better in quality and efficiency than any reference design.

Spillovers of the fruits of development

As mentioned above, Japanese phone makers are often the first in the world to adopt new components. In order to install components, several cycles of testing and problem fixing are needed. After a lengthy period of such effort, the component will become mature enough to be installed in a handset. However, the fruits of such efforts by the Japanese makers soon spill over to other mobile phone makers, because once the component becomes mature, component suppliers will consider selling it to others. For the supplier, it is better to have as many customers as possible in order to recover the initial investment and Japanese phone makers cannot prevent them from doing so. When the component is sold to others, it is generally cheaper than its initial price, and the quality more stable, because of learning-curve effects. Hence, the fruits of the development efforts of Japanese phone makers are often utilized by European and Korean phone makers at a much lower cost, and when the Chinese phone makers buy the components they will be even cheaper.[5]

Such technological spillover is inevitable in the vertically disintegrated structure of the mobile phone industry. Should Japanese phone makers want to reduce such spillovers, they must either require suppliers not to sell new components to others, or to integrate production through acquisition or in-house development. A large company such as Nokia, which occupies around 35% of the global handset market, can afford to integrate key component production: in fact, Nokia has integrated the design of key IC chips, for example. However, due to their relatively small sales volume Japanese manufacturers cannot easily bear the opportunity cost of losing global sales to suppliers.

Division of labour in development and production

There is a considerable difference in the division of labour of mobile handset production between Japan and China. In the case of Japan, most tasks are internalized within the phone maker itself, while Chinese phone makers rely heavily on subcontractors and suppliers.

The division of labour between firms in China has changed drastically since the emergence of Chinese phone makers. From when they began business activities in 1999 until around 2002, Chinese phone makers generally outsourced most development and production tasks to Korean and Taiwanese mobile phone manufacturers. After 2002, the role of Chinese phone makers in production became larger, but design was still outsourced to Korean design houses. Since 2003, however, Chinese phone makers have drastically reduced the volume of orders given to the Koreans, driving some of the latter to bankruptcy (Abe 2006). Instead, they have increased inhouse development and the orders they give to Chinese design houses. There were more than 60 independent design houses in China in 2005. Around one-half of the production by the Chinese phone makers is designed by domestic design houses, while the rest is designed by the phone makers themselves or by Taiwanese phone manufacturers.

The pattern of division of labour which is dominant in China in recent years is shown in Figure 2. The 'phone maker', which has its brand on the handsets, is only engaged in a part of product planning, wholesaling and a part of retailing. Most of the development activities, ranging from planning, design, trial production and evaluation are conducted by design houses. The end product of design houses are blueprints of the handset and a list of components. This material is then sold to the phone maker, which buys the components and delivers them, together with the blueprint, to 'electronic manufacturing services' (EMS) companies (independent electronic product manufacturers working as subcontractors), which then assemble the handsets.

The task of design houses is not necessarily limited to product design. Large design houses in China act as turnkey suppliers (Sturgeon 2002) that undertake many tasks for the sub-contracting firm. For example, some of the Chinese design houses provide printed circuit boards for the handset so that the phone maker can shorten the time to market. Some will contact component suppliers to ensure that particular catalogue components are currently available, or send engineers to the EMS companies to provide support for mass production. As most of the tasks of development and production are handled by design houses and EMS companies, the Chinese phone 'maker' can concentrate on the planning of product line-up and sales.

An important reason why Chinese phone makers outsource a certain part of their product development is that they need to release many models in order to compete with giant manufacturers like Nokia, which can easily release several dozens of models in China. The relationship between Chinese phone makers and design houses is not a fixed, long-term arrangement compared to the long-term customer-supplier relationship that is seen in Japan (Sako 1992). Chinese phone makers usually use two or three design houses, and the design houses in turn try to increase customers. Therefore, it is not unusual for

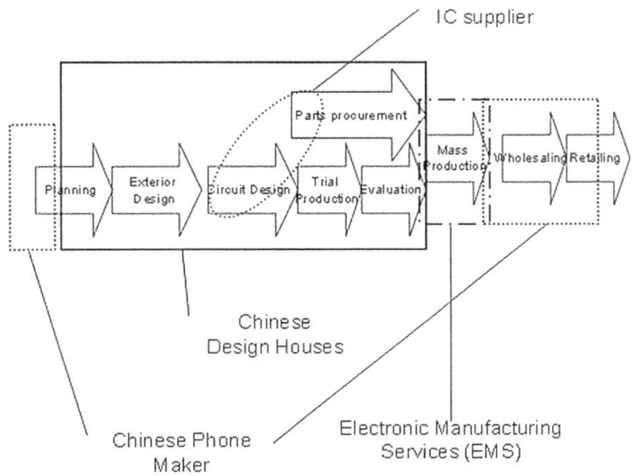

Figure 2. The division of labour within the Chinese mobile phone industry.

more than two phone makers to release very similar models at the same time in China, because they have bought the design from the same design house.

Design houses in China depend heavily on the IC suppliers platform and the reference design attached to it, so that circuit design and the selection of components are partly determined by the IC supplier. Chinese design houses, however, try to avoid depending on a single IC supplier by diversifying the source of platforms. This behaviour has opened up opportunities for new entrants. Some Chinese and Taiwanese IC suppliers have taken advantage of this and have entered business sectors once dominated by Western suppliers. The most prominent among the new entrants is the Taiwanese firm, Mediatek (MTK). Since MTK's platforms were cheaper and much easier to design a handset for than previous platforms, they were enthusiastically welcomed by Chinese phone makers and design houses. Mediatek's share among the platforms of Chinese-brand handsets rose from 13% in 2004 to 71% in 2005. The dominance of MTK's platforms, however, has intensified competition among Chinese phone makers. As MTK's platform contains not only basic operation software but also application software, all handsets that use it have almost the same functionality. It is difficult to differentiate one handset from another except for the case. Besides this, as MTK's platform is so easy to work with, more than 100 small businesses in China have started producing handsets using it. Though such firms are classified as 'illegal' producers under the production license system, they nevertheless produced more than 20 million handsets in 2005.

In the Japanese mobile phone industry, by contrast, the phone maker manages the entire manufacturing process, from planning to mass production (Figure 3). Some parts of the value chain, such as software development and mass production are, occasionally, outsourced to suppliers but under the close control and coordination of the phone maker. Compared with Figure 2, we can see that the position of Chinese 'phone makers' resembles that of service operators in Japan. Japanese firms tend to build fixed and exclusive relationships with their suppliers. Japanese phone makers, for example, typically will not try to diversify component suppliers but, instead, buy customized components from a single source. The supply relationship between the phone makers and the service suppliers is also relatively fixed and exclusive. Six out of twelve Japanese phone makers are exclusive handset suppliers to a single service operator, for example (Table 3).

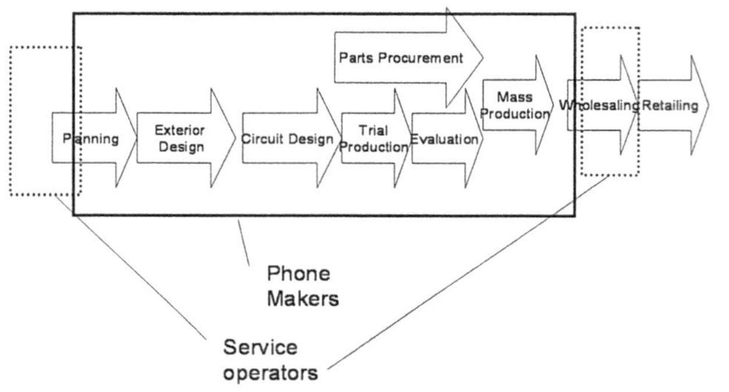

Figure 3. Division of labor within the Japanese mobile phone industry.

A comparison of the distribution system of Japan and China

In Japan, mobile handsets are technology-intensive products that require considerable time and cost to develop. They are released strictly according to the service operator's plan. Yet in China, handsets are developed more cheaply and rapidly, and they are released rather randomly in comparison. One reason for this difference is the fact that China is a rapidly growing market with a large disparity between regions and consumer segments. In such a volatile market, phone makers often have to resort to trial and error in order to detect and understand the underlying demand structure. The main reason, however, lies in the different levels of operator involvement in the distribution of handsets between the two countries.

Japan's bundle sales system

In Japan, all the handsets produced by phone makers carry the operator's brand and are sold to consumers through the operator. Retail shops never sell handsets alone: they are always bundled together with the operator's services. A handset is in effect a lure to attract the consumers to the service. Consumers are required to pay only a fraction of the real value of the handset, but they must at the same time subscribe to the service for at least 12 months. Japanese phone shops sometimes sell handsets at a price of only one Yen, but receive substantial commission from the service operator. An example was provided by one Japanese chain store selling mobile handsets which reported an instance of consumers paying 7800 Yen for a handset, and the store receiving 46,700 Yen as commission from the service operator. Operators gain because they can recover the commission they have paid from the subscriber's monthly fee.

Distribution channels in China

In China, operators are not involved much in the distribution of handsets. Mobile handsets are sold just like any other household electronic appliance. In the case of international brands such as Nokia and Motorola, handsets are distributed through large wholesalers. The wholesaler signs a contract with the phone maker to become the exclusive sales agent for some models, which are then sold to tens of thousands of retailers. Wholesalers hire sales staff at their branches and dispatch them to the retailers to help them sell the handsets to consumers. In the case of Chinese brands such as Bird and TCL, on the other hand, phone makers are directly involved in sales because large domestic wholesalers will not help them sell handsets. Phone makers sell handsets to retailers through their sales branch network in each province. Sales branches hire sales staff and assign them to retailers.

This sales system is one of the main factors that helped Bird and TCL to grow their market shares in China to become the first and second largest, respectively, by 2003 (Table 2). However, the system did not work well. Some of their sales branches failed to establish relationships with local wholesalers and retailers, forcing them to stockpile handsets in their warehouses. At the point of output from factories, Bird and TCL were indeed the top two sellers in China but sales volumes at the point of retailers ranked them third and fourth, or even lower. In 2005, Bird reformed the direct sales system and started using local wholesalers. TCL also drastically downsized their sales personnel (Li 2007), but that reform might have accelerated its decline of market share.

During the early years of mobile phone diffusion, the sales system in China was similar to the Japanese bundled sales system. However, since Chinese phone operators adopted the GSM standard, handset sales have been disconnected from phone service sales. The change is related to a technological feature of GSM handsets, in which the subscriber identity module (SIM) card, which records the subscriber's telephone number and other information, can be separated from the handset. When the two can be separated, those who have bought discounted handsets together with phone services can cancel the latter and use the cheap handset to subscribe to another service operator. If there are a lot of such informed consumers, a bundled sales strategy is not sustainable. Thus, bundled sales became virtually extinct in China. However, since around 2003, phone operators have restarted to bundle sales in order to attract phone users from their rivals. By 2005, bundled sales accounted for 11% of total handset sales in China.

A comparison of retailers

Mobile handset retailers in Japan and China are quite different in terms of size and the number of models sold. A handset shop in China is about twice the size of that in Japan, and sells around 200 models, which is more than double the number of models sold in a Japanese shop, typically. Secondly, the nature of competition that takes place at the retail level is different. In China, competition between phone makers takes place inside individual retail outlets, where each brand occupies one or a few showcases, each of which are staffed with sales people dispatched from the phone makers. In Japan, competition between service operators is visible at the retail level. Some outlets specialize in selling only one operator's handsets. In outlets that sell several operators' handsets, each operator occupies one showcase and sometimes, sales staff are provided by the service operators.

Table 4 compares some basic indicators for a number of representative outlets in Japan and China. There is a large difference in the number of employees at one shop. In China, there are more than 30 employees if the sales persons sent from phone makers are included. Table 4 also shows a striking difference in the price of handsets. The average value of handsets is more than 54,000 Yen in Japan, if commissions from the operators are included. This price zone belongs to the high end in China, which accounts for approximately 20% of China's market. The average retail price is less than 27,000 Yen even in Guangzhou and Shenzhen, two of the richest cities in China. Even the cheapest handset in Japan is not as cheap as this.

Discussion: Japanese phone manufacturers in China

As the aforementioned comparison shows, handsets in Japan exist only as a component of a bundled package of hardware and services, while in China they are independent

Table 4. Comparison of mobile handset retailers.

Name and location of retailer	Sakai (Japan)	Yihaotong (Guangzhou, China)	Anxun (Shenzhen, China)
Monthly sales per shop (units)	232	833	1000
Monthly sales per employee (units)	57	39 (19)	67 (33)
Price per unit (yen)	54474	27000	25350
Employee per shop	4	22 (43)	15 (30)
Sales amount per employee (million yen)	3.1	1.0 (0.5)	1.7 (0.8)

Notes: Figures in parenthesis include the salespersons hired by phone makers. The price per unit for Sakai includes the commission provided by the operator. Values in Chinese yuan are converted to Japanese yen at the exchange rate of 1 yuan = 15 yen.
Source: Author's interviews and various company materials.

commodities. In a sense, mobile phone makers in Japan can be regarded as component suppliers, while in China they are end-product makers. This means that to succeed in the Chinese market, Japanese phone makers need to acquire capabilities that are not needed in Japan. In Japan they only have to win the competition for service operators' orders, but in China they need to have the capability to overcome competition in consumer markets. In Japan, phone makers need to develop only a few very sophisticated handsets but in China they need to develop several dozens of models every year. In Japan, phone makers are not required to undertake distribution activities but in China, phone makers must learn how to establish and manage complex distribution channels and how to promote sales.

From their entry to China in 1995 until 2002, the operations of Japanese phone makers in China followed a typically highly centralized pattern; they released only a few models that were adapted from their models in Japan to match the GSM technology. They invested little in marketing, believing that a good product would open up a market by itself. In fact, some individual models, including Matsushita's 'GD88', which was one of the first handsets in China to have a camera, did sell well. Yet the Japanese quickly recognized that they could gain only tiny market shares in China. Japanese makers had only high-end models and with a small number of models, they only had a modest presence in retailer outlets. The pressure was strong for them to increase the number of models, especially middle- and low-end models, so that they could compete with European and Chinese brands.

Since 2003, the Japanese phone makers, especially Matsushita and NEC, began to increase the number of models offered in China. They learned from the Chinese manufacturers how to increase the line-up, and outsourced the development and production of handsets to Chinese design houses and Taiwanese manufacturers. By making use of outsourcing, NEC, for example, which formerly sold only two models in China, released seven models in 2003 and 32 models in 2004. NEC also hired a Chinese manager, who had formerly worked for Motorola, as the head of its mobile phone company in China, expecting that this would help transfer distribution management know-how in China. These efforts contributed to the expansion of NEC's market share in China from 0.2% in 2003 to 2.1% in 2005.

However, by autumn 2005, Japanese phone makers recognized that the cost of increasing market share in China was substantial. Their market shares expanded but so did their losses. The reasons why the new strategy failed can be summarized as follows. First, competition from Chinese makers became very severe in 2005 – large numbers of 'illegal' handsets using MTK's chips flooded the market, and this posed a major threat to low-end handsets. Even major Chinese brands such as Bird and TCL were making losses in 2005.

Second, as some Chinese wholesalers interviewed reported, the product line-up of Japanese manufacturers did not fit the tastes of Chinese customers and their distribution channels were not well organized. Around the end of 2005, both NEC and Matsushita decided to withdraw their mobile phone business from China. With the exception of Sony, who now operates as Sony Ericsson and remains one of the top brands in China, all the Japanese phone makers had given up their business in China by 2006.

Conclusions

The observations and insights expressed in this analysis are based on a relatively small number of interviews conducted during a narrow time frame, and the mobile phone industry is changing very rapidly, especially in China. Nonetheless, it is clear that, during the period under study, the Japanese and Chinese mobile phone markets each stand at opposite ends of a spectrum. In Japan, the market is strictly controlled by the four service operators, and handset manufacturers act as suppliers to the operators. Entry barriers are very high, and even global giants, such as Nokia, Motorola and Samsung, struggle in this market. In China, on the other hand, the influence of service operators on handset manufacturing is slight, and manufacturers sell handsets independently of service operators. Entry barriers are low, and this explains why there are so many phone makers in China. In Japan, handset manufacturers need to develop only a few models every year but, in China, manufacturers need to release several dozens of models every year to be ranked among the top brands. Mobile telephone markets in most other countries fall somewhere between these two extremes: arguably nowhere in the world is the control of operators as strong as in Japan, and nowhere in the world are manufacturers as free as in China.

This study has found that the reason why Japanese phone makers failed in China largely lies in differences in distribution structure and demand conditions between Japan and China. The centralized organization and innovation process, which is a common feature of Japanese manufacturing MNEs, made it difficult for them to adapt to China. They were required either to adopt a more decentralized approach, in which their Chinese subsidiaries managed innovation independently from the headquarters in Japan, or to allocate more resources for overseas market development within a centralized organization. After several years of struggle in China, NEC and Matsushita adopted the former approach, but they failed again. Samsung adopted the latter approach: the Korean company maintained a centralized organization, but because its domestic market is small the company allocated a large amount of resources for the development of handsets for overseas markets. The success of Samsung in China reveals that a decentralized approach is not a necessary condition for overcoming competition in China. At the same time, the reason for the failure of NEC and Matsushita's decentralization should not be attributed to the approach itself. After all, competition in China was tough for all players in 2005. Having said that, the lack of experience in managing a decentralized innovation process may have been a contributory factor. The fact that after a few years of experimenting with decentralization NEC and Matsushita hastily withdrew from China and returned to a centralized approach, suggests that they could not find a suitable way to manage a decentralized organization in that market. It would be interesting for further research to compare the market development strategy of Japanese mobile handset manufacturers in China with those they have used in other developing and transition economies in order to gauge to what extent the challenges faced were specific to the China context.

Some observers expect that the start of 3G mobile phone services in China, which is forecast (at the time of writing) to take place in 2008, will open up opportunities for

Japanese manufacturers to succeed in China. 3G services will enable operators to provide various services so there will be more technological requirements placed on handsets than the current GSM demands. Operators may resort to bundling sales of handsets and services to promote the use of 3G. In short, it is likely that in future the Chinese mobile phone market will contain a segment that resembles aspects of the Japanese market. Consequently, Japanese phone makers may be in a better position in future to exploit in China the capabilities they have developed in Japan.

Differences in the technical standard, however, may prevent the Japanese from taking full advantage of 3G: for example, the Chinese authorities are eager to let their indigenous standard Time Division Synchronous Code Division Multiple Access (TD-SCDMA) succeed in the competition among 3G standards. Since Japanese manufacturers are not involved in the development of this technology, they will be handicapped in competition among TD-SCDMA handsets. Moreover, the fact that Chinese authorities are setting a low price target for TD-SCDMA handsets will also make it difficult for the Japanese to adapt to the market, because they still do not have the capability to develop competitive low-end handsets.

On the other hand, it might be the Japanese side that is going to change. In 2006, a research unit organized by the Japanese government concluded that the government must consider restrictions on the bundling of handsets and services by the operators to enhance competition. If handsets and services are unbundled, there will be more opportunities for foreign manufacturers to sell their products in Japan, and Japanese manufacturers will be required to face stiffer competition in consumer markets and to act more like independent handset manufacturers.

Notes

1. The following mobile telephony technologies are referred to in this study. Personal Digital Cellular (PDC) is a second-generation digital mobile communications technology created by the dominant telephone operator, Nippon Telegraph and Telephone (NTT) and several Japanese mobile phone manufacturers. Global System for Mobile (GSM) communications (originally from Groupe Spécial Mobile) is a second-generation digital mobile communications technology created as a pan-European mobile phone standard by European telecommunication authorities. It was adopted by mobile phone operators in more than 220 countries and regions around the world. Total Access Communication System (TACS) is a first-generation analogue mobile phone system standard developed by Motorola on the basis of AMPS, or Advanced Mobile Phone System, the primary standard in the United States. The personal handyphone system (PHS) is a type of mobile phone system developed by Nippon Telegraph and Telephone (NTT), and is characterized by low transmission power and small cell, making it unsuitable for rural areas or for calling from rapidly moving vehicles. In addition to being operated in Japan by Willcom, it is operated by two telephone carriers in China. Time Division Synchronous Code Division Multiple Access (TD-SCDMA) is a technology originally proposed by Siemens, but is being commercialized by a Chinese research consortium led by the state-owned enterprise, Datang.
2. Japan accounted for 39% of the worldwide subscribers of W-CDMA (Wideband Code Division Multiple Access) at the end of 2006 and 28% of the worldwide CDMA1xEV-DO (Code Division Multiple Access, Evolution-data Optimized) subscribers.
3. All companies, including both Chinese and Japanese manufacturers, wanting to sell handsets in China need to have their handsets pass these certifications.
4. Quality certification and dye manufacturing are part of the handset development process in Japan, but because their relative importance in the whole process is much smaller than in the case of China, they are omitted in Figure 1.
5. If a non-Japanese manufacturer tries a new component first, then Japanese manufacturers can theoretically enjoy the fruits of component development cheaply, but this is rarely the case in practice.

References

Abe, M., 2006. Kankoku keitaidenwa tanmatsu sangyo no seichou. (The growth of mobile handset industry in Korea). *In*: K. Imai and M. Kawakami, eds. *Higashi ajia no IT kiki sangyo – Bungyo, kyoso, sumiwake no dainamikusu* (East Asian IT hardware industry – the dynamics of division of labour, competition, and co-existence). Chiba: IDE-JETRO.

Bartlett, C.A. and Ghoshal, S., 1998. *Managing across borders: the transnational solution*. Boston: Harvard Business School Press.

Cairncross, D., 1994. The strategic role of Japanese R&D centres in the UK. *In*: N. Campbell and F.N. Burton, eds. *Japanese multinationals: strategies and management in the global kaisha*. London: Routledge, 98–112.

Cheung, C., 2005. *Technology transfer and competition–the mobile handset industry in post-WTO China*. Hamburg: Deutscher Universitats-Verlag.

Editorial Committee, 2000, 2001, 2002. *Zhongguo dianzi gongye nianjian 2000, 2001, 2002* (China electronics industry yearbook). Beijing: Dianzi gongye chubanshe.

Fuji Kimera Research Institute, 2007. *2007 Jisedai keitai to ki debaisu shijo no shorai tenbo* (Future prospects of next-generation mobile phones and key device markets). Tokyo: Fuji Kimera Research Institute.

Funk, J.L., 1998. Competition between regional standards and the success and failure of firms in the world-wide mobile communication market. *Telecommunications policy*, 22 (4–5), 419–441.

Funk, J.L., 2002. *Global competition between and within standards: the case of mobile phones*. London: Palgrave.

Institute of Industrial Economics, ed., 2003. *Zhongguo gongye fazhan baogao 2003* (China industrial development report). Beijing: Jingji guanli chubanshe.

iSuppli, 2005. China handsets: consolidation underway. China Research Service, Topical Report, Q2.

Kimura, K., 2006. Chugoku keitai denwa tanmatsu sangyo no hatten. (The development of Chinese mobile handset industry). *In*: K. Imai and M. Kawakami, eds. *Higashi ajia no IT kiki sangyo – Bungyo, kyoso, sumiwake no dainamikusu* (East Asian IT hardware industry – the dynamics of division of labour, competition, and co-existence). Chiba: IDE-JETRO.

Li, J., 2007. TCL tongxun li huawei you duo yuan? (What is the difference between TCL and Huawei?) *Zhongguo dianzi shangwu*, 2, 14–17.

Sako, M., 1992. *Prices, quality and trust*. Cambridge University Press.

Sturgeon, T.J., 2002. Modular production networks: a new American model of industrial organization. *Industrial and corporate change*, 11 (3), 451–496.

Whitley, R., *et al.*, 2003. The changing Japanese multinational: application, adaptation and learning in car manufacturing and financial services. *Journal of management studies*, 40 (3), 643–672.

The impact of workgroup commitment on organizational citizenship behaviour, absenteeism and turnover intention: the case of Germany and China

J. Felfe[a] and W.H. Yan[b]

[a]*University of Siegen, Department of Psychology, Adolf-Reichwein-Straße 2, 57068 Siegen, Germany;* [b]*Department of Psychology, East China Normal University, Shanghai, China*

Introduction

Increasing processes of globalization and rising markets in Eastern Europe and Asia – particularly in Russia and China – have led to a growing number of Western organizations that engage in cooperations, joint ventures, or direct investments in these areas. Meanwhile, there are also a growing number of Asian companies that are strengthening their economic activities in Western countries. Both of them extend their management style to a foreign country. These enterprises are confronted with cultural differences and challenges in cross-cultural leadership when supervisors and subordinates or members of project teams come from different cultural backgrounds.

Though rapid changes in economic industrialization can be observed, China is still one of the most traditional and collectivistic countries in Asia. Therefore the management of different cultures is a challenge for organizations that engage in cross-cultural activities. Consequently, cross-cultural understanding, competence and training is needed to overcome cultural barriers and to avoid misunderstanding and conflict (Berry *et al.* 2002). In order to increase our understanding of cross-cultural differences in the organizational context, this study examines the impact of cultural differences on the relationship between commitment and relevant outcomes. Employees organizational citizenship behaviour (OCB) is an important factor for organizational success. Organ (1988, p. 4) defines OCB as representing 'individual behaviour that is discretionary, not directly or explicitly recognized by the formal reward system, and in the aggregate promotes the effective functioning of the organization'. OCB comprises altruism, courtesy, general compliance and civic virtue as sub-dimensions. These behaviours primarily depend on employees motivation and initiative. Employees do what needs to be done in order to accomplish organizational goals without any official or formal requirement. This is essential for the effective and efficient functioning of an organization. In the literature, these behaviours are also known as extra role behaviour or contextual performance (Felfe 2007).

From a western point of view, it is evident that employee commitment is an important factor for success in terms of performance and OCBs (Meyer *et al.* 2002). Yet how do different cultural contexts influence the role of commitment, and how should management consider culture in order to maintain and develop employee commitment? A growing number of current studies document the importance of research in this field (Chen and Francesco 2000, 2003, Donald and Siu 2001, Lee *et al.* 2001, Cheng and Stockdale 2003, Felfe *et al.* 2008a).

The present study goes beyond past research on the influence of culture on the commitment-outcomes linkage by proposing and testing the assumption that, in a collectivistic context, commitment to the workgroup may play a more crucial role than organizational commitment. In the past, most research in the field of commitment has been conducted in Western societies and most studies have only examined organizational commitment. It is a question of high theoretical and practical importance to what degree commitment to the workgroup improves organizational success in different cultural contexts.

Thus, the purpose of this research is to contribute to the large body of research addressing the meaning, the maintenance and the development of commitment in organizations. Managers in cross-cultural contexts need to know what the most relevant factors to improve commitment are, and what the specific impact of commitment on relevant outcomes is in the culture they engage with.

Literature review

Commitment in the workplace

As Meyer and Herscovitch (2001) stated, most of the definitions consider commitment to be a stabilizing force that gives direction to behaviour and binds a person to a course of action. In this sense, commitment towards an organization is 'a bond or linking of the individual to the organization' (Mathieu and Zajac 1990, p. 171). An increasing number of studies refer to the commitment concept of Meyer and Allen (1991), who introduced a three-component model that includes: (1) affective commitment; (2) continuance commitment; and (3) normative commitment (NC). Affective commitment means the emotional linkage between an employee and the organization. Attendance is characterized by common values, satisfaction of personal needs, identification with organizational aims combined with feelings of pride and attachment. Persons with a high degree of affective commitment stay in their organization because they want to. On the other hand, employees with a high amount of continuance commitment stay in their organization because they have to, or there are important reasons to. Rational reasons are recent investments or low alternatives. Their linkage is based on calculation including costs, investments and pay offs. Normative committed people feel an obligation to stay because of norms and values they share, or they stay because other important people tell them to do so. They would feel guilty if they left the organization and stay, even if they had to reject better alternatives. The multidimensionality of commitment can be regarded as a mind-set that takes different forms. The varying forms include desire, perceived costs, as well as the obligation to continue a course of action.

As two decades of research have shown, organizational commitment serves as an important predictor for several positive (satisfaction, in role and extra role performance, for example) and negative (such as role conflict, perceived work overload, absenteeism, intention to quit and turn-over) outcome variables on the individual level. Employees expressing high organizational commitment show more positive attitudes towards their jobs and are more likely to strengthen their effort and to improve their performance for the organization compared to others in the organization. Furthermore, they articulate less turnover intentions and show lower rates in absenteeism. Current reviews of conceptual and theoretical progress in the field of commitment are provided by Cohen (2003) and Meyer and Herscovitch (2001). Recent meta-analyses have confirmed previous results and provide a more comprehensive view on the empirical research in the field of commitment (Meyer *et al.* 2002, Cooper-Hakim and Viswesvaran 2005).

According to the multidimensional approach, Meyer *et al.* (2002) differentiate between the three components of commitment in their current meta-analysis. They show that affective organizational commitment, in particular, serves as an important predictor for several positive and negative outcome variables. Employees expressing high affective organizational commitment are more satisfied with their work, report higher job involvement and are more likely to engage in behaviours that strengthen the competitiveness of the organization. In contrast, employees with continuance commitment tend to develop negative attitudes, experience negative affects and are more likely to exert undesirable behaviours. The authors conclude that a specific behaviour (such as OCB) is more likely with primarily affective commitment, followed by NC and then continuance commitment. With respect to antecedents of commitment, besides organizational climate, organizational support and task content, transformational leadership plays a particularly important role for the development of commitment (Meyer *et al.* 2002, Felfe *et al.* 2004).

In the meantime, several studies have been conducted in Western Europe that confirm Meyer and Allen's three-components model (Vandenberghe *et al.* 2001, Felfe *et al.* 2005, Felfe *et al.* 2008b). To date, there have only been few studies that have examined organizational commitment in East Asian organizations. Results from China, Taiwan and South Korea show sufficient support for the three-component model of commitment (Lee *et al.* 2001, Chen and Francesco 2003, Cheng and Stockdale 2003). Thus, there seems to be some evidence that the model can also be transferred to Asian countries (Allen 2003, Vandenberghe 2003).

The different forms of commitment described above do not only exist towards employer organisations, but also towards other entities. Like other authors (Becker 1992, Cohen 2003), Meyer *et al.* (1993) postulated with their generalization thesis that commitment can be directed to any other target like the team, the supervisor, the occupation and certain aims (that is, subcomponents of the organization). Using confirmatory factor analysis they demonstrated that commitment to the occupation (account manager, engineer, teacher for example) and commitment to the organization, with each of the three components being regarded as distinguishable measures. Furthermore, hierarchical regression revealed that organizational and occupational commitment independently contributed to the prediction of work-related outcomes. These findings have been confirmed by Irving *et al.* (1997). Generally, targets of commitment can be abstract concepts as well as recognizable entities or domains, which are relevant for a person and important for the understanding of the behaviour of interest. Therefore, the commitment mind-set includes both a course of action and a target (Meyer and Herscovitch 2001). Accordingly, recent research extended the commitment concept to commitment on the part of the supervisor, the workgroup and top management

(Becker 1992, Cheng *et al.* 2003, Felfe *et al.* 2008a); to organizational change (Herscovitch and Meyer 2002); to the form of employment (Felfe *et al.* 2005, 2008b); and to customers (Stinglhamber *et al.* 2002), all in both private and public contexts. Employing factor and regression analyses, these studies demonstrated empirically distinguishable experiences of commitment toward these foci as well as improvement of prediction of outcomes when using multiple commitments. In line with these extensions of the commitment concept, the focus of this study is on commitment to the workgroup. The rationale for putting emphasis on this focus is grounded on the assumption that in a more collectivistic context, workgroup commitment, in particular, might be more relevant and predictive for outcomes than in a Western context.

Cultural differences and commitment

According to Berry *et al.* (2002), culture is the shared way of life of a group of people. Culture consists of shared motives, values, beliefs, identities, and interpretations or meanings of significant events that result from common experiences of members of collectives that are transmitted across generations. As it is impossible to cover the full range of cultural diversity, in this study the focus will be on the well-established dimension of individualism-collectivism that has been identified to be meaningful, particularly for the understanding of cultural differences between Eastern and Western countries (Triandis 1995, Trompenaars 2000, Hofstede 2001). According to Hofstede (2001), individualism-collectivism focuses on the degree to which society reinforces individual or collective achievement and interpersonal relationships. In individualistic societies, individual differences and motives are much appreciated and valued, whereas more collectivistic societies reinforce group-orientated values and behaviour. It is expected that everyone takes responsibility for group members and individual behaviour can be understood on behalf of the group and the social context. In a collectivistic context, leaders encourage group loyalty and group members are expected to subordinate individual interests and goals. In general, Asian societies are more collectivistic than Western societies (Hofstede 2001). Though rapid changes are taking place, China is probably still one of the most traditional and collectivistic societies in Asia. The findings of the recent GLOBE study (House *et al.* 2004) confirm previous findings (Hofstede 2001), for both dimensions of institutional and family collectivism.

From a theoretical point of view, there should be a strong relationship between culture and the impact of commitment. One reason why culture should determine the influence of commitment is that culture entails the basic values, norms and behaviour patterns that are also relevant in the organizational context. The general preference for the group and the propensity to build close relationships with a social entity, for example, should be related to the meaning of commitment to the organization and more so to the proximal social entity of the workgroup. Employees in a collectivistic context are expected to behave more on behalf of their group than employees in an individualistic context. Thus the long-term and close relationship to the organization plays a crucial role and has an important personal meaning. If, for any kind of reason, employees in a collectivistic context cannot develop considerable commitment to their social environment, they will probably lose motivation, reduce engagement and will develop thoughts about leaving the organization (turn-over intentions). Thus, commitment is a crucial precondition for employees behaviour in organizations, particularly in collectivistic contexts. Accordingly, in a less collectivistic context, where autonomy and independence are highly valued, employees' behaviour is not so much dependent on the relationship to others, and therefore commitment will not have as much of a dominating role.

Actually, there is some empirical evidence that cultural differences moderate the relationships between commitment and outcomes (satisfaction, OCB, experienced strain). Tan and Akhtar (1998), for example, found that NC had a stronger influence on experienced burn-out (feeling helpless, tired and emotionally exhausted) than affective commitment. They explain this finding by the precedence of a normative orientation over affective orientation in a collectivistic context. Results obtained by Lee *et al.* (2001) also underline the role of NC in Eastern organizations. They report higher correlations between NC and intention to leave in collectivist cultures than for samples in North America. They therefore concluded that NC might be more predictive in collectivist cultures, than it is in individualistic cultures. These findings indicate that NC may be more influential in collectivistic societies because the compliance of social norms is highly expected and supported. However, the empirical basis for these conclusions is limited as the sample was relatively small and restricted to the health sector. In their recent study on the influence of cultural differences on the relationships between organizational commitment and antecedences and outcomes, Felfe *et al.* (2008a) also found higher correlations between affective and normative organizational commitment and OCB and turnover intentions as outcomes in collectivistic samples (China and Romania), compared to a German sample. Moreover, they demonstrate that commitment variables were important predictors for positive and negative outcomes after controlling for other variables; and in support of the assumption of cultural differences, the amount of variance explained by commitment variables was higher in China and Romania than in Germany. However, they did not find differences between the affective and the normative component. In all, the results indicate that the cultural context may moderate the impact of commitment. However, the role of commitment to the workgroup as a specific focus has not been investigated in a cross-cultural context.

Commitment to the workgroup

Given the fact that employees are committed to both the workgroup and the organization, the question must be raised as to which focus of commitment is more influential for the employees' behaviour at the workplace. Riketta and Van Dick (2005) argue that workgroup commitment in general may be more powerful than organizational commitment because the workgroup as a proximal social entity might be more important in daily work life than the organization, and therefore should influence work-related behaviours more often or more directly. Thus, the identification with or commitment to the workgroup is supposed to be a more proximal and direct predictor, and organizational commitment is a more distal factor. Another rationale for this distinction is grounded in social identity theory (Tajfel and Turner 2003). According to this approach, individuals strive for a positive social identity. A positive image and distinctiveness of the in-group foster identification with the group and enhance the group members' self-esteem. The salience of the own team in daily work supports the self-categorization as a team member and the distinctiveness of the workgroup, rather than the categorization of the entire organization. In order to improve the image of the team, members will strive for better performance. Accordingly, Ellemers stated that 'people's willingness to exert individual effort on behalf of one's team, should depend on their commitment to that team which is not necessarily related to reported levels of commitment to the organization as a whole' (Ellemers 2001, p. 110). Thus, a reciprocal relationship can be assumed. Group members get more committed and identified on behalf of the success of the group, and contribute to the success of the group by providing extra effort. In particular, closer relationships can be expected with respect to group-related outcomes in comparison to criteria that are on the organizational level.

Results of a recent meta-analysis conducted by Riketta and Van Dick (2005) provided some empirical support for this assumption. Workgroup commitment was more strongly related to workgroup extra-role behaviour (averaged and corrected correlation: 0.30) than organizational commitment (0.20), whereas for organizational commitment a higher correlation was found with turnover intention (−0.48) than for workgroup commitment (−0.30). In an earlier study, Becker (1992) found that commitment to the workgroup contributed unique variance in intent to quit and pro-social organizational behaviours (helping colleagues for example) above and beyond the influence of organizational commitment. However, Stinglhamber *et al.* (2002) did not find evidence for additional explanation of variance in intent to quit for commitment to the workgroup. Also, Bentein *et al.* (2002) only found modest correlations for supervisor commitment and corresponding OCB facets, but no meaningful relationship for workgroup and organizational commitment. To sum up, in Western contexts workgroup commitment seems to be a slightly better predictor for workgroup extra-role behaviour, but organizational commitment is more predictive for the intent to quit.

Based on Confucian philosophy and along with collectivism, the social context plays a more crucial role in Asian societies. In comparison to a Western, more individualistic context, a collectivistic context puts more emphasis on interpersonal relationships. Employees in this context behave on behalf of the group rather than other factors because the membership to a group is an important facet of their self-concept. Therefore, it can be assumed that the workgroup is more influential for employees' behaviour and engagement in terms of OCB, or disengagement in terms of turnover intention and absenteeism as an objective measure. As mentioned before, Felfe *et al.* (2008a) have already found a stronger relationship between organizational commitment for Chinese and Romanian employees than for German employees. This effect of cultural influence should be replicated for workgroup commitment and, especially, the influence of workgroup commitment should be stronger than organizational commitment in a collectivistic context.

H 1.1: *There is a stronger relationship between workgroup commitment and outcomes in a collectivistic context than in an individualistic context.*

H 1.2: *Workgroup commitment explains more variance over and above organizational commitment and is more predictive for outcomes than organizational commitment in a collectivistic context than in an individualistic context.*

As pointed out above there is some empirical evidence that NC components may be as, or even more, influential in a collectivistic context than the affective components (Tan and Akhtar 1998) that have been found to be predominantly predictive in Western contexts (Meyer *et al.* 2002). Lee *et al.* (2001) report even higher correlations between NC and intention to leave for samples in collectivist cultures than for samples in North America, and therefore suggest 'that normative commitment might matter more in making turnover decisions in collectivist cultures than it does in individualistic cultures'. Supporting this suggestion, Meyer *et al.* (2002) found higher correlations between affective commitment and turnover intention within North America, whereas NC was related more strongly outside North America (Asia, Europe, South America). Moreover Meyer *et al.* (2002) found higher relationships between normative and affective commitment outside North America and suggested that in collectivistic cultures there might be less differentiation between general norms and individual motives. In a recent meta-analysis, Stanley *et al.* (2007) were able to confirm this assumption. They found that the correlation between affective and NC was higher in countries scoring higher on collectivism than in counties with lower collectivism. Therefore, the following hypothesis can be derived.

H 2: *Affective and normative components are more related in a collectivistic context.*

Bentein *et al.* (2002) addressed the question of how different commitment foci interact and found more support for a model which postulates that the proximal entity (workgroup) mediates the relationship between distal organizational commitment and outcomes, than for the alternative model which assumes that the local commitment influences outcomes via organizational commitment. Besides causality, it is an important question as to how close different foci are related. Organizational commitment and workgroup commitment may be relatively independent as pointed out by Ellemers (2001) or highly correlated, indicating that workgroup commitment might influence organizational commitment, or vice versa. At least both entities cannot be completely independent because the workgroup is part of the organization, or in other words, is 'nested' in the organization. It can be assumed that in a collectivistic context, nested entities are more closely related because people in this context are more willing to strive for consistent social identity. The workgroup might be more regarded as a part of the whole organization that knits all organizational units together (workgroup, department and company). Thus, it is more probable to have a similar relationship with the workgroup as with the organization. In a more individualistic context, however, employees are more ready to accept differences between levels of related social entities and they perceive their unit as more independent. Thus it is more probable to differentiate, such as having a favourable relationship with the workgroup while assuming a critical attitude towards the organization.

H 3: *Organizational and workgroup commitment are more related in a collectivistic context.*

Methodology

Design and procedure

This study is part of a bigger research project conducted to analyze the cultural influence on organizational commitment, its antecedences and consequences (Felfe *et al.* 2008a). In order to reduce the length of the questionnaire and, therefore, increase the willingness of the management to support the research project, only organizational commitment was addressed as the central focus in the main project. However, it was possible to include measures for workgroup commitment in two smaller samples of clerical workers. Data were gained in volunteer-based and anonymous surveys that were conducted in a German and a Chinese company. Questionnaires were administered to employees by the human resources departments and returned afterwards to the researcher. Confidentiality was guaranteed to the participants. The management was provided with a short feedback of the results. The instruments have been carefully developed. All items have been transferred with the translate-retranslate method by independent translators for forward and back translating. Before employing the instrument in China, the Chinese version had been tested by a group of bilingual Chinese students. Except for a few items that were modified afterwards, no systematic differences occurred between the German and the Chinese version of the questionnaire. According to our research question, correlations are expected to be moderated by cultural differences. Therefore, comparisons mainly of correlations and regression analysis are conducted for data analysis. As pointed out by Ryan *et al.* (1999) it is a precondition in cross-cultural research to ensure that the instruments used are equivalent. Accordingly it is not only sufficient to address the adequacy of translation but, also, it is required to establish measurement equivalence. Following Ryan *et al.* (1999), we employed a multiple-groups covariance structure analysis in order to test the assumption of equivalence. The invariance of factor loadings is an accepted standard for measurement equivalence.

Participants

Participants were 235 clerical workers from a German financial organization (59.1%) and from a Chinese industrial company with international ownership (40.9%). Most of them were women (59.1% women and 40.9% men). Men and women were not equally distributed to the samples. In the German sample, there were 71.2% women whereas in the Chinese sample, there were 41.7% women. The average age was 35.7 years (SD = 9.9). Participants in the Chinese sample were younger than their German colleagues (M = 32.3, SD = 9.1; M = 38, SD = 9.7, respectively). The German employees had been in their organization for 11.7 years (SD = 6.7), whereas the Chinese employees had been in their companies for only 5.4 years (SD = 3.3). All the participants held at least a bachelor degree. As only a few managers and supervisors participated in the Chinese survey, all supervisors were excluded from both samples in order to gain homogeneity with regard to the participants' level in the respective organization.

Measures

To measure commitment as a multidimensional concept, a German version (Felfe *et al.* 2008a) was employed that was adapted from the instruments developed by Stinglhamber *et al.* (2002) and Meyer *et al.* (1993). The scale ranges from 1 ('not at all true') to 5 ('completely true'). Sample items to measure affective and normative organizational commitment are 'I am proud to be part of this organization' and 'I would feel guilty if I left my organization now', respectively. Sample items to measure affective and normative workgroup commitment are 'I feel like "part of the family" at my team', and 'I owe a great deal to my team', respectively.

Following the procedure conducted by Stinglhamber *et al.* (2002), the dimensionality of the multiple components model was tested by confirmatory factor analysis. The fit of a one-factor model (1) was compared to a two-foci model (2), which then was compared to the theoretically postulated two foci x two-components model (3). Results revealed that there was empirical support for the theoretically postulated model (3) with four latent factors. The fit for the full model (3) was acceptable (Chi^2 = 522.12 (312), TLI = 0.91, IFI = 0.93, CFI 0.93, and RMSEA = 0.05), whereas the less differentiated models showed a clear decrease of fit. Measurement equivalence was examined with multi-group CFAs (Steenkamp and Baumgartner 1998). The unrestricted model (A) that freely estimated all parameters was compared to a model with fixed loadings (B). Following Ryan *et al.* (1999), invariance of loadings can be defined as the main criterion for measurement equivalence. Invariant loadings indicate metric invariance which means that people in different countries respond to the items in a similar way (Steenkamp and Baumgartner 1998). Ryan *et al.* (1999) suggest that statistical non-invariance should not lead to rejection of equivalence when the overall fit of a model is still acceptable. Accordingly, differences up to 0.04 for changes in fit indices are practically unimportant and can be accepted (Rahim and Magner 1995, Vandenberghe *et al.* 2001). The results show that the there is only modest loss of fit ($\Delta chi^2 = 28.73$ (16), p = 0.03; Δ TLI = 0.001, and Δ IFI = 0.01). Thus, the test for measurement equivalence of the commitment scales proves that loadings are invariant across countries. The internal consistencies (Cronbach's alpha) for the affective workgroup commitment (WCA) in Germany and China were good ($\alpha = 0.89$ and $\alpha = 0.92$, respectively), and were also sufficient for normative workgroup commitment (WCN) ($\alpha = 0.82$ and $\alpha = 0.78$, respectively). For the organizational affective commitment (OCA), the internal consistencies in Germany and China were good ($\alpha = 0.92$ and $\alpha = 0.90$, respectively) and were also sufficient for organizational normative commitment (OCN) ($\alpha = 0.82$ and $\alpha = 0.72$, respectively). Means and standard deviations are provided in Table 1.

OCB was assessed with a self-developed instrument based on the questionnaire used by Podsakoff *et al.* (1996). In this study we used items from the two subscales: conscientiousness/compliance and altruism. Sample items for altruism are 'If there are any questions or problems with work my colleagues mostly contact me', and for conscientiousness 'I often work longer than my colleagues'. The answer format ranges from 1 ('not at all true') to 5 ('completely true'). The internal consistencies (Cronbach's alpha) for the conscientiousness/compliance subscale were in Germany and China ($\alpha = 0.72$ and $\alpha = 0.59$ and for the altruism scale $\alpha = 0.63$ and $\alpha = 0.71$, respectively). Turnover intention was measured with three items. A sample item is 'I often think of quitting my present job'. The answer format ranges from 1 ('not at all true') to 5 ('completely true'). The internal consistencies (Cronbach's alpha) of the combined measure were acceptable in Germany and China ($\alpha = 0.77$ and $\alpha = 0.75$, respectively). To measure absenteeism, participants were asked to indicate how many days they were unable to come to work because of illness. Means and standard deviations are provided in Table 1. A test for measurement equivalence revealed that loadings for OCB scales and turnover intention were invariant across countries ($\Delta chi^2 = 16.48$ (16), p = 0.02; ΔTLI = 0.01, and Δ IFI = 0.03).

Data analysis

With *H 1.1*, a stronger relationship between workgroup commitment and outcomes was postulated in a collectivistic context than in an individualistic context. As can be seen in Table 1, in China the correlation between WCA and altruism is r = 0.24, and is r = 0.25 with conscientiousness. The correlation between WCN and altruism is r = 0.12, and r = 0.27 with conscientiousness. The correlations between WCA and WCN with outcomes were higher in the Chinese sample than in the German sample. Whereas correlations between workgroup commitment scales and OCB subscales range between r = 0.12 and 0.27 in China, the range is from r = −0.02 to 0.13 in the German sample. The negative correlations with turnover intentions are also higher in the Chinese sample (r = −0.58 and −0.55) than in the German sample (r = −0.15 for both components). As expected, the negative correlations with turnover intentions are also higher in the Chinese sample (r = −0.21 and −0.25) than in the German sample (r = 0.10 and −0.06).

To test these differences for significance, a series of hierarchical regressions was performed. The nationality of respondent was dummy coded with Germany = 0 and China = 1. Sex and age were entered first as control variables. The commitment scores were transformed to z-values. As shown in Table 2, the results of the regression analysis reveal that WCN negatively predicts turnover intention. WCA positively predicts altruism but not conscientiousness and negatively predicts turnover intention.

Table 1. Means, standard deviations and correlations.

	MGer	SDGer	MChi	SDChi	1	2	3	4	5	6	7	8	9	10
1. Sex						−0.17	−0.06	−0.16	−0.10	−0.18	−0.16	−0.06	0.13	0.15
2. Age	38.0	9.69	32.3	9.14	0.21		0.15	0.09	0.07	0.00	0.12	0.22	−0.07	0.19
3. OCA	3.87	0.89	3.21	0.96	0.14	0.33		0.78	0.63	0.56	0.14	0.08	−0.73	−0.13
4. OCN	2.98	0.95	2.98	0.84	0.05	0.31	0.60		0.56	0.64	0.07	0.07	−0.66	−0.21
5. WCA	3.50	0.91	3.21	0.98	0.06	0.10	0.28	0.29		0.76	0.24	0.25	−0.58	−0.21
6. WCN	2.54	0.95	2.79	0.88	−0.02	0.13	0.26	0.51	0.70		0.12	0.27	−0.55	−0.25
7. OCB Alt	3.55	0.64	3.74	0.67	−0.10	0.03	0.15	0.13	0.13	0.10		0.50	−0.02	−0.06
8. OCB Con	3.18	0.91	3.35	0.85	−0.16	0.03	0.14	0.06	−0.02	0.01	0.46		−0.08	−0.19
9. ToI	1.79	0.87	2.82	1.02	−0.12	−0.37	−0.64	−0.27	−0.15	−0.15	0.03	−0.05		0.17
10. Absenteeism	5.4	13.7	1.5	3.2	0.06	−0.06	0.03	0.10	0.10	0.06	−0.15	−0.07	0.01	

Note: Sex: male = 1, female = 2; OCA = organizational commitment affective, OCN = organizational commitment normative, WCA = workgroup commitment affective, WCN = workgroup commitment normative, OCB Alt = Organizational citizenship behaviour altruism, OCB Con = Organizational citizenship behaviour conscientiousness, ToI = turnover intention; German Sample (below diagonal), $r > 0.17$ ($p < 0.05$), $r > 0.22$ ($p < 0.01$), $r > 0.29$ ($p < 0.001$), $N = 139$; Chinese sample: (upper diagonal): $r > 0.20$ ($p < 0.05$), $r > 0.26$ ($p < 0.01$), $r > 0.35$ ($p < 0.001$), $N = 96$.

Table 2. Hierarchical regressions.

Commitment dimension	WCA								WCN							
Outcome criteria	Ocb Alt		Ocb Con		ToI		Absenteeism		Ocb_alt		Ocb_con		ToI		Absenteeism	
	beta	Δ R^2	beta	Δ R^2	beta	Δ R^2	beta	Δ R^2	beta	Δ R^2	beta	Δ R^2	beta	Δ R^2	beta	Δ R^2
Step 1		0.03*		0.03*		0.13***		0.01		0.03*		0.03*		0.13***		0.01
age	−0.17**		−0.15*		−0.11′		0.11		−0.17**		−0.15*		−0.11′		0.11	
sex	0.05		0.09		−0.32***		0.02		0.05		0.09		−0.32***		0.02	
Step 2		0.04**		0.01		0.25***		0.03*		0.02′		0.02*		0.24***		0.03′
age	−0.14*		−0.13′		−0.01		0.07		−0.13*		−0.12′		−0.03		0.07	
sex	0.06		0.11		0.18**		−0.03		0.07		0.11		−0.19**		−0.03	
country	0.13′		0.09		0.44***		−0.17*		0.13′		0.09		0.43***		−0.17*	
commitment	0.16*		0.07		−0.30***		0.05		0.08		0.10		−0.29***		0.04	
Step 3		0.01		0.01′		0.04***		0.01		0.01		0.01′		0.04***		0.01
age	−0.13*		−0.12′		−0.02		0.06		−0.13′		−0.11		−0.05		0.06	
sex	0.06		0.11		−.19***		−.03		.07		.11′		−.20***		−.03	
country	0.13′		0.09		0.43***		−0.18*		0.13′		0.10		0.42***		−0.17*	
commitment	0.05		−0.15		0.08		0.23		0.07		0.01		−0.12′*		0.11	
country x commitment	0.12		0.25′		−0.43***		−0.20		0.02		0.17′		−0.27***		−0.11	
R^2	0.07**		0.05*		0.41***		0.05*		0.05*		0.06*		0.40***		0.05′	

Note: sex: male = 1, female = 2; country: Germany = 0, China = 1; WCA = workgroup commitment affective, WCN = workgroup commitment normative; ′ = $p < 0.10$, * = $p < 0.05$, ** = $p < 0.01$, *** = $p < 0.001$.

Significant interaction effects indicate that the relationships between WCA and WCN and turnover intention are moderated by the country context. Moreover, the relationships between both commitment components and conscientiousness are moderated by country context ($p < 0.10$). For the relationship with altruism no interaction occurred.

There is no significant relationship between workgroup commitment and absenteeism after controlling for differences between countries, and the interaction effects fail to reach significance. This might be due to highly different absenteeism rates and a smaller variance in the Chinese sample. As it might be difficult to detect interaction effects with moderated regression analysis, additional z-tests were conducted in order to show that the correlations in both samples are different. In fact, these additional tests (Preacher 2002) revealed that the relationship between WCA and absenteeism was stronger in the Chinese sample ($Z = 2.316, p < 0.05$). The same was found for NC and absenteeism ($Z = 2.341$, $p < 0.05$). Thus *H 1.1* is clearly supported for turnover intention and partly supported for OCB and absenteeism.

H 1.2 firstly predicted that workgroup commitment explains more variance over and above organizational commitment and secondly, postulated that workgroup commitment is more predictive for outcomes than organizational commitment in a collectivistic context than in an individualistic context. In order to test the first criterion (which only refers to the amount of additional variance that can be contributed by workgroup commitment over and above organizational commitment and does not necessarily require that workgroup commitment is the stronger predictor), additional regression analysis was conducted. Organizational commitment was entered in the first step and the respective workgroup component was entered in the second step, predicting each outcome. In the German sample, workgroup commitment did not explain additional variance in outcomes, whereas in the Chinese sample, in four of the eight cases (two components x four outcomes), workgroup commitment systematically explained variance over and above organizational commitment (WCA: turnover intention: $\Delta R^2 = 0.02$*, conscientiousness: $\Delta R^2 = 0.06$*, altruism: $\Delta R^2 = 0.04$, $p = 0.055$, absenteeism: $\Delta R^2 = 0.03$, $p = 0.11$, WCN: turnover intention: $\Delta R^2 = 0.03$*, conscientiousness: $\Delta R^2 = 0.09$**, altruism: $\Delta R^2 = 0.01$, n.s., absenteeism: $\Delta R^2 = 0.02$, n.s.). Two further cases barely failed to reach the 5% level and the 10% level.

With regard to the second criterion, correlations were examined. As can be seen in Table 1, organizational commitment is not systematically related to the OCB scales in both samples. As predicted, workgroup commitments are systematically related to OCB scales in the Chinese sample – except for WCN and altruism – but not in the German sample. Compared to their respective organizational commitment components, WCA and WCN were more strongly related with conscientiousness ($z = 1.97, p < .05$; $z = 2.31, p < 0.05$, (comparison of correlated correlations according to Meng *et al.* 1992). Absenteeism was not systematically correlated with any commitment component in the German samples, whereas in the Chinese sample OCN is systematically related to absenteeism and correlations with both workgroup commitments are stronger. However, these differences were not significant. With regard to turnover intention, higher correlations were found for organizational commitment in both samples.

Thus *H 1.2 is* supported for conscientiousness and for the intention to leave with regard to the first criterion (explaining additional variance only in collectivistic context), but only supported for conscientiousness with regard to the second criterion (stronger predictor). However, in the German sample, the relationship between OCA and turnover intention is much higher ($r = -0.64$) than for WCA ($r = -0.15$), whereas in the Chinese sample the difference is much smaller (-0.73 and -0.58, respectively). Thus workgroup commitment is not more influential, but is nearly as influential as organizational commitment in a collectivistic context.

H 2 addressed the assumption that affective and normative components are more related in a collectivistic context. As can be seen in Table 1, the correlation between affective and normative components is higher for organizational commitment in the Chinese sample ($r = 60$ and 0.78, respectively). The test reveals a significant difference ($z = 2.602$, $p < 0.01$) (Preacher 2002). For workgroup commitment components, however, the differences are smaller ($r = 70$ and 0.76, respectively) and are not significant. Thus *H 2* is only confirmed for organizational commitment and not for workgroup commitment.

With *H 3* it was postulated that organizational commitment and workgroup commitment are more related in a collectivistic context. The comparison of correlations between both countries reveals a significant difference for OCA and WCA ($z = 3.37$, $p < 0.001$). As expected, the relationship between OCA and WCA is much stronger in a collectivistic context. For NC, the expected difference also occurred ($r = 51$ and 0.64) but was significant only at the 10% level ($z = 1.45$, $p = 0.07$). Thus *H 3* is clearly supported for WCA, and it is also supported for WCN on a 10% level of error probability.

Conclusions

The aim of this study was to examine the impact of cultural differences on commitment. Extending the body of previous research (Lee *et al.* 2001, Meyer *et al.* 2002, Cheng *et al.* 2003, Riketta and Van Dick 2005, Felfe *et al.* 2008a, Stanley *et al.* 2007), the question was raised if workgroup commitment might play an even more crucial role in collectivist than in individualistic contexts. Previous research that addresses cross-cultural issues in the field of workplace commitment has either focused on organizational commitment and omitted other foci that might be of specific relevance in collectivistic contexts, or was conducted only with samples of one cultural context. Therefore, it was the purpose of the present study to include multiple foci of commitment simultaneously and to directly compare their respective influence in different contexts. In the following section, the findings will be summarized and discussed. Referring to literature and on the basis of previous research, it was assumed that workgroup commitment components are more important with regard to their potential influence on relevant organizational outcomes in a collectivistic than in an individualistic context. Comparing employees from Germany and China, the results confirm this idea. In predicting turnover intention, absenteeism and conscientiousness as OCB subscales, the cultural context moderated the influence of WCA and WCN. This effect was not found for altruism. Generally, the results support the assumption that workgroup commitment is more meaningful in a collectivistic than in a more individualistic context. However, it has to be stated that this cultural influence is not consistent with all outcomes. No such effect was found for altruism and the expected failed to reach significance with absenteeism after controlling for country effects. This may be due to small sample size and a lack of statistical power. However, it can be concluded that at least workgroup commitment should be included when examining commitment in collectivistic contexts.

Going beyond the point that workgroup commitment exerts higher influence in a collectivistic context, the question was raised if these proximal commitments might be even stronger predictors than the well-established organizational commitment (Meyer *et al.* 2002). In a first step, it could be shown that workgroup commitment explained variance in outcomes over and above organizational commitment only in the collectivistic context. In a second step, the assumption of even higher influence of workgroup commitment was tested. This was only confirmed for workgroup commitment and conscientiousness. Both components were more strongly related to conscientiousness than the respective organizational commitment components. For turnover intention no such effect occurred. This result is in line with the meta-analytical findings of Riketta and Van Dick (2005) and underlines the suggestion to include workgroup commitment particularly in collectivistic contexts. At least they are supposed to improve the prediction of outcomes, but in some cases they may be even more influential than organizational commitment.

As norms and rules are characteristic for collectivistic contexts, it was expected that affective and normative components are more related in this kind of environment. It was suggested that in collectivistic cultures there might be less differentiation between general norms and individual motives and, therefore, they are more closely related. The results support this assumption only for organizational commitment. This finding is in line with previous research (Stanley *et al.* 2007). For workgroup commitment, no such relationship was found. One reason might be that employees in collectivistic contexts also differentiate when it comes to evaluating proximal entities, and do not with regard to distal entities.

It was assumed that in a collectivistic context nested entities such as the workgroup and the organization might be more closely related because people in this context are more willing to strive for consistent social identity. The results support this assumption. It can be argued that the workgroup might be more regarded as a part of the whole organization, whereas in a more individualistic context employees perceive their unit as more independent of the whole organization.

There are several limitations in this study and some of them require further research to be clarified or ruled out. Though most of the results mirror previous research, one must be careful in generalizing the results as the comparability of the samples may have been biased by unknown factors (such as different branches, size of organization, working conditions, salary). However, the effects of differences between types of organizations have been controlled in the regression analyses by the country variable. Due to small sample sizes there was a lack of power for more complex analysis (including more control variables). Also, the nationality of the ownership (German) of the Chinese organization may have lowered the expected differences. Moreover, in this study, cultural differences have not been measured directly. Therefore, it cannot be excluded that context differences may have been rather small. In order to enhance the validity of the results, our findings should be replicated with other samples. Future studies should also include more objective and independent outcome criteria (supervisors' performance assessments, sales and quality records).

Besides adding more samples, it is also possible to measure cultural influences on the individual level in order to make results more reliable (Triandis 1995, Clugston *et al.* 2000, Wasti 2003, Felfe *et al.* 2008a). Felfe *et al.* (2008a), for example, found that individual value orientations were related to organizational commitment and that collectivism moderated the influence of antecedences of organizational commitment. This could be shown for similar samples in different cultures (China, Romania and Germany). Highest correlations were found for collectivism in each country. Additionally, their results showed that after controlling for alternative variables (task content, climate), individual collectivism appeared to be the most influential predictor for commitment besides leadership. Obviously, the individual preference for the group and the propensity to build close relationships with a social entity is related to one's commitment to the organization.

Interestingly, a differentiated examination of the correlation patterns for the different components revealed that in Germany and China, highest correlations occurred for collectivism with NC and lowest with continuance commitment. This finding confirmed the theoretical assumption that from a collectivistic perspective, rules and norms play an important role. As we expected, the relationships between collectivism and the commitment components were stronger in China than in Germany. It was suggested that a cultural context that supports individual orientations towards the group will foster such a relationship by a process of reciprocity and reinforcement. Although correlations were somewhat lower, for uncertainty avoidance similar results were obtained. Interestingly, relationships with continuance commitment appeared to be relatively strong. This finding supported the assumptions of Clugston *et al.* (2000), who argue that persons who refuse to pursue their own goals to gain security and orientation experience high psychological costs. Thus commitment that is influenced by uncertainty avoidance in particular results in continuance orientated commitment. Again, it could be shown that the relationship between value orientation and affective commitment was influenced by the cultural context. We conclude that, from an overall perspective, collectivism seems to foster NC and affective commitment, whereas uncertainty avoidance is related to affective and continuance commitment. This individual level approach can be transferred to the examination of workgroup commitment and supervisor commitment in order to better understand their respective antecedences and outcomes in the light of cultural differences.

With regard to antecedences, Felfe *et al.* (2008a) addressed the question if leadership and task content had specific impacts on organizational commitment depending on the cultural context. Their results show that there is a closer relationship between leadership as antecedence and organizational commitment in China than in Germany, whereas the influence of task content is stronger in Germany than in China. Extending this approach, it seems a promising research perspective to examine specific antecedences of workgroup commitment in different cultural contexts.

Moreover, research suggests that not only Asian countries but also Eastern European countries are more collectivistic than Western European countries (Hofstede 2001, House *et al.* 2004, Littrell and Valentin 2005). Accordingly, the results obtained by Felfe *et al.* (2008a) for a Romanian sample were similar to the findings for the Chinese samples in many points. To shed more light on the role of multiple commitments in Eastern European countries, additional studies are required.

Implications

For organizational practice, different implications result from the present study. Probably one of the most striking findings of this research is that in comparison to Germany, workgroup commitment is more powerful in a collectivistic context. Employees in this cultural environment are more willing to behave on behalf of the group. Therefore, it is recommended to analyze their specific antecedences in order to maintain and improve workgroup commitment. Even more, as organizational and workgroup commitment are more closely linked to each other, it can be expected that organizational commitment can be positively influenced by the enhancement of workgroup commitment. This is important because Felfe *et al.* (2006) have already shown that the level of OCA within Chinese organizations is relatively low compared to German samples. Thus, workgroup commitment could be a key factor to increasing overall commitment. Whereas recommendations for management that are based on findings in Western organizations focus on the enhancement of OCA (Meyer *et al.* 2002), in China other foci such as the workgroup and NC should be particularly addressed. As Riketta and Van Dick (2005) have shown, team climate (that is the quality of the interaction between group members) in particular is related to workgroup commitment. Therefore, it is recommended to management and leaders in cross-cultural settings to engage in actions that help to improve the team climate (enhance mutual understanding, foster communication between members, support informal contact). To pursue this issue, teams can undergo systematic team building and team development processes. Goal clarity, a shared vision, cohesion, social support, chances for participation, sufficient information and communication, for example, are all relevant factors for fostering both effective and satisfactory teamwork and a good team climate. The assessment of weakness and strength is an important starting point for development processes. Appropriate tools have been developed by West and colleagues (Anderson and West 1996). Moreover, leadership is supposed to be an important factor for the functioning of a team. The concept of transformational leadership (Bass 1998) is a particularly promising approach to enhance team effectiveness and team climate. Consequently, executive training and individual coaching programmes may help leaders to develop their leadership behaviour in order to be successful team leaders.

References

Allen, N.J., 2003. Examining organizational commitment in China. *Journal of vocational behavior*, 62, 511–515.

Anderson, N. and West, M.A., 1996. The team climate inventory: development of the TCI and its applications in teambuilding for innovativeness. *European journal of work and organizational psychology*, 5, 53–67.

Bass, B.M., 1998. *Transformational leadership. Industrial, military, and educational impact.* Mahwah, NJ: Lawrence Erlbaum Associates Inc.

Becker, T.E., 1992. Foci and bases of commitment: are they distinctions worth making? *Academy of management journal*, 35, 232–244.

Bentein, K., Stinglhamber, F., and Vandenberghe, C., 2002. Organization-, supervisor-, and work-group-directed commitments and citizenship behaviors: a comparison of models. *European journal of work and organizational psychology*, 11, 341–362.

Berry, J.W., *et al.*, 2002. *Cross-cultural psychology: research and applications.* 2nd ed. Cambridge: Cambridge University Press.

Chen, Z.X. and Francesco, A.M., 2000. Employee demography, organizational commitment, and turnover intentions in China: do cultural differences matter? *Human relations*, 53, 869–887.

Chen, Z.X. and Francesco, A.M., 2003. The relationship between the three components of commitment and employee performance in China. *Journal of vocational behavior*, 62, 490–510.

Cheng, B.S., Jiang, D.Y., and Riley, J.H., 2003. Organizational commitment, supervisory commitment, and employee outcomes in the Chinese context: proximal hypothesis or global hypothesis? *Journal of organizational behavior*, 24, 313–334.

Cheng, Y. and Stockdale, M.S., 2003. The validity of the three-component model of organizational commitment in a Chinese context. *Journal of vocational behavior*, 62, 465–489.

Clugston, M., Howell, J.P., and Dorfman, P.W., 2000. Does cultural socialization predict multiple bases and foci of commitment? *Journal of management*, 26, 5–30.

Cohen, A., 2003. *Multiple commitments in the workplace: an integrative approach.* Mahwah, NJ: Lawrence Erlbaum Associates Inc.

Cooper-Hakim, A. and Viswesvaran, C., 2005. The construct of work commitment: testing an integrative framework. *Psychological bulletin*, 131, 241–259.

Donald, I. and Siu, O., 2001. Moderating the stress impact of environmental conditions: the effect of organizational commitment in Hong Kong and China. *Journal of environmental psychology*, 21, 353–368.

Ellemers, N., 2001. Social identity, commitment, and work behavior. *In*: M.A. Hogg and D.J. Terry, eds. *Social identity processes in organizational contexts*. Philadelphia: Psychology Press.

Felfe, J., 2007. Besonderes Engagement bei der Arbeit [Extraordinary engagement at work]. *In*: H. Schuler and K.H. Sonntag, eds. *Handbuch der arbeits- und organisationspsychologie* [*Handbook of work- and organizational psychology*]. Göttingen: Hogrefe, 246–253.

Felfe, J., Schmook, R., and Six, B., 2006. Die Bedeutung kultureller Wertorientierungen für das Commitment gegenüber der Organisation, dem Vorgesetzten, der Arbeitsgruppe und der eigenen Karriere [The relevance of cultural value orientations to organizational, supervisor, team, and career commitment]. *Zeitschrift für personalpsychologie*, 5, 94–107.

Felfe, J., Tartler, K., and Liepmann, D., 2004. Advanced research in the field of transformational leadership. *Zeitschrift für personalforschung* [*German journal of human resource research*]. *Special research forum*, 18, 262–288.

Felfe, J., *et al.*, 2005. Commitment gegenüber Verleiher und Entleiher bei Zeitarbeitern: Bedingungen und Konsequenzen [Contingent employees' commitment to agency and client organization: antecedents and consequences]. *Zeitschrift für personalpsychologie*, 4, 101–115.

Felfe, J., Yan, W., and Six, B., 2008a. The impact of individual collectivism on commitment and its influence on OCB, turnover, and strain in three countries. *International journal of cross-cultural management*, 8, 211–237.

Felfe, J., *et al.*, 2008b. Does the form of employment make a difference? Commitment of traditional, temporary, and self-employed workers. *Journal of vocational behaviour*, 72 (1), 81–94.

Herscovitch, L. and Meyer, J.P., 2002. Commitment to organizational change: extension of a three component model. *Journal of applied psychology*, 474–487.

Hofstede, G., 2001. *Culture's consequences: company values, behaviors, institutions, and organizations across nations*. 2nd ed. Beverly Hills, CA: Sage Publications.

House, R.J., *et al.*, 2004. *Leadership and organizations: a 62 nation GLOBE study*. Thousand Oaks, CA: Sage Publications.

Irving, P.G., Coleman, D.F., and Cooper, C.L., 1997. Further assessments of a three-component model of occupational commitment: generalizability and differences across occupations. *Journal of applied psychology*, 82, 444–452.

Lee, K., *et al.*, 2001. The three-component model of organizational commitment: an application to South Korea. *Applied psychology: an international review*, 50, 596–614.

Littrell, R.F. and Valentin, L.N., 2005. Preferred leadership behaviours: exploratory results from Romania, Germany, and the UK. *Journal of management development*, 24, 421–442.

Mathieu, J.E. and Zajac, D.M., 1990. A review and meta-analysis of the antecedents, correlates, and consequences of organizational commitment. *Psychological bulletin*, 108, 171–194.

Meng, X.L., Rosenthal, R., and Rubin, D.B., 1992. Comparing correlated correlation coefficients. *Psychological bulletin*, 111, 172–175.

Meyer, J.P. and Allen, N.J., 1991. A three-component conceptualization of organizational commitment. *Human resource management review*, 1, 61–89.

Meyer, J.P. and Herscovitch, L., 2001. Commitment in the workplace toward a general model. *Human resource management review*, 11, 299–326.

Meyer, J.P., Allen, N.J., and Smith, C.A., 1993. Commitment to organizations and occupations: extension and test of a three-component conceptualization. *Journal of applied psychology*, 78, 538–551.

Meyer, J.P., *et al.*, 2002. Affective, continuance, and normative commitment to the organization: a meta-analysis of antecedents, correlates, and consequences. *Journal of vocational behavior*, 61, 20–52.

Organ, D.W., 1988. *Organizational citizenship behaviour*. Lexington, MA: Lexington Press.

Podsakoff, P.M., MacKenzie, S.B., and Brommer, W.H., 1996. Transformational leader behaviors and substitutes for leadership as determinants of employee satisfaction, commitment, trust, and organizational citizenship behaviors. *Journal of management*, 22, 259–298.

Preacher, K.J., 2002. Calculation for the test of the difference between two independent correlation coefficients (Computer software). Available from: http://www.quantpsy.org [Accessed May 2005].

Rahim, M.A. and Magner, N.R., 1995. Confirmatory factor-analysis of the style of handling interpersonal conflict: first-order factor model and its invariance across groups. *Journal of applied psychology*, 80, 122–132.

Riketta, M. and Van Dick, R., 2005. Foci of attachment in organizations: a meta-analytic comparison of the strength and correlates of work group versus organizational identification and commitment. *Journal of vocational behavior*, 67 (3), 490–510.

Ryan, A.M., *et al.*, 1999. Employee attitude surveys in a multinational organization: considering language and culture in assessing measurement equivalence. *Personnel psychology*, 52, 37–58.

Stanley, D.J., *et al.*, 2007. Cross-cultural generalizability of the three-component model of commitment. *22nd annual Society for Industrial and Organizational Psychology (SIOP) conference*, April, New York.

Steenkamp, J.M. and Baumgartner, H., 1998. Assessing measurement invariance in cross-national consumer research. *Journal of consumer research*, 25, 78–90.

Stinglhamber, F., Bentein, K., and Vandenberghe, C., 2002. Extension of the three-component model of commitment to five foci. *European journal of psychological assessment*, 18, 123–138.

Tajfel, H. and Turner, J.C., 2003. The social identity theory of intergroup behavior. *In*: M.A. Hogg, ed. *Social psychology - volume IV intergroup behavior and societal context*. Thousand Oaks, CA: Sage Publications.

Tan, D. and Akhtar, S., 1998. Organizational commitment and experienced burnout: an exploratory study from a Chinese cultural perspective. *International journal of organizational analysis*, 6, 310–333.

Triandis, H.C., 1995. *Individualism and collectivism*. Boulder, CO: Westview Press.

Trompenaars, F., 2000. *Riding the waves of culture – understanding cultural diversity in business*. 2nd ed. London: Nicholas Brealey.

Vandenberghe, C., 2003. Application of the three-component model to China: issues and perspectives. *Journal of vocational behavior*, 62, 516–523.

Vandenberghe, C., *et al.*, 2001. An examination of the cross-cultural validity of a multidimensional model of commitment in Europe. *Journal of cross-cultural psychology*, 32, 322–347.

Wasti, S.A., 2003. Organizational commitment, turnover intentions and the influence of cultural values. *Journal of occupational and organizational psychology*, 76, 303–321.

Competitiveness, localization and Japanese companies in China: realities and alternate approaches

H. Itagaki

Faculty of Economics, Musashi University, 1-26-1, Toyotama-kami, Nerima-ku, Tokyo 176-5984, Japan

Introduction

China at present, particularly in its large cities, is experiencing unprecedented mobility in the workforce, especially amongst the younger generation. The authority of Shanghai recently reported that the average length of service in the city is only one and a half years for employees under 30, and two years and three months for employees in their 30s (Tanaka 2006). This movement stems from severe competition and a strong orientation toward success among younger talented people, as well as a short-term employment contract system under the reform of the old regime represented by state-owned companies. Against this backdrop, many companies face serious difficulties in maintaining steady management of their Chinese operations. Taiwanese electronics manufacturing services (EMS) companies, for example, have re-transferred their research and development (R&D) facilities from China to Taiwan since around 2003. Some US global electronics companies which procure products from Taiwanese EMS companies have also followed their trading partners.

Export-oriented companies can exercise this choice. However, for companies whose major target is the Chinese market, the more investment increases, the more significant both R&D and corporate strategy functions become in China. This will in turn increase the necessity for recruiting talented human resources locally. In this situation, Japanese companies can expect to face more serious difficulties than their US or European counterparts. This is due to two closely related factors. The first has to do with the style of work. The style of work can be defined as the extent of demarcation of job areas, of the manner of information-sharing and problem-solving methods that correspond to the strengths and weaknesses of the demarcation of job areas. American companies, in general, standardize job categories and clarify decision-making authority on the basis of defined job descriptions. This system enables companies to manage corporate organizations without serious problems when there is a high turnover of employees (Kagono *et al.* 1985). On the other hand, Japanese companies generally do not standardize job categories but rather allocate work tasks flexibly to individual employees (Kagono *et al.* 1985, Jacoby 2005). Pucik (1999) demonstrated that American executives of Japanese-affiliated companies in the US often complained about the lack of clarity of performance objectives and the quality of performance feedback that they received. This seems to stem from different understandings about the style of work between Japanese expatriates and American executives. There is a strong possibility that Japanese-affiliated companies will experience a similar set of challenges in China.

The second reason why Japanese companies may face more serious difficulties is related to human resource management practices. Many American companies abroad, under the standardizing of jobs and authority, select superior personnel and promote them early to higher or top positions (localization of managers), reward them with high remuneration if they can demonstrate good performance and, if not, fire them (Shiraki 2006, Tanaka 2006). In contrast, Japanese multinational enterprises (MNEs) have often been cited for their expatriate-intensive management abroad or lag in localization of managers (Bartlett and Yoshihara 1992, Kopp 1999, Pucik 1999). As long as this management style continues, young ambitious people are unlikely to be attracted to Japanese-affiliated companies (Seki and Fan 2004), and this may hamper business development abroad.

Research framework and research questions

Even though Japanese MNEs have long been criticized by scholars and the media for their slow progress in the localization of managers, expatriate-intensive management persists. This tendency may have stemmed from the fact that the majority of Japanese MNEs began their foreign activities later than their Western counterparts. However, in the case of China, this reason cannot be applied, as the entry to China by major Japanese and Western firms occurred more or less at the same time, that is, after China's declaration of a 'socialistic market economy' and the introduction of the 'Open Door Policy' as part of the dismantling of the planned economy which began in 1978 (Marukawa 1999). Other than the development stage explanation, there exist two further interesting interpretations. Kopp (1999) explains that expatriate-intensive management abroad by Japanese MNEs is a mirror image of rigid differentiation of categories of core regular employees (*seishain*) and peripheral employees (non-*seishain* or temporary workers) at home. In other words, Japanese expatriates correspond to *seishain* and American white-collar staff to non-*seishain*. However, in view of the fact that the average ratio of Japanese expatriates to total employees at Japanese affiliates in the US is around 2%, this explanation is not appropriate even as a similitude. Furthermore, this interpretation cannot explain the reason why Japanese-affiliated companies have sent a considerable number of local employees to train in Japan at pecuniary and time costs, or why most Japanese affiliates in the Association of Southeast Asian Nations (ASEAN) countries did not layoff, but trained and educated regular employees in the midst of the Asian economic crisis in the late 1990s (Itagaki 2002). Pucik (1999) ascribes the lag in the localization of managers to the situation where in the 'no-growth environment in Japan, Japanese expatriate positions in Japanese foreign affiliates are very valuable, as they provide places for the surplus Japanese managerial workforce'. However, this explanation is apparently in contradiction to the fact that the ratio of Japanese expatriates to total employees has not decreased considerably, even after Japanese companies executed large-scale personnel reduction at home in the late 1990s and early 2000s. Therefore, these two explanations are not adequate answers.

The question then is why Japanese MNEs do not standardize jobs and adopt fast-track strategies like US multinationals? Japanese manufacturing companies have practiced a work style and human resource management system that is in contrast to those of US companies at home, and these practices have sustained international competitiveness in some manufacturing sectors. If Japanese MNEs altered their practices considerably at affiliates abroad, they would probably suffer a weakening in their competitive edge. They need to transfer their essential elements of work style into host countries. This task is not easy, however, and takes considerable time. It requires the presence of Japanese expatriates who possess the required work style for a considerably longer duration since they started operations abroad. This is just one fundamental reason why the ratio of Japanese expatriates has decreased so slowly (Itagaki 2002).

Regarding the specific context of China in the localization or transplantation of human resource management (HRM) practices, Seki and Fan (2004) and Shiraki (2006) attempt to explain reasons for the lag in localization of managers in Japanese affiliates in China, by attributing it to the attitude of Japanese MNEs. However, their arguments do not consider the linkage between HRM practices and the core competence of Japanese companies. Takeuchi *et al.* (2003), applying the resource-based theory of the firm, make a useful analysis of the relationship between core competence and HRM practices of Japanese companies, and international transfer of these practices to Chinese and Taiwanese affiliates. However, their arguments are optimistic about the international transferability of HRM practices. Their examination lacks a viewpoint of 'institutional complementarity' between HRM practices and organizational features, including work style. As Aoki (1994) insists, there exists institutional complementarity among corporate subsystems, such as HRM practices. Here, institutional complementarity means that the functions of subsystems and elements of the whole managerial system are sustained and reinforced by each other. These subsystems have been developed under the peculiar circumstances of the home countries of MNEs. It is not an easy task for MNEs, in general, to transfer their HRM practices into host countries where managerial circumstances are different. Japanese MNEs, in particular, face difficulties in the transplantation of their HRM practices for these reasons. The aim of this study is to explore the types of difficulties that Japanese firms experience in the specific context of China and to consider some possible solutions. In addressing this important issue, the study is structured as follows: first, we clarify the elements of competitiveness of some Japanese manufacturing sectors and examine the characteristics of the work style and human resource management practices which underpin the competitive edge of Japanese MNEs. Then the international scope of these practices is explored and key challenges identified. These challenges are contextualized for the case of China along with several proposed adaptation approaches, based on findings obtained during extensive field research in Japanese affiliates. This is followed by conclusions, managerial implications and recommendations for further research.

Literature review: core competences of Japanese manufacturing

It is only natural that Japanese manufacturing companies have strengths in some sectors and products, and weaknesses in others. Representative products that demonstrate international competitiveness are electronic durable goods such as digital cameras, flat panel TVs and DVD recorders, passenger cars, various kinds of components and materials for electronics products and automobiles, and production equipment including machines for manufacturing integrated circuit (IC) chips. On the other hand, mobile phones and desktop computers account for only a very small share of Japanese businesses in world markets. This gives rise to the assumption that the same characteristics of management result in the promotion of competitive strength for some product sectors but not for others. Before going directly to the problem, we wish to consider elements that make some Japanese products competitive by taking a look specifically at passenger cars and parts and materials.

The competitive strength of Japanese passenger car manufacturers lies in both the areas of R&D and manufacturing. In R&D, the capability to achieve total optimization is critical, as passenger cars require an optimal combination and fine-tuned adjustments of a great number of parts and materials from the design stage onwards (Fujimoto 2003). Furthermore, Japanese auto manufacturers have succeeded in these areas in a shorter period than their US and European counterparts (Clark and Fujimoto 1991, Fujimoto *et al.* 2002). The essential ability required in this task is coordination and cooperation in devising optimum solutions for the whole and parts of that product which are satisfactory to relevant inhouse sections, as well as to procurers and suppliers (Asanuma 1997).

Competitiveness of Japanese auto makers, in terms of manufacturing, stems from their capability to achieve three goals simultaneously at a high level: a wide variety in production, high quality and high efficiency (Fujimoto 2003). In contrast, under the traditional American mass-production system these three goals were caught in a trade-off relationship. Even today Japanese car manufacturers surpass their counterparts in the US in in-process defect ratios, man hours for production of equivalent models, and the number of models produced in one factory (Liker *et al.* 1999). Such a production system requires a number of elements to be in place, including multi-skilled engineers and workers, incremental and continuous *Kaizen* (work-place 'quality' improvement) activities, and coordination and cooperation among different sections in one company and between car makers and suppliers of both components and equipment (Ishida *et al.* 1997).

Other representative product lines of Japanese manufacturers, which demonstrate strong international competitiveness, are various kinds of parts and materials, and production equipment. Typical examples are parts and materials for mobile phones and consumer electronics durables, high-tension steel sheets for automobiles, and microscopic miniature bearings. These products cannot be readily copied because they require a deep extraction of fundamental technology and know-how in both products and manufacturing processes that have accumulated within and between companies (Itagaki 2008). These kinds of technologies and know-how are built and refined through a long process of trial and error, and close exchange of information between R&D and manufacturing divisions and between producers and their customers.

From the above examination, we can infer that the source of a Japanese company's competitive edge lies in the high level of problem-solving capability based on a long-term accumulation of knowledge and know-how within and between companies, and the coordination and combination of jobs, divisions and companies (Itagaki 2008). The coordination and combination are characterized by a horizontal information exchange in which information does not necessarily flow along managerial lines of the corporate hierarchy (Aoki 1988), and by the importance of middle managers who often play key roles in direct inter-divisional coordination (Nonaka 1988). The concept of 'administrative network' presented by Lifson (1992), is similar to this horizontal information exchange. However, Lifson (1992) strongly emphasizes the importance of informal and individual networks. While information does not necessarily flow along managerial lines of the corporate hierarchy, there is a horizontal information exchange that can be seen as the formal network in Japanese companies. Of course, horizontal information exchange embraces informal networks and problem-solving emphasized by Lifson (1992).

Coordination and combination between jobs, divisions and companies are built on the basis of the work style generally observed in Japanese companies. This work style is characterized fundamentally by low barriers between jobs, which are, in turn, sustained by a long-term orientation toward business, employment and the trade relationship (Itagaki 2008). Low barriers between jobs – that is, weak demarcation – represent the style of work where tasks are allocated to individual employees flexibly, instead of allocating employees to clearly defined jobs and authorities (Kagono *et al.* 1985). Section heads have the authority to allocate tasks to younger subordinates, and these allocations of tasks change in a flexible way according to circumstances. This work style enables job rotation from one section to another, through which multifunctional skills and knowledge are developed and acquired (Koike 1988). Multifunctional skills and knowledge are the basis of teamwork between divisions. Job rotation can be considered as a kind of training cost for the company, since it decreases work efficiency temporarily as a result of allocating workers to unfamiliar task areas. Companies cannot afford to bear this kind of training cost if employees quit their jobs frequently. Coordination, combination and information sharing between companies also require a long continuum of business relationships (Itagaki 2008). Thus teamwork between jobs, divisions, and companies necessitates a continuity of operations, employment and trade over a long period.

This work style has been supported by the salient pay and promotion system generally observed in large Japanese companies (Koike 1988). The pay and promotion mechanisms are represented by an inhouse qualification system formed and established in large Japanese companies since the country's period of high economic growth. The system does not grade jobs but grades employees by age, length of service, and performance evaluation (ability rating). The qualifications or ranks in the system determine the basic salary or wage for each employee. This also applies to the promotion system, as some specific qualifications are indispensable prerequisites for some specific managerial positions, such as section and division heads. Firstly, this system is suitable for the style of work in Japanese companies, since it does not base salaries or wages on specific jobs per se (Koike and Inoki 1990). Secondly, it is superficial to interpret Japanese corporate pay and promotion systems as being solely seniority-based, since they include performance evaluation of individual employees (Ishida 2003).[1] Evaluation of work performance naturally stimulates competition among employees. However, it also encourages cooperation among employees, as a review of ability includes such elements as cooperative behaviour, coordination capability, and ability to educate and train younger colleagues (Ishida 2003). Thirdly, of course, it facilitates long-term service by employees, because length of service is a factor in determining the employee's rank. Fourthly, the system brings in slow promotion or 'late selection for promotion' (Koike 1988). Most of the large Japanese corporations do not, for the most part, differentiate ranks among employees in the same generation until a certain age, and after that they gradually widen the gap between the ranks of those employees.

This slow promotion system has two effects. One is that, coupled with the ability rating mentioned above, it encourages both competition and cooperation among employees (Ito 1994). So long as employees have an orientation toward management participation and promotion, they have an expectation of the possibility of promotion to higher positions within the corporate hierarchy. This stimulates competition among employees for a long period. At the same time, slow promotion affords employees the leeway to cooperate with their colleagues (Koike 1988). The other effect is that it is a suitable mechanism for the manufacturing industry. It takes a long time for the formation of skills in the manufacturing industry, and this is not only for Japanese companies. One Chinese picture tube maker once adopted a fast-track promotion policy in order to attract talented people. However, the company revised it to a system that sets a minimum number of years for staying in each position. The reason is that many fast-track managers lacked skills and knowledge required in their managerial positions.[2]

As already mentioned, Japan also has manufacturing sectors that do not demonstrate competitiveness in world markets. A typical example is desktop computers, where Japanese electronics companies account for only a very small share of the world market. To compete with rivals successfully in this industry requires that companies demonstrate various kinds of problem-solving capabilities. The interfacing of parts and components of desktop computers are so standardized that long-term coordination between makers and suppliers is not required. Instead, an adept logistic capability for tapping into and organizing good suppliers, which can provide parts of moderate quality at a reasonable price, is crucial (Fujimoto 2003). Some US computer makers in particular have strong capabilities in this field through their close relationships with EMS companies, especially from Taiwan. Generally speaking, US companies are superior at integrating heterogeneous elements into whole organizational units by standardizing the jobs and roles of individual organizations.

Findings: difficulties faced by Japanese-affiliated companies abroad

Japanese MNEs have mainly focused their international activities on the assembly of finished products, as well as parts and components (Abo 1994a, Itagaki 1997). R&D activities abroad have been limited because most Japanese companies need to avoid duplication of investment. Manufacturing activities utilizing deep extraction of technology are also limited, as they require close communication with R&D divisions. As mentioned, the competitive edge of Japanese assembly plants lies in their ability to achieve the three goals of wide product variety, high quality and high efficiency, simultaneously, at a high level. Liker *et al.* (1999) demonstrated that Japanese car manufacturers surpass their US counterparts in in-process defect ratios, man-hour for production of equivalent models, and the number of models not only in domestic plants but in US plants, too.

To achieve satisfactory performance, Japanese MNEs have transplanted various kinds of methods and devices developed in their domestic operations, such as just-in-time techniques within a factory, total quality control (TQC), total productive maintenance (TPM) and other techinques, to their affiliated companies abroad (Abo 1994a, 1994b, Itagaki 1997, 2008, Kumon and Abo 2004). These methods are, in a sense, 'visible' so that they are relatively smoothly transferred. These methods cannot function effectively, however, without the aforementioned work style. It is not an easy task to transfer all aspects of the work style into host countries where the scope of job demarcation is different, or where at least time is required for its adequate transfer. To maintain their competitive edge, Japanese MNEs have 'resolved' this problem by sending to the host country operation, a relatively large number of Japanese expatriates who possess the necessary elements of the work style. This is the fundamental reason for the lag in the localization of managers at Japanese-affiliated companies abroad (Itagaki 2002).

Since a work style based on a weak demarcation of individual job descriptions supports the methods that directly lead to the high performance of plant operations, there is a strong possibility that the standardization of jobs and adoption of fast-track promotion decreases the competitive strength of Japanese-affiliated companies. In China, the situation seems to be worse than in other host countries. This is due not only to the short-term view of Chinese people toward their employment in a certain company, but also due to the methods of Japanese companies themselves. Rapid development and expansion of Chinese business have compelled Japanese companies to achieve satisfactory performance immediately after their start of plant operations. Under this pressure, many Japanese MNEs have dispatched a considerable number of Japanese expatriates to China instead of training and fostering local talent based on a long-term perspective (Tanaka 2006). Yet this may engender a 'vicious cycle' in which expatriate-intensive management is likely to lead to capable people not being attracted to Japanese-affiliated companies which causes, in turn, the need for Japanese expatriates and a concomitant lag in the localization of managers.

In the case of subsidiaries whose main objective is to manufacture products for export to Japan or third countries, this vicious cycle may not cause serious results. During fieldwork, one director of a leading electronics company said that 'the company did not delegate discretional power regarding strategies to their subsidiaries abroad'.[3] In fact, there are many Japanese subsidiaries abroad whose function is almost the same as domestic assembly plants in Japan (Itagaki 1997, Liker *et al.* 1999). In those cases, Japanese MNEs can be practical about the existence of Japanese expatriates as a necessary cost to maintain their competitiveness (Itagaki 2002). As for R&D activities or affiliates whose main targets are oriented towards Chinese market, however, the story is quite different. R&D bases need talented Chinese engineers, since they are required to coordinate and negotiate with local suppliers. These are considerably difficult tasks for Japanese engineers. If the main mission of an affiliate is to produce and sell products to the Chinese market, strategic thinking appropriate to the Chinese environment is essential. Accompanying the expansion of investment that targets the Chinese domestic market and an increase in the significance of R&D activities in China, Japanese-affiliated companies will be forced to attract more talented resources locally.

Naturally, the situation differs from area to area. Even among industrialized and urbanized parts of China, the northern region, including Dalian and Tianjin, does not have a workforce with a high rate of mobility, as a number of interviews at Japanese affiliates revealed. In fact, some Japanese MNEs have established R&D facilities at Dalian and Tianjin. However, in recent Chinese contexts, low mobility of the workforce implies the scarcity of migration from other areas. It was reported that this makes it difficult for companies to recruit talented people from wide areas.

How then can Japanese MNEs in China escape their dilemma? In the next section, some attempts and practices of Japanese-affiliated companies to keep talented managers and engineers will be examined as a means of circumventing the dilemma of maintaining a competitive edge and, at the same time, localizing management.

Discussion: three approaches to reconciling the competitiveness/localization dilemma

Discussions in this section are based on a series of interviews that took place from August 2005 to October 2007 in China. Interviews were conducted with Japanese expatriates and senior Chinese managers in 35 Chinese affiliates of Japanese MNEs. Interviews were semi-structured, as designed questionnaires and free questions were used jointly.

Since the objective of the field survey was to examine broader aspects of management, three 'typical' cases regarding the localization of HRM practices by Japanese MNEs are introduced and discussed below.

Prior to an examination of specific cases, it is important to discuss the issue of salaries paid to employees by Japanese affiliates and their Western counterparts, since the difficulty of Japanese affiliates in recruiting talented people has been frequently ascribed to their lower wage and salary system (see NSS 2005). Actually, many Japanese expatriates interviewed agreed that their employees were frequently headhunted with the incentive of higher salaries by their Western counterparts. However, it is superficial to assume that salaries paid by Japanese affiliates are much lower than those of their US or European counterparts in China. It is certain that some local managers and engineers in Western global companies earn much higher salaries. However, high earnings are not always ensured, as interest accounts are carried forward as a considerable portion of payment (Tanaka 2006). Moreover, employment relations themselves are often uncertain in those companies. While fast-track promotions result in higher salaries for employees in many Western multinationals at least until a certain age, HRM in Japanese affiliates is characterized by slow promotion, though the speed of promotion in China is considerably faster than in Japan. This slow promotion leads to a slower increase in salary. Ma (2000), however, shows that Japanese MNEs in China surpass their western counterparts in terms of average salary paid to employees aged 40 years or over. A further, more recent, survey reports that the salaries of people in China who can conduct business discussions in Japanese are higher than those who can only use English (NSS 2005). In addition, employment relations in Japanese MNEs are often far more stable than in Western firms. Consequently, it is possible to argue that the difference between JMNEs and Western multinationals is not an issue of the amount of salary itself but the manner of payment (Tanaka 2006).

Some Japanese-affiliated companies are able to retain talented employees successfully, and their turnover ratios are low. By introducing such cases, we will next examine what elements can lead to successful outcomes.

Model 1: road map of promotion

The regional headquarters of two leading Japanese electronics companies located in Beijing, prepared salary tables by job category that reflected the average market price of each job. On the basis of the salary table, the company devised a road map of promotion in which each employee is able to realize his/her abilities and experience required for promotion to some specific managerial position. The companies also prepared programmes to educate and train their personnel by job categories and by career stage. The companies believe that their systems can attract capable people who wish to work and can demonstrate their abilities under stable circumstances.

Model 2: opportunities to acquire advanced technology or to do satisfying jobs

A joint venture of a leading Japanese manufacturer of lighting systems for passenger cars located in Shanghai, set up an engineering centre within its plants in 2001. The centre has over 150 engineers, including R&D engineers, die designers and production engineers. Though the salary level set in the company is, at most, slightly higher than average for the industry, nevertheless the turnover ratio is as low as 0.5% per year, which is extremely low in Shanghai. The most important reason for the low turnover ratio is attributed to the opportunity to learn and acquire the latest technology. The company sends R&D engineers frequently to Japan, since the technological advancement of this industry in Japan is very rapid. To quit the company means that employees lose the opportunity to learn about the latest technology and may acquire only well-established knowledge in subsequent employment.

Another joint venture of a leading Japanese electronics company has an R&D centre with 200 engineers in the same location as its factory in Dalian. The R&D centre designs DVD players, which the Chinese factory solely produces for distribution in the worldwide production networks of the company. The salaries paid are only on a par with the average level in the area, but the turnover ratio of the engineers is nevertheless low. The company believes that satisfying jobs can help to retain talented local engineers.

Model 3: academic opportunities

An electronics component factory located in Beijing also benefits from retaining good human resources. The reason is the opportunity the firm gives for staff to further their academic careers. The company has an evening university programme run jointly with a famous university in Beijing. After employees get credits, they can be treated in the same way as graduates of the university. This is an attractive programme for young people who have the ability to go to university but for some reason are unable to attend as full-time students. The company also offers its own MBA programme to employees in cooperation with the university. After completion, of course, those employees are treated as MBA holders.

Managerial implications

The above cases provide some important clues as to how Japanese companies can escape the dilemma faced in maintaining competitiveness and, at the same time, localizing management. These cases suggest there are at least three means by which Japanese companies can recruit and retain capable people in China, whilst avoiding losing their own competitive edge. Firstly, Japanese affiliates need to find and recruit talented local personnel who are suited to the Japanese work style. Japanese affiliates should contrive to attract intelligent people who take a long-term perspective and prefer a work place where they can exercise their capabilities steadily to earn an immediate high-paying salary. Secondly, Japanese companies need to demonstrate clearly and concretely that working in their companies is beneficial to employees' career prospects. This is especially crucial in an environment where there is enthusiasm for progress and a desire among employees to upgrade their status, as both individuals and members of society. In addition to this, China is a society where people prefer explicit explanations to tacit understandings and the management of Japanese companies is advised to bear this in mind when communicating to local staff (Qiu 1997). Thirdly, the best way to retain capable employees is not always to reward achievement with money but with challenging and satisfying jobs. Actually, this is an essential element underpinning the success of Japanese companies at motivating talented employees in Japan (Takahashi 2005).

Conclusions

Scholars of international strategic human resources management (Li 2003, Takeuchi *et al.* 2003) have discussed the relationship between the core competencies of MNEs and HRM practice. This current study lies within this research stream. However, earlier research lacks a consideration of the linkage between features of corporate organisation, including work style (the subject of this study) and the core competencies of the firm. Therefore, this work does not take sufficient account of the difficulties associated with the international transfer of HRM practices and core competencies related to features of corporate organization. This is because the arguments that underpin this body of work lack the viewpoint of institutional complementarity, as discussed here. The present study is a tentative attempt to bridge the gap between international strategic HRM and institutional complementarity.

In terms of the localization of managers, the next challenge for Japanese affiliates in China will be to find and foster key persons more conscientiously and deliberately. A key person is defined as a manager or an employee who is acquainted with the strategy, organization, and the work style of the Japanese company at which he or she is working, who will exercise leadership by 'translating' the characteristics of the strategy and work organization into the 'language' that local employees can understand, and who will motivate his or her colleagues and subordinates. There are some companies which 'fortunately' encounter and foster this kind of manager. From now on, Japanese affiliates will be required to foster key persons taking a longer viewpoint. It will become increasingly important for candidates of key positions in Chinese affiliates of Japanese MNEs to have demonstrable experience of having fulfilled important tasks with experienced Japanese employees, as frequently as possible. It is also useful to send these candidates to the headquarters or to other business units in Japan for on-the-job training at important stages of their career development. The reason many Japanese employees develop a certain work style is not that they are Japanese. Instead, they acquire skills and know-how about the manner of work by working with their superiors and seniors. A Chinese vice president of a leading Japanese electronics company emphasized the significance of experience in working at Japanese companies or working closely with Japanese colleagues to perform important tasks. Many Japanese companies have already sent a number of Chinese employees to Japan. In many cases, however, Japanese companies are required to send them in order to introduce new products or new equipment. Of course, such experience is important. However, Japanese-affiliated companies should send employees abroad for training based on a long-term employment perspective in future, too.

Even if Japanese-affiliated companies can foster the development of key persons, they cannot execute all work tasks required by the company. The fewer the number of employees acquainted with a certain work style, the more that standardization of work is required. It will become crucial for Japanese-affiliated companies to recognize what mission, which tasks, and to what extent jobs can be standardized. The degree to which Japanese affiliates in China standardize jobs over time remains to be investigated.

Acknowledgements

Field research was funded by Grant-IN-AID for Scientific Research (Project Number: 15330045, 2003-2005 and Project Number: 19402032, 2007-2009), Musashi Open Research Centre Project: 2003-2007, and by the Visiting Scholar Programme of Musashi University.

Notes

1. Performance evaluation of in-house qualification systems does not rate the result of specific work but work behaviour: that is, the ability to execute work and attitude toward work.

Therefore, an in-house qualification system is an ability-based pay system. A number of Japanese companies have introduced so-called merit-based wage systems since the 1990s. However, in many cases the pay systems are actually based on employee ability. In those cases, we cannot differentiate between recently introduced merit pay systems and established in-house qualification systems. Furthermore, a merit system in which the results of the work of each employee is rated, requires the standardization of work. As discussed above, the standardization of jobs contradicts much of the manner of work in Japanese companies. This is why many Japanese companies have re-evaluated the usefulness of so-called merit-based pay systems. For more detailed discussion, see Itagaki (2008).

2. This information was collected in interview with a Chinese picture tube maker in Shanghai in August 2004. The parent company is owned by the local state administration and operates several joint ventures with Japanese electronics manufacturers.
3. Source: interview held at the headquarters of the company in August 2006.

References

Abo, T., ed., 1994a. *Japanese management and production systems and the US* [in Japanese]. Kyoto: Minerva Shobo.

Abo, T., ed., 1994b. *Hybrid factory: the Japanese production system in the United States*. New York: Oxford University Press.

Aoki, M., 1988. *Information, incentives, and bargaining in the Japanese economy*. Cambridge: Cambridge University Press.

Aoki, M., 1994. The contingent governance of teams: analysis of institutional complementarity. *International economic review*, 35 (3), 657–676.

Asanuma, B., 1997. *Japanese corporate organizations: mechanism for innovative adaptation: structure and functions of long-term trading ties* [in Japanese]. Tokyo: Toyo Keizai Shinposha.

Bartlett, C. and Yoshihara, H., 1992. New challenges for Japanese multinationals: is organization adaptation their Achilles heel? *In*: V. Pucik, N. Tichy, and C. Barnett, eds. *Globalizing management: creating and learning the competitive organization*. New York: John Wiley & Sons, 276–299.

Clark, K.B. and Fujimoto, T., 1991. *Product development performance: strategy, organization, and management in the world auto industry*. Boston: Harvard Business School Press.

Fujimoto, T., 2003. *Capacity-building war – why are Japanese automakers so strong?* [in Japanese]. Tokyo: Chuokoron-Shinsha Inc.

Fujimoto, T., *et al.*, 2002. Computerization and corporate organizations: from the perspectives of architecture and organizational capabilities. *In*: M. Okuno, T. Masahiro, K. Takemura, and J. Shintaku, eds. *Electronic society and market economy* [in Japanese]. Kita-Kyushu: Shinseisha, 97–134.

Ishida, M., 2003. *Social science of work – frontiers in labor studies* [in Japanese]. Kyoto: Minerva Shobo.

Ishida, M., *et al.*, 1997. *Lean production system in Japan: case of automotive industry* [in Japanese]. Tokyo: Chuou Keizaisha.

Itagaki, H., 1997. *The Japanese production system: hybrid factories in East Asia*. London: Macmillan Press.

Itagaki, H., 2002. Japanese multinational enterprises: paradox of high efficiency and low profitability. *Asian business and management*, 1 (1), 101–124.

Itagaki, H., 2008. Management system and strategy of the Japanese companies: its reality and future. *In*: T. Kawamura, ed. *Hybrid factories in the U.S. under the global economy*. New York: Oxford University Press (forthcoming).

Ito, H., 1994. Japanese human resource management from the viewpoint of incentive theory. *In*: M. Aoki and R. Dore, eds. *The Japanese firm: sources of competitive strength*. New York: Oxford University Press, 233–264.

Jacoby, M.S., 2005. *The embedded corporation: corporate governance and employment relations in Japan and the United States*. Princeton: Princeton University Press.

Kagono, T., *et al.*, 1985. *Strategic vs evolutionary management: a US-Japan comparison of strategy and organization*. Amsterdam: North-Holland.

Koike, K., 1988. *Understanding industrial relations in modern Japan*. London: The Macmillan Press.

Koike, K. and Inoki, T., eds, 1990. *Skill formation in Japan and Southeast Asia*. Tokyo: University of Tokyo Press.

Kopp, R., 1999. The rice-paper ceiling in Japanese companies: why it exists and persists. *In*: S.L. Beechler and A. Bird, eds. *Japanese multinationals abroad: individual and organizational learning*. New York: Oxford University Press, 107–128.

Kumon, H. and Abo, T., eds, 2004. *The hybrid factory in Europe: the Japanese management and production system transferred*. London: Palgrave.

Li, J., 2003. Strategic human resource management and MNE's performance in China. *International journal of human resource management*, 14 (2), 157–173.

Lifson, T.B., 1992. The management integration of Japanese business in America. *In*: S. Kumon and H. Rosovsky, eds. *The political economy of Japan: volume 3: cultural and social dynamics*. Stanford: Stanford University Press.

Liker, J.K., Fruin, W.M., and Adler, P.S., eds, 1999. *Remade in America: transplanting & transforming Japanese management systems*. New York: Oxford University Press.

Ma, C., 2000. *Labour matters of foreign affiliated companies in China* [in Japanese]. Tokyo: JETRO.

Marukawa, T., 1999. *Dynamics of emerging market: Chinese economy at transition era*. Tokyo: Nihon Boeki Shinkokai Ajia Keizai Kennkyujo.

Nikkei Sangyo Shinbun, 2005. The salary of Chinese who are proficient in Japanese is going up. May 10, p. 17.

Nonaka, I., 1988. Toward middle-up-down management: accelerating information creation. *Sloan management review*, 29 (3), 9–18.

NSS, *See* Nikkei Sangyo Shinbun.

Pucik, V., 1999. When performance does not matter: human resource management in Japanese-owned U.S. Affiliates. *In*: S.L. Beechler and A. Bird, eds. *Japanese multinationals abroad: individual and organizational learning*. New York: Oxford University Press, 169–188.

Qiu, Y., 1997. *Structure of thought of Chinese* [in Japanese]. Tokyo: Chuoukouronsha.

Seki, M. and Fan, J.T., 2004. *Localization of Japanese affiliated companies in China* [in Japanese]. Tokyo: Shinhyouron.

Shiraki, M., ed., 2006. *Human resource management toward China shift* [in Japanese]. Tokyo: Hakutoshobou.

Takahashi, N., 2005. *Strategy of 'management to rear': path to post merit system*. Tokyo: Kodansha.

Takeuchi, N., Wakabayashi, M., and Chen, Z.G., 2003. The strategic HRM configuration for competitive advantage: evidence from Japanese firms in China and Taiwan. *Asia Pacific journal of management*, 20 (4), 447–480.

Tanaka, N., 2006. Shanghai Jihou: is it wrong the way of salary payment by Japanese affiliated companies? *Nikkei Business Online*, 6 June. Available from: http://business.nikkeibp.co.jp

CONCLUSIONS AND IMPLICATIONS

The changing role of China in the transformation of corporate Japan

Adam R. Cross[a] and Sierk A. Horn[b]

[a]Leeds University Business School, Maurice Keyworth Building, University of Leeds, Leeds LS2 9JT, UK; [b]Department of East Asian Studies, School of Modern Languages and Cultures, University of Leeds, Leeds LS2 9JT, UK

This conclusion to the special issue, 'Cross-cultural Management Practices in East Asia: Lessons for Japanese MNEs', examines how Japanese firms are responding to, and are affected by, increasing engagement with the Chinese economy. In addition to the three specific themes identified *a priori* to be of greatest concern to the transformation of corporate Japan (namely marketing and distribution, inter-corporate networks and human resources management), two additional themes can be discerned. These relate to institutional evolution and the challenges of localization. It is concluded that Japanese firms can be shown to demonstrate flexibility in their engagement with China within this analytical framework.

Introduction

In the wake of the longest recession Japan has experienced in the post-war era, the case for major reform of the Japanese economic system in general, and of the Japanese corporate system in particular, is generally considered incontrovertible by scholars and Japanese policy-makers alike. Indeed, many of the measures advocated by supporters of reform have already been implemented by a significant number of Japanese firms, not only large, internationally-oriented ones, such as Toyota, Canon, Yamaha, Hitachi and Mitsubishi but numerous small- and medium- sized companies as well (*The Economist* 2007c). For this reason alone, it is important for scholars to revisit conventional wisdom concerning the performance and competitiveness of Japanese firms. The task for international business scholarship, in particular, is to keep abreast of how Japanese multinational enterprises (MNEs) are now responding to the ongoing challenges of globalisation in light of the changes to organisational structures and management practices that have been undertaken. Collectively, the studies in this special issue contribute towards this task.

It would, of course, be shortsighted to attribute the trigger of corporate reform solely to deregulatory measures in Japan and other internal forces. 'Gaiatsu' – or pressure from abroad – has long played an important role in the (albeit often slow) evolution of Japanese corporate practice, and this continues to be in evidence today. In January 2007, a workshop took place at the University of Leeds to examine one particularly prominent (and, arguably, predominant) force for change, namely the rise of China in the regional and global economy. As noted in the 'Introduction' to this special issue, when the workshop was conceived a large amount of research on the activities of Japanese firms in China, especially in the field of international business, concentrated mainly on explaining sub-national location choice, typically using econometric modeling and data drawn from surveys of Japanese firms reported in Toyo Keizai's annual publication *Japanese overseas investment* (*Kaigai Shinshutsu Kigyô Sôran*), combined with province-level data published by the National Bureau of Statistics of China and other official sources. While this research has been helpful in identifying how the foreign direct investment (FDI) strategies of Japanese MNEs in China have evolved over time in response to location-specific factors such as incremental market opening, regional economic growth, differential labour costs, agglomeration externalities and other effects, this literature pays little attention to how the performance, management practices and strategic development of Japanese firms, both within and outside China, are being influenced by their engagement with the Chinese economy. Our intention with this special issue is to open a new chapter of research which examines in an explicit way the effect of China on the transformation of corporate Japan. Various facets of this topic are explored in the contributions from a number of different, though inter-related, perspectives.

In this conclusion, we assess and discuss the individual and combined contributions made by the studies included here within the context of the three underlying themes we establish in the 'Introduction', namely marketing and distribution, inter-corporate networks and human resources management. Before we do this, however, it is informative first to reflect upon a number of recent developments that illustrate what might be described as the Janus face of China's economic rise, and which have the potential to shape our understanding of how Japanese firms are now approaching their engagement with China.

The most obvious manifestation is the continued growth of the Chinese economy and its rate of integration with the global economy. Statistics show that China's gross domestic product (GDP) has consistently grown by between 7% and 12% per annum since 1992. In 2007, China for the first time contributed more to the growth of global GDP than did the USA (*The Economist* 2007a). A number of indicators point to the level of integration of China with the global economy. For example, together, China and Hong Kong SAR (Special Administrative Region) accounted for more merchandise exports in dollar terms than any other economy in 2007; and in 2006 they were host to the world's third largest stock of FDI (UNCTAD 2007). Capital outflows from China are also on the rise (Buckley *et al.* 2007b). Recently, although the World Bank has revised downwards the size of the Chinese economy in dollar terms following the adoption of a new method for calculating purchasing power parity (PPP), statistics show that China's GDP is presently the world's second largest. A number of commentators suggest that China will overtake the US as the world's largest economy (in PPP terms) by 2018 (*The Economist* 2007d). Of course, caution is required when simply extrapolating present day trends into the future: much the same was predicted for the Japanese economy during its 'economic miracle' period. Nevertheless, it is clear that China is poised to become (at least) an important engine of growth for the world economy. As noted in the 'Introduction', given its geographic proximity, economic complementarity and the competitive advantages of many of its firms, especially with regard to brand equity and innovatory and technological capability, Japan – an export nation 'par excellence' – is particularly well placed to exploit the opportunities that China now presents. The role of China as an important source of growth for Japanese firms, and for the Japanese economy in general, is brought into particularly sharp relief when juxtaposed against the evident slowdown of a number of industrialized economies, not least the USA, following the global financial crisis which began in August 2007 amid concerns surrounding American sub-prime mortgage lending and other factors. Much of the recent recovery of the Japanese economy has been export-led, with the US continuing in its traditional role as a prime market for Japanese goods (*The Economist* 2008). For this reason, Japan is especially vulnerable to a slowdown in the US economy: indeed, year-on-year trade statistics show that in September 2007 Japanese exports to the US fell by 9.2%, the largest monthly decline in four years (*The Economist* 2007b). Clearly, the ability to readjust internationalization strategies away from slowing industrialized economies and to tap upswings in the business cycles of developing countries in Asia (such as China) will be instrumental to the future performance of many Japanese firms. This is one facet to the Janus face of China's rise.

The contrary facet is multidimensional and is encapsulated in the concept of 'China risk'. Such risk is manifested in various ways, each with the potential to lessen the attractiveness of China as a target market or production base relative to other locations, not only for Japanese firms but for all nationalities of MNEs. At a political level, the international response to China's stance towards issues such as Tibet, ethnic minorities and human rights has been conspicuous by its silence in diplomatic and corporate circles, despite, for example, numerous public demonstrations around the world in the run-up to the Beijing Olympics in 2008. Cross-strait relations, regional militarism, and the increasing willingness of China to use its economic weight in regional agreements and rules-setting concerning, for example, trade, investment, environment and security, are further possible sources of future political tension in the region, especially should the national interests of Japan be challenged. At an economic level, the sustainability of China's recent economic growth has been questioned, with upward pressure on the Renminbi, inflationary pressures, dramatic stockmarket corrections and a growing threat of trade sanctions and other protectionist measures vis-à-vis the USA (Yoshida and Ito 2006) all being highlighted as possible sources of economic uncertainty (*The Economist* 2007a). At a societal level nationalism in China is resurgent, with one outcome being increasingly frequent boycotts of foreign goods (some of which is purported to have been government sanctioned). Economic slowdown, rising unemployment (following reform of the State sector) and rising commodity prices (especially food prices) are further potential precursors to social upheaval in China. Some of this risk is already reflected in international business trends. For example, annual aggregate FDI flows to China declined (by 4%) for the first time in seven years in 2006, with rising production costs and labour shortages in the coastal regions being cited as key contributory factors (UNCTAD 2007, see also Delios *et al.* in this special issue). Japanese firms also have to confront a number of additional challenges that are less relevant to other nationality firms, not least in relation to: (i) negative country-of-origin effects (anti-Japanese sentiment remains evident in many parts of Chinese society) (JETRO 2005); and (ii) the problems of localizing firm specific advantages which have evolved primarily to strengthen competitiveness in technologically advanced home markets. The twin notions of China as a key source of growth for corporate Japan and 'China risk' have come to represent two extreme points of view around which oscillate debates concerning the types of new business frameworks that will emerge in East Asia as a consequence of China's rise.

With this backdrop in mind, it is important for scholarship to generate fresh insights and understanding of the changes underway in Japanese firms, at plant level and in the parent organisation, vis-à-vis China's growing regional centripetal force. Given the rapidity of economic change in East Asia and the heterogeneity of China, amongst other things, this is no easy task. Our overarching objective in compiling this collection has been to demonstrate that China is indeed acting as an important agent provocateur, if not a catalyst of change, for Japanese firms not least by serving as an increasingly accessible market and by continuing to be an important low cost production location. When selecting studies for inclusion, we prioritized those by Asian scholars and scholars based in Asia, and also those that were informed primarily by qualitative methodologies and extensive fieldwork. This is because we wanted to avoid an analysis overly dominated by Euro- or US-centric viewpoints and to provide a fresh and, perhaps more importantly, a varied look at the position of China in the strategies of Japanese MNEs from a micro-level perspective. As such, the overall contribution of this special issue can be summed very quickly: it underscores the current and future importance of China for corporate Japan.

The contributions address a range of issues that help to improve our understanding of Japanese firms in China. As such, the special issue contributes in a number of ways to the burgeoning literature on the internationalization of developed economy MNEs to emerging markets (Meyer 2004, Ramamurti 2004, see Wright *et al.* 2005 for a survey). A number of questions have been answered, and some have not, while further questions have been raised. In addition to the general and recurrent thematic thread of corporate transformation and change running through all of the contributions, a further two specific themes that connect many of the contributions are also in evidence: namely (i) institutional and regulatory change as key determinants of the corporate strategies and behaviour of firms; and (ii) the challenges of localization and adaptation. In the 'Introduction', we categorize and discuss these challenges under three main headings, namely marketing and distribution, inter-corporate networks and human resources management (HRM). Although it can be argued that this categorization is somewhat arbitrary, and it is certainly not exhaustive, it does serve as a helpful starting-point for understanding what aspects of the transformation of corporate Japan are most likely to be shaped by China's growing economic presence in East Asia. It is indicative of where future research should profitably focus attention. Of course, it is inevitable that the evolution of, and interactions between, the Chinese and Japanese economies will produce outcomes that are difficult to envisage within current frameworks of understanding. This strengthens our fundamental contention that the subject requires ongoing scrutiny and investigation. With this proviso in mind, we now consider the contributions made by the research presented in this special issue.

Corporate transformation

Two of the contributions inform our understanding of the types of changes being implemented by Japanese MNEs to improve domestic and international competitiveness levels. In his study, Peter Buckley compares the management styles and practices of Japanese MNEs today to those of the mid-1980s, when their international expansion was in its heyday. Buckley argues that a sizeable number of Japanese firms have successfully moulded their business models, corporate networks and HRM systems – all well established in the literature as key contributors to the success of the 'J-system' (both at home and abroad) – to confront the economic realities of globalization. In this respect, it can be argued that a significant number of Japanese MNEs have demonstrated an equivalent degree of flexibility and adaptability as their Western counterparts, although, because their administrative heritage differs, so their starting points differ. Nonetheless, as Peter Buckley asserts, Japanese MNEs continue to be distinctive in a number of important respects, not least with regard to the insularity of internal capital markets, upper management labour markets and knowledge management and innovation systems. This, it is argued, has given rise to *hybridity* amongst Japanese MNE, with management practices (insofar as this can be generalized) falling somewhere between the classic 'international' (or ethnocentric) and 'global' (or geocentric) approaches to international management and strategy (Perlmutter 1969, Ghoshal and Nohria 1993, Segal-Horn and Faulkner 1999). It remains to be seen whether such hybridity is transitory or optimal, given the evident home-country embeddedness of many Japanese firms. In this respect, comparative research on the performance of hybrid versus traditional ('J-type') MNEs that have adopted and incorporated fewer Western-style management practices and processes would be informative. Such research would also illuminate the growing literature on the evolution of corporate governance in Japan (see, for example, Shibagaki 2000, Jürgens 2003, Yoshikawa *et al.* 2006, Aoki *et al.* 2007) with the addition of the important international dimension.

The contribution by Tim Goydke also demonstrates that Japanese corporatism is changing. Goydke examines the transformation of Japanese MNEs from a comparative standpoint, but instead of adopting a longitudinal perspective, an intra-industry comparison is made. This is done by investigating the transformation of two firms from distinctive institutional settings, namely Japan Post and Deutsche Post, with the privatization of the former informed by that of the latter, as the study reveals. Inevitably, the issues discussed in these studies can only be a snapshot of the evolving nature of the 'J-system'. Nonetheless, they inform the literature on corporate governance and organizational change among Japanese firms. While the jury is still out on what elements of the Japanese management system will endure over the coming years, ongoing reforms indicate that Japanese firms are demonstrating – once again – an ability to adapt to external challenges of globalization in many important respects.

Institutional and regulatory evolution

In the 'Introduction', we make the case that China represents an ideal lens through which to investigate the strategic responses of firms to regulatory change in emerging markets. The contribution by Delios *et al.* supports this proposition by relating the inbound FDI behaviour of Japanese firms to institutional change in China. This macro-level analysis is further complemented by two contributions that reveal the effect of institutions on the market entry and development strategies of Japanese firms in China at a micro-level. As we elaborate below, the entry of Toyota Group to China, which is examined in the study by Faith Hatani, was delayed by the inability of the core firm to obtain formal approval for local production because of the stipulations of the country's ninth five-year plan, which concerned the development of the domestic automobile industry. Similarly, in Tomoo Marukawa's investigation of the entry of Japanese mobile telephone manufacturers to China, regulations concerning local content requirements promoted the competitiveness of indigenous manufacturers in particular market segments. Two further studies allude to the influencing role of institutions in emerging markets, but in the specific context of Japanese internationalization. As discussed in the 'Introduction', a large proportion of Japanese FDI to China has historically gravitated towards locations with significant amounts of prior investments by Japanese and other nationality MNEs. It can be argued that the agglomerative behaviour of firms is a response, at least in part, to the problems of under-developed market institutions because agglomeration externalities help compensate firms for inefficient labour markets and inefficient intermediate and final product markets. However, as shown by the contributions of both Sierk Horn and Delios *et al.*, Japanese MNEs have demonstrated greater willingness in recent years to invest away from traditional investment 'hotspots' in China. Institutional theorists may characterize this development as a response to the transition towards more market oriented institutions in China, although this theoretical relationship is not explored explicitly by the contributors to this special issue in such terms. Nonetheless, a number of ramifications for research on business in emerging markets can be identified. First, within the international business strategy literature there is a debate concerning which theoretical approaches and methodologies offer greatest explanatory power when studying business in emerging market contexts (Wright *et al.* 2005). Four conceptual perspectives have been used in previous research, namely transaction cost theory, agency theory, resource-based theory, and institutional theory (Hoskisson *et al.* 2000, Peng *et al.* 2001). The contributions presented here suggest that it is the institutional theory approach that has particular resonance for our understanding of Japanese business in China, especially compared with the resource-based theory: after all, Japanese firms in both the automobile and telecommunications industries hold substantial core competencies in technology-related capabilities, knowledge and learning which, it can be argued, were insufficient in helping Japanese firms to build their competitiveness in this market. Second, the contributions reveal that case study methodologies that focus on particular industries and firms are particularly informative in revealing *how* institutions matter to international business in emerging country settings. This is because such methods enable scholars to discern the nuanced responses of firms to institutional and regulatory change over time in a way that can be difficult to achieve convincingly with analyses of macro-level economic data. Three, the contributions highlight the importance for research on foreign business strategy in China to take full and proper account of institutional change, especially in longitudinal studies, particularly as China continues to adopt a more market-oriented economy as a consequence of its World Trade Organisation (WTO) accession conditions and other stimuli. Finally, the contributions point to the importance of the concept of 'insider' and 'outsider' firms in countries where institutions are in transition. In some important respects, for example, it can be argued that the Toyota Group was a latecomer to China because it was an 'outsider firm' and, as such, was unable to influence policy formulation and implementation in its favour in the 1990s, unlike other global players in the automobile industry, as Faith Hatani discusses. This highlights the importance of firms establishing good relations with government agencies at national and sub-national levels in emerging countries, especially when, for whatever reason, laws and regulations are opaque or are applied inconsistently. In the case of China, a capacity for relationship-building is commonly encapsulated in the familiar concept of '*guanxi*' (see Buckley *et al.* 2006), although it is of course important in other emerging market contexts, too. Indeed, it is not uncommon for Japanese firms to now employ a designated 'political office' charged with dealing with government agencies and officials in China. It follows that it is important for research on foreign business strategy in China and other emerging markets to continue to scrutinize the moderating role of firms' relationships with governments and institutions on market entry and development performance.

Marketing and distribution

A substantial body of literature has grown to demonstrate that adaptation and localization are fundamental to the success of international business activities (for a discussion see Tallman and Yip 2001). However, this exposes one of the weaknesses commonly attributed to Japanese MNEs, which is that they can often find it difficult to design appropriately nuanced international marketing strategies. Reasons cited include the predominantly home-market orientation of Japanese firms (Collinson and Rugman 2008), their reluctance to decentralize key activities and functions to local markets (which Peter

Buckley also notes in his contribution) and the pursuit of geocentric as opposed to polycentric (or multidomestic) strategies. The familiar trade-off is that the adoption of a 'global strategy' and a focus on high-income consumers allows developed country MNEs to generate substantial scale economies in production and marketing, but at the cost of responsiveness to local market conditions (Segal-Horn and Faulkner 1999). A number of studies point to the limitations associated with firms simply extending strategies used globally to emerging market contexts (London and Hart 2004, Wright *et al.* 2005). The main criticism is that such an approach does not allow for the creation of business models that adequately address the specific demands of lower income consumers. Investigation of the extent to which Japanese firms have revised and adapted their approaches to international marketing and market servicing in response to idiosyncrasies associated with the Chinese business environment provides a useful addition to this literature. Three of the contributions tackle this issue directly, and reveal contrasting findings. Taken together, they illustrate a multifarious spectrum of localization efforts among Japanese firms, ranging from a high degree of intercultural awareness and adaptation on the one hand, to inflexibility and insensitivity to local market peculiarities on the other. This illustrates the shortcomings of assuming a homogenous corporate response of Japanese firms to the challenges of globalization, and that performance and behaviour are highly contingent upon industry and firm-specific factors.

In his contribution, Sierk Horn highlights the special challenges faced by Japanese firms in China besides those experienced by MNEs in general, especially with regard to persistent anti-Japanese sentiment (that is, negative country-of-origin effects). Historically, this has been seen as a significant constraint on the sales of some Japanese brands and has hampered the ability of Japanese affiliates to recruit skilled staff, amongst other things. Nonetheless, a number of Japanese firms are shown to have adapted their business models successfully to address Chinese consumers (especially upper and middle income consumers) through the use of a variety of highly focused market segmentation techniques. These have been directed towards particular consumer types (early adopters, for example); demographic groupings (young professionals); geographic locations (metropolitan and urban areas), and product offerings (typically high-end, luxury products). Success is also attributed to the compression of product life cycles and accelerated product launches in response to high demand for novelty and innovation in target market segments. A strong case is made that Japanese firms have accomplished this by deviating from familiar brand and marketing strategies used at home. To this extent, Japanese MNEs seem to have avoided the pitfall, as advanced in the international strategy literature (see Wright *et al.* 2005), of simply extending to China those strategies and techniques traditionally used in domestic or industrialized country markets. This flexibility demonstrates that Japanese MNEs do have the capability of adjusting familiar business models when servicing international markets and such learning, if transferred to other parts of the organization, may act as an important stimulus to the transformation of marketing practices in domestic and other markets.

The contribution by Tomoo Marukawa, by contrast, offers an interesting and important counterview and provides partial support for the body of research that argues that Japanese firms find it difficult to localize their international marketing strategies, for reasons discussed above. In a study of the performance of Japanese mobile telephone manufacturers in China, it is shown that, despite the possession of both technological advantages and early-mover status, Japanese firms in this industry have found it difficult to establish a significant market position in China and, in some instances, this has led to market retreat. Tomoo Marukawa attributes this to an inability, or disinclination, to develop the specific capabilities needed to compete effectively with indigenous manufacturers and other nationality firms in China. This inflexibility is due, it is argued, to an over-reliance on product superiority and technological leadership, insufficient decentralisation of new product development and related functions to China, and an inability to establish appropriate distribution-related capabilities. In short, to be successful in China, Japanese manufacturers in this industry were required to acquire capabilities not needed in Japan. In some respects, this finding is surprising, given that novelty and high customer responsiveness are key success factors in mobile telecommunications, especially in Japan, which is generally considered to be in the vanguard of technological innovation in the industry. One explanation is that Japanese telecommunications companies have focused their marketing efforts mainly on domestic markets, because this is where technological innovation is most intense and where local players are required to be highly flexible in order to remain competitive. To this extent, the case of Japanese telecommunications companies in China provides further evidence of the difficulty that Japanese firms can experience in realigning corporate priorities away from home to overseas markets (even those with substantial opportunities), and that decentralisation of decision-making, flexibility and commitment to market are capabilities that are not acquired quickly by some Japanese MNEs. While this may be an industry-specific effect, it nevertheless offers a cautionary perspective on the extent to which organizational learning in emerging market contexts is effective as Japanese MNEs seek to transform and adapt their international marketing practices.

The case study by Tim Goydke on the internationalisation of Japan Post reports a somewhat mixed picture, with aspects of both market focus and inflexibility found. Despite the disadvantage of latecomer status following its relatively recent privatization, Japan Post has been successful in carving out a market niche by focussing on the provision of specific services (in this case, express delivery) and by concentrating on specific geographic markets, mainly in the Asia Pacific region, where China plays a pivotal role. However, by targeting Japanese customers primarily, a certain inflexibility to the company's international marketing approach is revealed. This, in turn, alludes to the enduring nature of the dependency of Japanese firms on agglomeration externalities (in this case, close relations with Japanese customers) in the internationalisation process. The example of Japan Post, however, should not overshadow the emergent phenomenon demonstrated by many Japanese firms of overcoming agglomeration dependencies, as the contribution by Delios *et al.* highlights. They suggest that regional diversification of Japanese FDI in China, and the concomitant expansion of production and sales networks away from traditional investment locations in the Yangtze and Pearl River Delta regions, indicates that investing firms are increasingly willing to loosen their linkages with established networks and territories in response to changes to the competitive environment and other factors. As the authors point out, key variables for this trend are industry affiliation and the level of technological development of the host region.

To sum up the contributions to our theme of marketing and distribution, it is clear from the studies that the willingness and ability of Japanese firms to localize their marketing efforts in emerging economies such as China are influenced by both exogenous and endogenous factors. A willingness to engage and expand at the local level (as evidenced by decentralisation, flexibility, and adaptability) can be hindered by firm and industry-specific exigencies, while location factors (such as location-industry mix, local government initiatives, socio-demographics) also predetermine to a great extent how flexible Japanese firms are prepared to be. Research that investigates the performance of Japanese firms away from traditional agglomerations in China and their ability to localize production and management systems in China is likely to generate valuable insights for our understanding of how they are developing and refining their international marketing skills and business models outside of familiar developed country contexts.

One topic we consider important to our understanding of the strategies of developed country firms in emerging countries (see the 'Introduction') is not addressed directly by the contributors, however. This concerns the servicing of low income consumers ('marketing to the poor'). In many respects, the success of Japanese firms reported in the contributions is a product of successful targeting and market skimming of middle and high income consumer segments, with lower income, mass-market segments relinquished (voluntarily or under external pressure) either to domestic competition or East Asian competitors (especially South Korean and Taiwanese firms). While a focussed strategy clearly has many advantages in China, the corollary is that indigenous manufacturers (or other companies) may be given sufficient competitive 'space' in low-end market segments to establish strong market positions, and this may be used as a base from which to expand into higher income consumer segments in future, both in China and more widely. Already, there is a body of literature to suggest that the competitiveness of Chinese firms is improving as a direct consequence of the demonstration and spill-over effects of FDI (see Buckley *et al.* 2002, 2007a). We believe this has several important implications for both future research and management practice. Firstly, it is important to raise understanding of the types of business models that developed country firms are adopting to address middle and low income consumers in emerging countries such as China; and, second, it is important to understand how and in what ways the competitiveness of indigenous Chinese firms is changing, and how this might impact the competitive environment of markets both within and outside China. Already, a number of Japanese firms such as Toyota and Shiseido have started to extend their product and brand portfolios to appeal to a much broader customer base. This is likely to bring them into more direct competition with other foreign players in East Asia and beyond. It will be interesting to see just how Japanese firms fine-tune their business models in response.

Inter-corporate networks

One of the most discussed particularities of Japan's industrial structure and economic 'catch-up' in the post-war era is the keiretsu (a generic term within which is subsumed a range of mainly vertically and horizontally organised groupings of firms). That keiretsu companies have undergone substantive change has been heavily commented upon since the late 1990s (Park and Kim 2003, Yoshikawa *et al.* 2006). The challenges associated with the international extension and integration of supply chains of Japanese MNEs in general, and their FDI activities in emerging markets in particular, have also received some attention in the literature (Itagaki 1997, Yusuf *et al.* 2004). While corporate alignments are changing substantially (not least in light of corporate restructuring in Japan itself), the role of suppliers in inter-firm networks is in the process of being redefined. Several of the contributions raise our understanding of this process within a specific country context.

The contribution by Faith Hatani shows that 'enforced' organisational adaptation can be proactively turned into a virtue and, as such, it provides a further illustration of the adaptability and flexibility of Japanese firms as they expand their operations to countries such as China. However, the stimulus here relates less to changes in Chinese consumption patterns and more to the evolving institutional setting. The case of Toyota reveals atypical entry behaviour by a keiretsu firm, in that the entry of the core firm is preceded by that of group member and supplier firms in a process that is termed 'pre-clusterization'. The study highlights the enduring nature of keiretsu structures in some quarters of Japanese industry (despite the trend for corporate restructuring noted in the 'Introduction' and in Peter Buckley's contribution). However, it suggests that the deployment of this structure can be adapted to cope with the particular regulatory environment experienced by the core firm in evolving emerging market settings. In this case, group suppliers invested well in advance of the core firm in response to both encouragement from Toyota and the availability of various investment incentives provided by the Chinese authorities. Of course, it remains to be seen whether this was a 'one-off' strategic response necessitated by the evolutionary nature of regulatory conditions of a particular industry in China during a specific period of time, or whether similar examples of such organisational flexibility and adaptation can be demonstrated for other keiretsu firms in China or in other countries where incremental market opening is found. When viewed alongside the contributions by Delios *et al.* and Sierk Horn, this study provides some evidence that, with respect to production networks, Japanese MNEs have not fully abandoned agglomeration dependency in China, which prior literature shows has historically been an important source of competitive advantage. Nonetheless, it could be argued that China presents Japanese MNEs with an opportunity to trial new forms of inter-firm systems and buyer-supplier relationships. The study of Toyota in China illustrates an example of such experimentation: here, group suppliers are not only ready to accept a higher risk on market entry but, as first-movers, they are also instrumental in helping to establish a new dimension to the keiretsu structure in a specific country context. It will be important for research to continue to investigate the new types of inter-firm relationships into which Japanese firms enter, both in Japan and in different country and industry settings, as the corporate transformation process progresses.

Human resources management

A number of studies point to the localization of HRM as a key success factor for MNEs (see Dowling and Welch 2004). As discussed in the 'Introduction', the Japanese employment system contrasts in many important respects to Anglo-Saxon work practises, which tend to emphasise meritocratic systems in which individual results-orientation is given preference over group performance. In the case of China, there are strong reasons for revisiting these issues for Japanese firms, most notably because of the (seemingly) better fit between Western style HRM practices and characteristics of the Chinese labour market (such as mobility of labour, for example). Although they have differing standpoints, the contributions by both Hiroshi Itagaki and Felfe and Yan reveal the potential gains to Japanese firms of actively pursuing the localization of HRM policies and practices. The contribution by Hiroshi Itagaki, for example, points to the importance of Japanese firms reflecting local expectations and changes to recruiting and promotion processes through the introduction of measures that encourage transparency, job motivation and staff retention, amongst other things. In order to address staff retention issues in particular this also means the removal of 'glass ceilings' to the promotion of local employees, and the adoption of initiatives such as the possibility of education and training elsewhere within the organisation, especially at the headquarters in Japan. At the same time, the selection (and preparation) of qualified Japanese expatriates with the competence to identify and promote key local personnel is likely to become of increasing importance. Given the shortage of suitably skilled personnel in some quarters of the Japanese economy, the ability of Japanese firms to tap into local expertise in China and to develop effective cross-functional and cross-border teams is likely to become all the more significant to corporate success. If the internationalization of Japanese HRM continues to proceed with an emphasis on localization of employment and recruitment practices in countries such as China, and if this is accompanied by increased 'permeability' to the influx of skills and expertise of foreign employees across the organization as a whole, this may help to further ameliorate rigidities in Japanese labour relations. Beyond the immediate implications for improving our understanding of how HRM practices are evolving in emerging markets, the relationship between localization and transformation of corporate Japan points to the need for further research on how effective Japanese firms are at absorbing and learning from foreign employees.

Meanwhile, the contribution by Felfe and Yan demonstrates that commitment of employees to the workgroup is of particular importance to the performance of organizations in collectivistic societies such as China, compared to more individualistic contexts (in this case Germany). The implication of this finding is that raising workgroup commitment raises commitment to the organization as a whole. This finding is of special relevance to Japanese firms in China, who often experience difficulties in recruiting and retaining skilled staff, as the contribution by Itagaki also acknowledges. In their recommendations to senior management, Felfe and Yan suggest that actions that help to improve team climate, and that facilitate mutual understanding, communication and informal contact, can also make an important contribution to raising team effectiveness for the benefit of the organization as a whole. The importance of workgroup commitment in China (arguably a cornerstone of Japanese HRM practice), demonstrates that Japanese firms need to carefully balance the supposed gains of adopting Anglo-Saxon work practices against established and familiar management systems when extending their operations into Asia.

Concluding remarks

The purpose of this special issue has been to directly establish the theoretical relationship between corporate transformation in Japan and the engagement of Japanese firms with the Chinese economy. Despite receiving less attention in mainstream international business literature than in their heyday of the 1990s, many Japanese MNEs are key international players and Japan remains a major source of FDI for many developing countries. Following Deng Xiaoping's Open Door policies and a careful commitment to the promotion of foreign trade and inward investment, China has quickly emerged as a key destination of Japanese FDI in East Asia. Japanese companies have recently complemented their traditional portfolio of activities (primarily labour-intensive, low value added, assembly production) with market-seeking and technology intensive investments. Not only are Japanese MNEs in the process of rapidly rolling out their sales networks across China, they are also increasing their activities by localising research and development. With respect to numbers of production and R&D affiliates, Japanese firms have established a presence in China that is on a par with their activities in North America, Europe and Southeast Asia. At the same time, and as the contributions to this special issue show, intensification of their engagement with China has created substantial challenges for Japanese firms. Examined collectively, the contributions show that there is neither a characteristically Japanese nor a uniquely Japanese response to the rapidly evolving Chinese market. As for other nationalities of firms, Japanese MNEs are required to adapt to the particularities of the Chinese market – especially in relation to institutional change, complexity and market heterogeneity – and some have demonstrated sufficient flexibility in adjusting their business models and localizing management techniques and practices accordingly, while others have not. If we accept the common assumption that internationalization is key for the survival of Japanese firms, and for the expansion of the Japanese economy as a whole, then the ability of Japanese MNEs to find the right balance between continuity and change of the J-system becomes paramount. The approach of Japanese firms to China is a case in point, as illustrated by the key themes of this special issue. In addition to playing a major role in the regional integration of the Japanese economy as a production location and target market, China also serves as a useful experimental setting for advancing our theoretical understanding and knowledge of the ongoing internationalization efforts of Japanese MNEs in other parts of the developing world. As such, it is likely that future research on Japanese firms in China will make important contributions to the international business strategy and marketing literatures. In particular, it is important that scholarship continues to advance our understanding of how corporate reform and business innovation processes are being fine-tuned by Japanese firms in light of Asia's economic integration, with China as a new or complementing gravity centre. After all, Japanese firms remain key players on the international business stage.

However, it is important to recognize that China represents only one, albeit a very important, growth opportunity for Japanese firms as they strive to defend and promote their competitive advantages abroad. Japanese firms have recently (re)intensified their regional involvement in Southeast Asia, a process in which bilateral and multilateral trade and investment agreements are playing an important facilitating role (Dent 2008). In many respects, Japanese firms are leading the way in establishing extensive cross-border production networks in the region and this is leading to the emergence of completely new production patterns and cross-border production networks. Given both 'China risk' and the challenges of operating in China, especially away from familiar business agglomerations and production networks, it will be interesting to see if, how and to what extent China will be integrated in Southeast and East Asian production networks vis-à-vis other attractive production locations, such as Thailand and Vietnam. In terms of markets, another important aspect for research to consider concerns the role that other large emerging markets and smaller developing countries will play in the international strategy of Japanese firms. India is a case in point. Although Japanese MNEs have had a presence in India for several decades, inbound FDI from Japan has only recently begun to accelerate, with Japanese manufacturers now investing in significant numbers in more economically advanced locations such as Bangalore and Chennai. It will be interesting to see whether the behaviour and performance of Japanese firms in China as portrayed in this special issue (such as agglomeration followed by decentralization and responses to institutional change) are mirrored in other emerging country research contexts or whether China is a special case in the internationalization of Japanese MNEs.

In the early 1980s, the former US Ambassador to Japan, Mike Mansfield, commented that '[t]he US-Japan relationship is the most important bilateral relationship in the world, bar none.' Recent rapprochement at the political level between Japan and China will set the course for further intensification of the already strong linkages between these two economic powerhouses. The official visit to China of Japan's current prime minister, Yasuo Fukuda (son of Takeo Fukuda, the 67th prime minister of Japan who re-established diplomatic ties with China in 1978), and his meetings with the Chinese president, Hu Jintao, and Premier of the State Council, Wen Jiabao, in December 2007 point towards a further (re)warming of Sino-Japanese relations. While neither country is in the position yet, politically, to admit to strong economic ties (Gurtov 2007), Japan arguably may soon come to outgrow Mansfield's 'most important relationship' with a nascent economic triumvirate of China, Japan and the USA as one plausible scenario (Dollar 2007). China and Japan already account jointly for around 22% of the world's GDP (on a PPP basis), 22% of the world's population, and 29% of the world's labour force. Together, they also occupy around 13% of world exports and 11% of world imports (World Bank 2007b). If the breadth and depth of Sino-Japanese business connexions do expand further, this may see the world's economic epicentre gravitating towards a dynamic East Asia with these two countries at its axis. Much will depend on how successful Japanese firms are at adapting their business models and strategies in response to China's rise. The challenge for research is to continue to refine our understanding of the adaptation process and the subsequent performance of Japanese firms.

References

Aoki, M., Jackson, G., and Miyajima, H., eds, 2007. *Corporate governance in Japan: institutional change and organizational diversity*. Oxford: Oxford University Press.

Buckley, P.J., Clegg, L.J., and Tan, H., 2006. Cultural awareness in knowledge transfer to China – the role of guanxi and mianzi. *Journal of world business*, 41 (3), 275–288.

Buckley, P.J., Clegg, L.J., and Wang, C., 2002. The impact of inward FDI on the performance of Chinese manufacturing firms. *Journal of international business studies*, 33 (2), 637–655.

Buckley, P.J., Clegg, L.J., and Wang, C., 2007a. Is the relationship between inward FDI and spillover effects linear? An empirical examination of the case of China. *Journal of international business studies*, 38 (3), 447–459.

Buckley, P.J., Clegg, L.J., Cross, A.R., Liu, X., Voss, H., and Zheng, P., 2007b. The determinants of Chinese outward foreign direct investment. *Journal of international business studies*, 38 (4), 499–518.

Collinson, S. and Rugman, A.M., 2008. The regional nature of Japanese multinational business. *Journal of international business studies*, 39 (2), 215–230.

Dent, C., 2008. *East Asian regionalism*. London: Routledge.

Dollar, D., 2007. Asian century or multi-polar century? [online]. World bank policy research working paper 4174, March. Available from: www.wds.worldbank.org/.../IW3P/IB/2007/03/20/000016406_20070320112343/Rendered/PDF/wps4174.pdf [Accessed 25 April 2008].

Dowling, P.J. and Welch, D.E., 2004. *International human resource management: managing people in a multinational context*. 4th ed. Cincinnati, OH: Thomson Learning.

Ghoshal, S. and Nohria, N., 1993. Horses for courses: organizational forms for multinational corporations. *Sloan management review*, Winter, 23–35.

Gurtov, M., 2007. Options for reconciling China and Japan. *Asian perspectives*, 31 (1), 169–175.

Hoskisson, R.E., Eden, L., Lau, C.M., and Wright, M., 2000. Strategy in emerging economies. *Academy of management journal*, 43 (3), 249–267.

Itagaki, H., ed., 1997. *The Japanese production system*. Basingstoke: Macmillan Press.

Japan External Trade Organization, 2005. Special survey of Japanese business in China – impact of the April anti-Japan demonstrations [online]. Tokyo: JETRO. Available from: www.jetro.go.jp/en/stats/survey/pdf/2005_04_biz.pdf [Accessed 18 April 2008].

JETRO. *See* Japan External Trade Organization.

Jürgens, U., 2003. The transformation of corporate governance systems in Japan and Germany: the end of Rhenian capitalism? *In*: S.-J. Park and S. Horn, eds. *Asia and Europe in the new global system*. Basingstoke: Palgrave Macmillan, 66–73.

London, T. and Hart, S.L., 2004. Reinventing strategies for emerging markets: beyond the transactional model. *Journal of international business studies*, 35 (5), 269–296.

Meyer, K.A., 2004. Perspectives on multinational enterprises in emerging economies. *Journal of international business studies*, 35 (4), 259–276.

Park, S.-J. and Kim, W.-P., 2003. Ohno Daiichi and Carlos Ghoshn: Zum Paradigmenwechsel von Unternehmensstrategien in Japan [Ohno Daiichi and Carlos Ghoshn: paradigm shifts in corporate strategies in Japan]. *In*: W. Dorow and H. Groenewald, eds. *Personalwirtschaftlicher Wandel in Japan* [*Changes in Japanese human resource management*]. Wiesbaden: Gabler, 95–113.

Peng, M.W., Lu, Y., Shenkar, O., and Wang, D.Y.L., 2001. Treasures in the China house: A review of management and organizational research on Greater China. *Journal of business research*, 52, 95–110.

Perlmutter, H.V., 1969. The tortuous evolution of the MNC. *Columbia journal of world business*, 4, 9–18.

Ramamurti, R., 2004. Developing countries and MNEs: extending and enriching the research agenda. *Journal of international business studies*, 35 (4), 277–283.

Segal-Horn, S. and Faulkner, D., 1999. *The dynamics of international strategy*. London: International Thomson Business Press.

Shibagaki, K., 2000. Recent arguments on corporate governance in Japan. *In*: A. Holzhausen, ed. *Can Japan globalize?* Heidelberg: Physica-Verlag, 99–105.

Tallman, S.B. and Yip, G.S., 2001. Strategy and the multinational enterprise. *In*: A.M. Rugman and T.L. Brewer, eds. *The Oxford handbook of international business*. Oxford: Oxford University Press.

The Economist, 2007a. China's economy: how fit is the panda? 29 September, 87–89.

The Economist, 2007b. Japan's wobbly economy [online], 14 November, Economist Intelligence Unit Viewswire. Available from: www.economist.com/displayStory.cfm?story_id=10129726 [Accessed 25 April 2008].

The Economist, 2007c. Business in Japan (special report): JapAnglo-Saxon capitalism, 1 December, 18–19.

The Economist, 2007d. Recalculating China's GDP: clipping the dragon's wings, 22 December, 98.

The Economist, 2008. Decoupling 2: Japan – unable to fend for itself [online], 24 January. Available from: http://www.economist.com/displaystory.cfm?story_id=10567586 [Accessed 25 April 2008].

UNCTAD, 2007. *World investment report: transnational corporations, extractive industries and development*. United Nations Conference on Trade and Development. New York and Geneva: UN.

Wright, M., *et al.*, 2005. Strategy research in emerging economies: challenging the conventional wisdom. *Journal of management studies*, 42 (1), 1–33.

Yoshida, Y. and Ito, H., 2006. How do the Asian economies compete with Japan in the US market? Is China exceptional? A triangular trade approach. *Asia Pacific business review*, 12 (3), 285–307.

Yoshikawa, T., *et al.*, 2006. Financial and product market integration: responses of Japanese firms. *Management international review*, 46 (5), 529–555.

Yusuf, S., Altaf, M.A., and Nabeshima, K., eds, 2004. *Global production networking and technological change in East Asia*. Oxford: Oxford University Press.

Index

Page numbers in *Italics* represent tables.
Page numbers in **Bold** represent figures.

Acon 111
Adjustment Period (1994-2000) 7, 8
administrative network 165
Aeon 110, **111**
ageing population 12
agglomeration: benefits 14
Ahearne, G.H.: and Shinada, N. 31
Akthar, S.: and Tan, D. 148
Allen, N.J.: and Meyer, J.P. 145, 146
ANA Cargo 74
Aoki, M. 2
Apple Computer 83
Asian Financial Crisis (1997) 46
assembly plant: Toyota 90
Association Asian Nations (ASEAN) 11, 163
automobile: manufacturer 13

Beamish, P.W.: and Inkpen, A. 18; and Jiang, R. 18
Beijing: Tianjin 46
Benetton 83
Berry, J.W. 147
birth rates 12
Bohai Bay: Yangtze River Delta 14
brand awareness 13
brand owner 28
bubble economy: Japan 2
Buckley, P.J. 18; and Ghauri, P.N. 26
bundle sales system: Japan 138
business models 20
business relations 2

cabinet decision: postal reform 67
Canada 42
Central Europe 98
cheap labour: exploitation 30
children and young adults: consumer 107
China 11; consumer price index (CPI) 43; degree of urbanization 110; distribution channel 138; economic environment 52; foreign activity 52, 54; foreign direct investment (FDI) *4-5*; foreign firms 103; homogenous employment system 17; individualistic 107; international activity 39, 57; Japanese entries *41*; Japanese foreign subsidies 40; Japanese-owned production 16; joint ventures (JV) 89; manufacturers 130; market 118; mobile phone brands *15*; mobile phone handsets *127*; mobile phone industry 128-9; phone manufacturer 139; population density 110; product development 133; six regions 46; State Council 53; World Trade Organisation (WTO) 102
Chinese brands 113
Chinese economy 5, 42
Chinese manufacturer: design period 134
Chinese Yuan 44, *45*, 46
circuit design 134
city/province in China: consumer price index (CPI) *43*; nominal wage rate index *44*
Coasean decision 26
commitment: workgroup 148-50; workplace 145-7
communication: word-of mouth 106
competitiveness: market 103
consumer 118; children and young adults 107; Chinese 106, 115; experts 108-9; middle-aged adults 108; middle-aged Chinese 109; salarymen 109; young Chinese 107; young professionals 108
consumer goods: manufacturer 13, 103
consumer market 104; Chinese 103

consumer price index (CPI): China 43; city/province in China *43*
consumerscapes 111
contract manufacturers 27
coordination: knowledge 56
Cornett, M. 64
corporate governance: economy 26; Japan Post 78; privatisation 64-5
corporate transformations: institutional change 20
corporations 13
cost advantages 42
cost competitiveness 44
cost effectiveness 96
counterfeiting 16
country of origin (COO) 11
Courier, Express, Parcel (CEP): market 72

decision-making process 30
Delios, A.: Beamish, P. and Juan, Z.X. 18; and Henisz, W. 85
Denso Corporation 90
design period: Chinese manufacturer 134
Deutsche Bundespost 71
Deutsche Post 61, 62, 69; internationalisation strategy 75; Japan Post 72
Deutsche Post World Net (DPWN) 71
DHL 61, 76
distribution channel: China 138
distribution system 138
division of labour 136; mobile phone industry **137**
Dodgson, J.: *et al* 63-4
duality: older age clusters 114

East Asian economic integration 18-20
economic environment: China 52
economic gravity 110
economic growth policy 1
economic industrialisation 145
economic integration 2
economic linkages: increased 2
Economic and Technology Development Zones (ETDZs) 14
economy 25, 26; corporate governance 26; global economy 26
electronics manufacturing services (EMS) 162
Ellis, P. 87
emerging markets 85; idiosyncratic environment 83; success 86
employees 168
expatriate managers 30
experts: consumer 108-9
exploitation: cheap labour 30; markets 63
export: -orientated companies 162; Chinese 38
Express Mail Service (EMS) 72

Felfe, J.: and Yan, W.H. 19
financial services: relative domestic focus 31
financial transnational corporations: top-50 *32*
firm specific advantages (FSAs): Japanese firms 12
firms 13; Japanese 12
flexibility 7
foreign activity 51-2; China 52, 54
foreign companies 39, 54
foreign direct investment (FDI): China *4-5*; inbound *7*; industry concentration *48-9*; Japan to China 39; Japan's outward *9-10*; Japanese 14; Japanese trends 3-12
foreign firms: China 103
foreign investors 38, 53, 87
foreign markets: Japan Post 72-5
Forsgren, M. 84
France 42

General Motors (GM) 88
geographic proximity 20
German Postal Law (1998) 71
Germany: postal administration 69-70; postal privatisation 70
Ghauri, P.N.: and Buckley, P.J. 26
Glaser, B.: and Strauss, A. 87
global competition: manufacturing firms 63
global economy: economy 26
global factory 18, 26-7; components 27; globally distributed production *27*; information structure 27-8, 28, **29**; key problem 30; manager 28; off-shoring 26
global network 75
global strategy 85

Global System for Mobile (GSM) 124; Samsung 126
globalisation 35
globally distributed production: global factory *27*
Godydke, T. 19
government 64; Japanese 65; reform 66
Gradual development period (1984-1991) 6
graduates: Chinese *113*

Haak, R. 63
handset development: typical schedule **133**
Hatami, F. 19
Henan 46
Henisz, W.: and Delios, A. 85
Hianen 46
Hofstede, G. 115, 147
Horn, S. 114
hub and spoke strategies **28**
Hubeui 46
human resource management (HRM) 17-18, 19, 20, 164

idiosyncratic environment: emerging markets 83
industry concentration *50*; foreign direct investment (FDI) *48-9*
information structure: global factory 27-8, 28, **29**
Inkpen, A.: and Beamish, P.W. 18
innovation systems 33
institutional change: corporate transformations 20
institutional theory approach 3
intermediate products 55
international activity: China 39, 57
international business: literature 55; models 1; research 56
international joint ventures (IJVs) 27
internationalisation 19, 34; Deutsche Post 75; literature 63; process model 84-5; service suppliers 63; theory framework 55
investment flows 46
investment regime: liberalisation 6
isolationist inward-looking perspective 15

J-system reform 20
Japan: bubble economy 2; bundle sales system 138; outsourcing demand 57; postal administration 69-70; seclusion period (1638-1858) 3; service operators 131, *132*
Japan Post 65-6, 71, 74, 76, 78; All Nippon Airways (ANA) 73; corporate governance 78; Deutsche Post 72; foreign markets 72-5
Japanese entries: China *41*
Japanese firms: firm specific advantages (FSAs) 12
Japanese foreign subsidies: China 40
Japanese investments 3
Japanese Post: phases of transformation 68
Japanese Postal Savings Bank 65
Japanese-owned production: China 16
joint ventures (JV) 88, 169; China 89
Jun'ivhiro, Prime Minister K. 61

keiretsu structure 15
knowledge coordination 56
knowledge management policies 34
Koizumi, J. 66; postal reform 67; reform package 67

La Porta, R. *et al* 64
La Poste 74
labour cost 18
labour shortages 18
liberalisation: investment regime 6
Lieberman, M.B.: and Montgomery, D.B. 86, 97
lifestyle: products 115
Linden, S.: and White, G. 97
liquid crystal displays (LCD) 16
literature: internationalisation 63
local cultures: world culture 30
local firms 124
local municipal government 53

Malaysia 42
management 5; effects 30; systems 3
management style: Japanese 25-6; non-core employees 2, 26
manager: global factory 28
manufacturer 133; automobile 13; China 130; consumer goods 13, 103; Japanese 12

manufacturing firms: global competition 63
market: China 118; competitiveness 103; exploitation 63; information 116; liberalisation 102; orientation 103
Matsushita 130; NEC 140, 141
Mazda 41; retail sales 104
Mediatek (MTK) 137
Meiji period (1868-1911) 5
member firms: organizational theory 96
Meyer, J.P.: and Allen, N.J. 145, 146; multidimensional approach 146
Ministry of Internal Affairs and Communications (MIC) 69
miracle economy 2
mobile phone brands: China *15*
mobile phone handsets: China *127*
mobile phone industry: China 128-9
mobile telephony market 19
modus operandi 20
MOFCOM data 6, 8
MOL 74, 76
Montgomery, D.B.: and Lieberman, N.B. 86, 97
Motorola 18
multidimensional approach: Meyer, J.P. 146
multinational bank (MNB) 55
multinational firms: models *32*
municipality 47

national debt 66
natural monopoly: theory 62
NEC: Matsushita 140, 141
Netherlands 42
network members: relational linkages 96
network-based entry 86-7
new business model 62
new plants 39-40
new policy zones 54
Nippon Express 74, 76
Nissan 41, 109
non-core employees: management style 26
non-financial transnational corporations *32*
North, D.C. 85

off-shoring 55; data 56; global factory 26; value chain 8-9
older age clusters: duality 114
Open Door Policy 163
Open Export Zones (OEZs) 6
Opinion 129-31
optimum location 28
organisational citizenship behaviour (OCB) 144, 145
organisational theory: member firms 96
orientation: market 103; production 103
Original Equipment Manufacturers (OEMs) 27
outsourcing 55, 56; arrangements 16; demand in Japan 57
Ozawa, T.: four stages 34

passenger car manufacturer 165
Peak Period 7
phone makers: China 139; Japanese 135; outsource 136
policy makers 52
political relations 1
population density: China 110
post-WTO accession period 11
postal administration 61, 62; Germany 69-70; Japan 69-70
postal express market **73**
Postal Life Insurance 61
postal privatisation 78; Germany 70
postal reform: cabinet decision 67; Koizumi, J. 67
postal savings: comparisons **70**
Postal Savings Bank 61, 68
postal service sector 63
pre-clusterisation 83, 84, 87, 96, 98; framework *95*; Toyota 91, 92; virtual assembly plants 89
pre-war period 5
privatisation 66; corporate governance 64-5; process 66, 68
product development 131; China 133
product diffusion 105
product groups 62
production: orientation 103
products: lifestyle 115
proprietary knowledge 16
province-industry mix 47
Pucik, V. 163
purchasing behaviour 13

quasi-internationalisation 28

recruitment: retention 20
reform: government 66
reform package: Koizumi, J. 67
regionalism 46-7
relational linkages: network members 96
relative domestic focus: financial services 31
research & development (R&D) 26, 123, 162
retail sales: Mazda 104
retailers 116
Riketta, M.: and Van Dick, R. 149
rural-urban income divide 105

Sagem 130
salarymen: consumer 109
Samsung: GSM market 126
Schwartz, S. 114
Science Council 26
seclusion period (1638-1858): Japan 3
Seiko 110
service operators: Japan 131, *132*
service suppliers: internationalisation 63
Shanghai 162
Shanghai Automotive Industry Corporation (SAIC) 88
Shinada, N.: and Ahearne, G.H. 31
Shiseido 104
Sino-Japanese economic ties 3
small and medium enterprises (SMEs) 34
social status 105
socio-demographic diversity 106
socio-demographic variables 106
socio-economic disparity 105
Sony Ericsson 130
South Korea 42
Special Economic Zone (SEZ) 46, 89
State Council 3; China 53
state monopolies: transformation 62-3
state-owned enterprises (SOEs) 52
Steenkamp, J.B.: *et al* 114
Strauss, A.: and Glaser, B. 87
subsciber identity module (SIM) 139
subsidiary role 51, 52
Suntory Tea 110
suppliers: Toyota 89
supply clusters: Toyota **91**

Tan, D.: and Akthar, S. 148
technological spillover 135
technology standards 124
Tiananmen Square 6
Tianjin: Beijing 46
TNT 74, 76
Total Access Communication System (TACS) 128-9
total productive maintenance (TPM) 167
total quality control (TQC) 167
Toyota 15, 41, 89; assembly plant 90; entry process **94**; pre-clusterisation 91, 92; suppliers 89; supply clusters **91**
Toyota Group 84, 88, 98
Toyota Motor 83
Trade Related Aspects of Intellectual Property Rights (TRIPS Agreement) 53
transformation: state monopolies 62-3
transnationality index 31

underdeveloped market institutions 85
United Kingdom (UK) 11
United States of America (USA) 11, 42

value added activity 51
value chain: off-shoring parts 8-9
Van Dick, R.: and Riketta, M. 149
virtual assembly plants: pre-clusterisation 89
Volkswagen (VW): poor performance 86

Wakasugi, R. 14
Weick, K.E. 87
Western economics 38
White, S.: and Linden, G. 97
work style 166
workgroup commitment 19, 148-50
workplace commitment 145-7
World Bank 13
world culture: local cultures 30
World Trade Organisation (WTO) 1, 53; China 102

Yan, W.H. 86; and Felfe, J. 19
Yangtze River Delta: Bohai Bay 14
young professionals: consumer 108

zombie firms 31

For Product Safety Concerns and Information please contact our EU
representative GPSR@taylorandfrancis.com
Taylor & Francis Verlag GmbH, Kaufingerstraße 24, 80331 München, Germany

www.ingramcontent.com/pod-product-compliance
Ingram Content Group UK Ltd.
Pitfield, Milton Keynes, MK11 3LW, UK
UKHW050234200926
475702UK00020B/3034
9780415845410